MW01405624

Contemporary Film Music

Lindsay Coleman • Joakim Tillman
Editors

Contemporary Film Music

Investigating Cinema Narratives and Composition

palgrave
macmillan

Editors
Lindsay Coleman	Joakim Tillman
Melbourne, Australia	Stockholm, Sweden

ISBN 978-1-137-57374-2   ISBN 978-1-137-57375-9 (eBook)
DOI 10.1057/978-1-137-57375-9

Library of Congress Control Number: 2017931555

© The Editor(s) (if applicable) and The Author(s) 2017
The author(s) has/have asserted their right(s) to be identified as the author(s) of this work in accordance with the Copyright, Designs and Patents Act 1988.
This work is subject to copyright. All rights are solely and exclusively licensed by the Publisher, whether the whole or part of the material is concerned, specifically the rights of translation, reprinting, reuse of illustrations, recitation, broadcasting, reproduction on microfilms or in any other physical way, and transmission or information storage and retrieval, electronic adaptation, computer software, or by similar or dissimilar methodology now known or hereafter developed.
The use of general descriptive names, registered names, trademarks, service marks, etc. in this publication does not imply, even in the absence of a specific statement, that such names are exempt from the relevant protective laws and regulations and therefore free for general use.
The publisher, the authors and the editors are safe to assume that the advice and information in this book are believed to be true and accurate at the date of publication. Neither the publisher nor the authors or the editors give a warranty, express or implied, with respect to the material contained herein or for any errors or omissions that may have been made. The publisher remains neutral with regard to jurisdictional claims in published maps and institutional affiliations.

Printed on acid-free paper

This Palgrave Macmillan imprint is published by Springer Nature
The registered company is Macmillan Publishers Ltd.
The registered company address is: The Campus, 4 Crinan Street, London, N1 9XW, United Kingdom

Dedicated to my dear music and piano teacher, Mrs Bonni-Belle Pickard

Acknowledgements

This book is possible thanks to two individuals: Joakim Tillman and Chris Penfold. Joakim started out as a contributor and, in one interaction after another, I could clearly see this book would only be a lesser volume without his being my direct collaborator. It has been an honour and a privilege to work with him. Chris Penfold is the true originator of this book's format. I had some notion of writing the theory chapters myself for the entire book, but Chris pointed out that the interviews were with sufficient personages to attract true experts to write individual chapters. Probably this was the best advice I received that entire year!

I would like to give very special thanks to Jack Dubowsky. Similarly to Joakim and Chris, Jack was a big part of what made this book work. I am so grateful to him for his wonderful insights, and ongoing support. Thank you so much, Jack.

The contributions of Joakim, Jack and Chris were invaluable in terms of the project's inception, yet it is the composers, and other contributors, who have made this book a tangible reality. I thank all of the interviewed composers for their kindness and candour, their support of this project, long in gestation. For the contributors, I thank every one of them for their patience with cuts and redrafts, their skill and dedication as researchers and musicologists, and their tireless commitment to promoting a greater understanding of film music.

For their assorted assistance I would like to thank Peter Golub, Rajiv Menon, Lina Aboujieb, and of course my little family, my wife Sarah and our little daughter, Audrey. Daddy gets up every day for work because of the two of you!

Lindsay Coleman

I'm incredibly grateful to all the contributors, not only for their outstanding essays, but also for their diligent and committed work. I would like to thank Lina Aboujieb at Palgrave for her invaluable guidance and help in the production of the book. My deepest thanks go to Lindsay, first for approaching me to write an essay for this book, and then for the even greater confidence of asking me to join him as a co-editor. It has been a very rewarding collaboration, and I'm looking forward to future projects with Lindsay. Finally, I'm extremely grateful for the patience and support of my wife, Åsa, and our two sons, Daniel and Oscar.

Joakim Tillman

Contents

1 **Introduction**   1
   Lindsay Coleman and Joakim Tillman

2 **A.R. Rahman Interview**   17
   Lindsay Coleman

3 **The 'Alternate Space' of A.R. Rahman's Film Music**   27
   Felicity Wilcox

4 **Zbigniew Preisner Interview**   57
   Jonathan Godsall

5 **Music by Zbigniew Preisner? Fictional Composers and Compositions in the Kieślowski Collaborations**   63
   Jonathan Godsall

6 **Carter Burwell Interview**   87
   Lindsay Coleman

7   Burwell and Space: Inner, Outer, Environmental
    and Acoustical   97
    Andrew Waggoner

8   Rachel Portman Interview   119
    Lindsay Coleman

9   Eero Tarasti and the Narratological Construction
    of Rachel Portman's *Emma*   125
    Lindsay Coleman

10 Dario Marianelli Interview   139
    Lindsay Coleman

11 Solo Instruments and Internal Focalization
    in Dario Marianelli's *Pride & Prejudice* and *Atonement* 155
    Joakim Tillman

12 Mychael Danna Interview   187
    Lindsay Coleman

13 Mychael Danna: Music as Metaphor   195
    Peter Golub and Katy Jarzebowski

14 John Williams and Contemporary Film Music   221
    Emilio Audissino

15 Musical Syntax in John Williams's Film Music Themes   237
    Konstantinos Zacharopoulos

Index   263

Notes on Contributors

Emilio Audissino is a film historian. He is currently finishing up a post-doctoral research project at the University of Southampton, UK, concerning the application of neoformalism and gestalt psychology to the analysis of music in films. He holds a Ph.D. in the history of visual and performing arts from the University of Pisa, Italy, and specializes in Hollywood cinema, film style, film dubbing, and film music. He is the author of *John Williams's Film Music:* Jaws, Star Wars, Raiders of the Lost Ark *and the Return of the Classical Hollywood Music Style* (Madison: University of Wisconsin Press, 2014), the first English-language monograph on Williams.

Lindsay Coleman is a film academic, and an independent documentary producer. His most recent books include *Sex and Storytelling in Modern Cinema* (London: I. B. Tauris, 2016), and *The Philosophy of Pornography: Contemporary Perspectives* (Scarecrow, 2014). In addition to these, he is working on a series of books on cinematography, film editing, musical composition for films, and visual effects in modern cinema. He is also working on documentary projects on Hollywood film editing, and Australian cinema.

Jonathan Godsall is currently Lecturer in music at Plymouth University. He completed a Ph.D. in musicology at the University of Bristol in early 2014. Jonathan has overlapping research interests in screen music, musical intertextuality, and musical reception, with publications to date addressing the use of pre-existing music in film. He also performs as a drummer and percussionist in various contexts.

Peter Golub has taught composition at UCLA, Bennington College, and Reed College. Since 1998 he has been the Director of the Sundance Film Music Program, where he runs the yearly Composers Lab, an intensive workshop for aspiring film composers. His film scores include: *Frozen River* (2008), *Wordplay* (2006), and *The Great Debaters* (2007) (co-composed with James Newton Howard). He has scored numerous Broadway productions. He was awarded the Classic Contribution Award by BMI, and is a member of the Academy of Motion Picture Arts and Sciences.

Katy Jarzebowski is a film composer currently based in Los Angeles, CA. In 2014, she was selected as a composer fellow for the Sundance Music and Sound Design Lab, at Skywalker Sound. Katy studied music composition and film studies at Yale University, and completed her master's degree in film scoring at NYU, where she was awarded the Elmer Bernstein Award and the Sorel Women Composer's Award. Her work includes numerous scores, notably for *After Spring*, a documentary produced by Jon Stewart, which premiered at Tribeca Film Festival (2016), and follows the lives of Syrian refugees at the Zaatari refugee camp in Jordan. Katy is forever grateful to her parents for being unapologetically militant cinephiles, and her grandparents for passing their musical genes over one generation to the next; she thanks them every day for their enthusiastic support.

Joakim Tillman is Assistant Professor of musicology at Stockholm University, where he teaches courses in music analyses, nineteenth- and twentieth-century music (including film and game music), and opera. He has recently completed a research project about Wagnerian influences in Late Romantic Swedish opera, and his current research focuses on the film music of Elliot Goldenthal, James Horner, and Hans Zimmer. His research has appeared in numerous scholarly journals and edited volumes, including the article '*Topoi* and Intertextuality: Narrative Function in Hans Zimmer's and Lisa Gerrard's Music to *Gladiator*' in *Music in Epic Film: Listening to Spectacle*, ed. Stephen C. Meyer (New York: Routledge, 2017).

Andrew Waggoner is Professor of Composition in the Setnor School of Music of Syracuse University. Called '*the gifted practitioner of a complex but dramatic and vividly colored style*' by the *New Yorker*, his music has been commissioned and performed by the Los Angeles Philharmonic; the JACK Quartet; and the Academy of St Martin-in-the-Fields, among many others. He has been awarded the Lee Ettelson Composer's Award from Composers Inc., a Guggenheim Fellowship, and the Roger Sessions Prize for an American composer by the Liguria Studies Center in Bogliasco, Italy. In 2009 he received an Academy Award from the American Academy of Arts and Letters.

Felicity Wilcox lectures in music and sound at the University of Technology Sydney. She was awarded her Ph.D. in composition from Sydney Conservatorium of Music in 2013. Her research and practice in interdisciplinary music is informed by her professional background as a screen composer. Under the alias Felicity Fox, she has composed scores for many award-winning Australian film and television productions, receiving multiple ARIA, AFI and APRA/AGSC awards and nominations, and many national and international television broadcasts, and screenings in major film festivals. Along with commissions for over 60 screen credits, Felicity has been commissioned to compose new concert works for Vivid Festival Sydney, Decibel New Music Ensemble, Ensemble Offspring, Ironwood, Halcyon Ensemble, the Australia Piano Quartet, the Sydney Symphony Fellows, and the Australia Ensemble. Since 2015, she has served as a director of the Australian Guild of Screen Composers.

Konstantinos Zacharopoulos is a film composer and musicologist. He is currently a Ph.D. candidate focusing on John Williams's film music (1975–today) at the Department of Music Studies, National and Kapodistrian University of Athens. He has won, among others, the Jerry Goldsmith Award for 'Best music for short film' in 2008 (Úbeda, Spain) and film credits include the score for *Cornered* (2009), a horror film starring Steve Guttenberg and James Duval.

List of Figures

Fig. 5.1	*No End* melody, Jacek's piano version. Music by Zbigniew Preisner. © Copyright 1985 Amplitude Publishing. Used by permission	70
Fig. 5.2	'L'Estaca' (first two phrases, transposed from A minor into G minor for ease of comparison). © Copyright 1968 by Lluis Llach Grande; SEEMSA, Alcalá 70, 28009 Madrid (Spain). Used by permission	71
Fig. 5.3	Refrain from 'Holy God' ('Święty Boże', traditional Polish church song)	71
Fig. 5.4	Van den Budenmayer funeral music in *Blue*. Music by Zbigniew Preisner. © Copyright 1994 MK2 SA, Chester Music Limited. All Rights Reserved. International Copyright Secured. Used by permission of Chester Music Limited	73
Fig. 5.5	Second Van den Budenmayer theme in *Blue* (as initially heard in Julie's version of the *Song*). Music by Zbigniew Preisner. © Copyright 1994 MK2 SA, Chester Music Limited. All Rights Reserved. International Copyright Secured. Used by permission of Chester Music Limited	74
Fig. 5.6	Main theme, Van den Budenmayer *Concerto in E Minor* from *Véronique*. Music by Zbigniew Preisner. © Copyright 1991 Delabel Editions SARL/New Music BV. Used by permission of Sony/ATV Music Publishing (Germany) GmbH	74
Fig. 5.7	Cadential melody, Van den Budenmayer song from *Decalogue IX*. Music by Zbigniew Preisner. © Copyright 1989 Amplitude Publishing. Used by permission	74

Fig. 5.8	Olivier's theme from *Blue*. Music by Zbigniew Preisner. © Copyright 1994 MK2 SA, Chester Music Limited. All Rights Reserved. International Copyright Secured. Used by permission of Chester Music Limited	75
Fig. 5.9	*Requiem for My Friend*, 'Kai Kairos', bars 84–87. Arranged by Zbigniew Preisner. © Copyright 1996, Chester Music Limited. All Rights Reserved. International Copyright Secured. Used by permission of Chester Music Limited	78
Fig. 15.1	'Main Theme' from *Superman*. Adapted from 'Superman March' from *Superman* (mm. 19–26), © 1978 Warner-Tamerlane Publishing Corp, Hal Leonard Signature Edition, 04490228	240
Fig. 15.2	'Remembrances Theme' from *Schindler's List*. Adapted from 'Three Pieces from *Schindler's List*, Remembrances' (mm. 14–21), © 1993 by Music Corporation of America Inc., Hal Leonard Signature Edition, 04490011	241
Fig. 15.3	'Basket Game Theme' from *Raiders of the Lost Ark*. Adapted from '*Raiders of the Lost Ark*, The Basket Game' (Excerpt) (mm. 3–11), © 1981 Bantha Music and Ensign Music Corporation (in the piano folio the final bar is 10, but in the handwritten score it's 11 due to the time signature change)	242
Fig. 15.4	'Main Theme' from *Presumed Innocent*. Adapted from John Williams 'Anthology, Remembering Carolyn (A Theme from "Presumed Innocent")' (mm. 9–16), © 1990 Warner-Tamerlane Publishing Corp, © 1991 Warner-Bros Publications Inc. VF1774	244
Fig. 15.5	'Yoda's Theme' from *The Empire Strikes Back*. Adapted from '*Star Wars* Suite for Orchestra, IV. Yoda's Theme' (mm. 3–10), © 1980 Warner-Tamerlane Publishing Corp & Bantha Music, Hal Leonard Signature Edition, 04490057	246
Fig. 15.6	'Irish Theme' from *Far and Away*. Adapted from 'Suite from *Far and Away*' (mm. 5–28), © 1992 Songs of Universal Inc., Hal Leonard Signature Edition, 04490190	247

CHAPTER 1

Introduction

Lindsay Coleman and Joakim Tillman

The twenty-first century is a strange time for films. Franchises upon franchises, a dwindling art house, piracy, one-off gimmick films propagating film series which last eons, and nostalgia, nostalgia, nostalgia. Mix in the increasing narrative power of animated films, the growing thematic sophistication of genre works, and the diminishing returns of filmdom's acknowledged auteurs, and one is left with a strange beast, a reanimated Frankenstein of cinema, torn apart and reassembled, torn apart and reassembled, endlessly. Yet, as always, film's essential components remain unchanged: a camera, actors, lights, editing, costumes, a set or location, sound and music. For a film to be without music is certainly possible, yet such instances are rare enough to raise an eyebrow, and qualify as an artistic exemption. Rather, in our present era, films are frequently overorchestrated, the running times of their musical accompaniments running into 70, 80, 100 minutes of screen time, and this often for films whose running time rarely exceeds that. Film music, depending on who

---

L. Coleman (✉)
Nunawading, Australia

J. Tillman
Stockholm, Sweden

© The Author(s) 2017
L. Coleman, J. Tillman (eds.), *Contemporary Film Music*,
DOI 10.1057/978-1-137-57375-9_1

you talk to, is either so indelible films cannot do without it, or so dispensable that it has been rendered musical wall paper. These strange times for cinema have spilled over, equally, into the odd adventures of the musical score in this new century.

Film music has seemingly also crossed into an afterlife of ubiquity, paired with an equal lack of specificity. In 1998, millions purchased James Horner's score to *Titanic* (James Cameron, 1997), for the express purpose of reliving the many evocative moments of that film. Now, film music is as likely to play in the background of a supermarket as it is to be on our iPhone. In such a period it might pay to begin with the most welcome aspects of this odd epoch. The definition of a 'generic', or 'conventional', film score has itself become an outmoded term. Where once the likes of Maurice Jarre would compose sweeping, melodic, clearly orchestral scores for *Doctor Zhivago* (David Lean, 1965), or *Lawrence of Arabia* (David Lean, 1962), the modern filmgoer might see a major release, such as *The Social Network* (David Fincher, 2010), and be confronted by a dense sound design that combines atmospherics, hard-to-place tonalities, and the childlike melodics of 'Hand Covers Bruise', a now universally recognized musical theme from the film. You may not know the title, but you have surely heard it, in film trailers, commercials, or humming in the background as you do your shopping. The emotional, but also nebulous, nature of this track is by-in-large emblematic of the Oscar-winning score for this film. Music accompanies the film, but rarely comments on it. As such, with the exemption of the Wendy Carlos-influenced 'In the Hall of the Mountain King', picture and music rarely directly intersect in *The Social Network*. Rarely does music expressly accompany an actor's performance, as it might have perhaps in George Fenton's memorably melodramatic score to *Dangerous Liaisons* (Stephen Frears, 1988), the precise emotional inflections of John Malkovich's portrayal of a sexual predator and seducer mapped with utter precision to Fenton's music. Rather, the music sets a contemplative tone, refusing to editorialize, both melodically warm, and electronically cold. It is a perfect fit for the stylized thematic ambiguity of the film. Is *The Social Network* a Horatio Alger tale, or is it a twenty-first century *Citizen Kane* (Orson Welles, 1941), a tale of spiritual desolation? The film's score has few answers in this respect. We are sucked into a tale with no clear heroes or villains, not even an emotional resolution in its final, Rosebud-esque, image. Fittingly, the film music of *The Social Network* is indeed music, but *only just*. In *The Piano* (Jane Campion, 1993), lead character Ada's improvisatory piano-playing is translated into the non-diegetic score, Michael Nyman's piano-based soundtrack echoing back to Ada's playing. In *The Social Network* there is no connection between incident and accompaniment, the one directly provoking the other. Music rarely syncs smoothly with events, or even emotional transitions within a scene. The first iteration of 'Hand Covers Bruise' in the soundtrack *does* feature the now-famous melody, yet it is offset by a rising-to-fortissimo sonic boil of ambient sounds. It is aligned neither with the incomplete musical sequence featured in Herrmann's score for *Psycho* (Alfred Hitchcock, 1960), nor with the simple melody of 'Lara's Theme' in *Doctor Zhivago*. It begins with what might almost be classified as an anti-theme, so rudimentary is the piano phrase; 'childlike', the film's director David Fincher observes on the film's DVD commentary track,[1] which is then so quickly subsumed by an escalating-to-incoherent fortissimo musical background mix that the 'score' is transfixed in a compositional no-man's-land. And, yet, this realm is by no means unpleasant. In a story whose inception is found in a key moment of social alienation for its hero, then finishes in what might be characterized as a moment of deluded hope that a keystroke might liberate him from said alienation, composers Atticus Ross and Trent Reznor always need to play hide-and-seek with an audience, not seeking an editorializing musical accompaniment, or any kind of emotional fanfare in this particular story. By conventional measure it is an odd score, for an equally odd hero.

Similarly, at the highest level of contemporary moviedom, the superhero firmament of Marvel and DC Comics, an inveterate punk sensibility is invested into one of the biggest, most bombastic scores of, in turn, the biggest movies of the past 15 years. So claims one of its composers, Hans Zimmer,[2] whose work on *The Dark Knight* (Christopher Nolan, 2008) is none of the things one might expect in the score of a summer blockbuster. Even though there are highly dissonant sections, the music is clearly anchored in D minor (without comparison the most frequently-used key in all of Zimmer's film music). Only intermittently does the Batman theme chime in for a series of bars. It is a score prone to long breaks of silence, or perhaps near-subliminal drones. Little in the score seems to commend itself to conventional notions such as 'character themes', 'romantic interludes', an 'overture'. Rather, Zimmer seems to trust the audience to respond instinctually to the music, the desperate intercutting of the film's many narrative strands bolstered by a score which might seem nebulous, but in fact represents the similarly desperate narrative pulse of this dark masterpiece. Almost devoid of the famously hummable theme of Danny Elfman's original *Batman* score (Tim Burton, 1989), 'Descent into a Mystery', the audience has the momentary sense of a theme evolving, a spasm of heroism, which is then overtaken as quickly by the crashing, electric-guitar soundscapes which represent the nihilism of the Joker, heavy with feedback and distortion. It might be worth noting, therefore, that the most identifiable, comforting sound of the film's hero is not an evolved theme but, rather, a noted feature of the film's soundscape, the rhythmic beating of a giant wing, a giant bat. This represents not only the melding of sound design with score, but much more than that it represents a creative 'sting' which exists outside of the diegesis, while simultaneously ringing a thematic bell which resonates throughout the entire score.

These two scores, *The Dark Knight* and *The Social Network*, represent not necessarily the 'best' of contemporary film scores. Similar ingredients to those that make these scores succeed are found in the films which followed on for the films' respective directors, Christopher Nolan and David Fincher. Yet, cult audiences aside, no one seems to be clamouring for the rhythmic chanting of *The Dark Knight Rises*, nor for the electronic overtures of *The Girl With the Dragon Tattoo* (David Fincher, 2011), or *Gone Girl* (David Fincher, 2014), to filter out into the wider culture. They exist as touchstones for wider trends. Trent Reznor was certainly not the first film composer to originate from an electro/house background. Orbital (working with Michael Kamen) and the band Massive Attack predate *The Social Network*, in the films *Event Horizon* (Paul W. S. Anderson, 1997), and *Danny the Dog* (Louis Leterrier, 2005). However, a film need no longer be ghettoized by taking an overtly electro, non-orchestral approach to its score. *Hanna* (Joe Wright, 2011), scored by The Chemical Brothers, represented a break for director Joe Wright from his successful collaborations with Oscar-winner Dario Marianelli (to whom he has since returned). While the score itself received negligible attention, this itself was significant, having been released in the year following *The Social Network*. The score was judged neither 'good' enough to warrant major praise, nor unconventional or surprising enough to warrant outside attention, and this for a film by an award-winning director, with an equally good cast, elevating a B-movie to B-plus/A-minus sophistication. The film was good, even very good. Its action and drama were complemented by a heavily electro score, which merited no major commentary. This, in itself, is a hope many composers put forward, that their music be incidental to the scenario. An 'electro score', after *The Social Network*, had become just plain 'score'. In short, the work of The Chemical Brothers, successful pop stars of the Dance world, succeeded, and they in turn succeeded as film composers, because the perception was that that their work had successfully served the film's drama. Equally, for *The Dark Knight*, a certain kind of score has now evolved, a Hans Zimmer-type score. Hans Zimmer did compose *The Dark Knight* with James Newton Howard, yet his compatriot has admitted that Zimmer's identification with, and passion for, the Batman narrative place him in a prime position with respect to influence on, and authorship of, the film.[3] Not only has Zimmer himself continued to compose superhero scores cut from the same cloth as *The Dark Knight*—*Man of Steel* (Zack Snyder, 2013), *The Amazing Spider-Man 2* (Marc Webb, 2014), *Batman v Superman: Dawn of Justice* (Zack Snyder, 2016)—but he has fostered a generation of new composers whose scores bear the Zimmer Batman imprint. Names come to mind such as Junkie XL, Harry Gregson-Williams and Henry Jackman. In turn, the scores they have produced, frequently for superhero movies, seem averse to the anthemic features, let us say, of John Williams, in his franchise heyday. Schoolchildren do not hum the theme for *Captain America: Civil War* (Anthony and Joe Russo, 2016) as they once did the music from *Star Wars* (George Lucas, 1977), *Raiders of the Lost Ark* (Steven Spielberg, 1981), and *E.T.* (Steven Spielberg, 1982), despite that film's ubiquity. Yet, arguably, Zimmer has nevertheless fostered his own unique cult, one rooted in a studied—depending on your frame of reference—sense of self-parody. The Zimmer blast, the Zimmer sting, the mammoth Zimmer chord, all have become not only expected tropes of his own scores, but are found in the symphonic scores of the vast majority of blockbusters to appear since *The Dark Knight*.

While the 'Zimmer' touch is ubiquitous, intriguingly the question as to its quality is extremely difficult to answer. In an era in which Zimmer himself confesses to there being 'too much music' in film, ironically artistic freedom can devolve into self-parody. Caught in a unique scenario, in which each score must in turn accompany films with ever more majestic budgets, Zimmer must set his own standards of artistic achievement. In doing so he periodically adopts a style, less of minimalism, more of 'poverty of means'. Here is his description:

> 'I'm not interested in the massive heroic tunes anymore. Now, I'm interested in how I can take two, three, or four notes and make a really complex emotional structure. It's emotional as opposed to sentimental. It's not bullshit heroic; it has dignity to it.'[4]

An interesting project, perhaps underarticulated, it has inadvertently prompted a style so easily parodied that it has found itself on an episode of *South Park*. Arguably, also, this approach has little more to guide it to its stated outcome of 'emotional complexity' than Zimmer's own hopes, and—perhaps at moments in his now-notorious score for *Inception*

(Christopher Nolan, 2010)—well-honed instincts. Music critic James Southall sums up Zimmer's position, as a pre-eminent composer of this period of film music history, thus:

> 'There's no inherent problem with simple music—but simplicity itself is not enough to establish an emotional connection. There's good simple music and bad simple music, just as there's good complex music and bad complex music. This is really, really bad simple music, puerile and banal throughout. If you were a youngster back in the 1990s who quite enjoyed Media Ventures film scores, then I imagine the music you might write for some sort of school project might sound something like this.'[5]

The freedom afforded the composer of the modern score has truly become a double-edged sword, equally as capable of beckoning popular parody as it perhaps is of evoking its own conceptual counterpoint to the narrative.

In short, composers find themselves in a position of the greatest possible freedom in, arguably, an era with less and less use for what they offer: musical accompaniment to a two-hour narrative, frequently inclusive of set pieces one might otherwise find in a videogame. It is also an era where what they do offer has become absorbed by the culture to the degree that a piece may be ubiquitous, yet also entirely non-specific. John Williams may evoke Korngold's score for *The Adventures of Robin Hood* (Michael Curtiz and William Keighley, 1938) frequently, yet there is never any doubt as to which score you are humming, and what the precise shorthand means as you zip through the opening bars of the *Indiana Jones* March. 'Hand Covers Bruise' has doubtless affected on a powerfully emotional level as many people as did the theme from *Superman* (Richard Donner, 1978), yet in the service of what? As background, perhaps, to your friend's edited clips of their visit to Bali, or maybe played beneath a slideshow of a happy couple who have just got married, running at their wedding reception. Film music is very much a part of our lives, and perhaps less a part of our viewing lives. We remember, as we listen to 'Hand Covers Bruise', that we first heard it in a good movie, but we also remember that we heard it with that great new Hecklett Packard commercial, or maybe we remember how much it sounds like the music on that new Apple commercial, doubtless a piece functioning as a pastiche of the original Reznor/Finch track. That first blush of emotion, tied as it was to a tale of success, alienation, loneliness, determination, has now been refracted through many, many other iterations. Sometimes, 'Hand Covers Bruise' can be presented as wistful, other times as romantic, other times as emotionally self-assured. Just as film music depends on the images it is found with when we first encounter it, so too do its many further entrances into our lives, with brand-new pictures which in turn recontextualize, time and again, our emotional response to it. Like so many other anthemic pieces of music, 'Hand Covers Bruise' has become a temp track for *our* lives, a piece emotionally fulsome enough to cover the necessary bases for an ever-expanding range of visuals, and attendant scenarios, which populate our social media profiles, and our many viewing experiences on an evolving range of platforms. In turn, as we move from one iteration to the next, our relationship to the original piece of music becomes more and more predicated on that most recent iteration to which we have just been exposed. In the end, film music becomes, literally, world music.

Freedom in composition, then, may be both liberating and reductive in its effects. Christopher Nolan has described the work of Zimmer as that of 'a minimalist composer with a maximalist production sense' creating 'simple and specific pieces'.[6] While this certainly may have been Nolan's intent, and effective, it has also aided in the generation of a paradigm where, due to what I would argue is often a mismatch in approaches, the score itself is rendered sufficiently oppressive as to warrant parody, likely not the result either Zimmer or Nolan were hoping for. Yet, running parallel to this new freedom, is a wilful repetition and recycling. In the franchise era we now find ourselves a part of, many of the brightest lights of film composition find themselves returning, time and again, to the same narrative. John Williams has scored seven *Star Wars* (1977–2015) films, three *Harry Potter* (2001–2004) films, four *Indiana Jones* (1981–2008) films, and so forth. Howard Shore has now scored six mammoth films based on the world of J. R. R Tolkien. In effectively being major contributors to the sound worlds of these narrative universes, these inventive composers are nevertheless compelled to aid sonically, and thematically, in the continuity of these works. This results in, simply, repetition. On TheOneRing.net, a website dedicated to all aspects of filmed Tolkien, the writer admits to much of the same frustration listeners have at the first *Hobbit* (Peter Jackson, 2012) film's score, offering an apologia for the second film's soundtrack:

> 'A lot of folks noted (or if you prefer, complained about) the lack of new motifs in *An Unexpected Journey*. "Give us a hook, just something new to whistle!", the people seemed to cry.

On first listen, the Standard Edition of the soundtrack for *The Hobbit: The Desolation of Smaug* (2013) doesn't introduce that many new hooks. There does seem to be one for Bard, and perhaps a short baroque moment of harpsichords on 'Thrice Welcome' that might introduce the Master of Laketown (or maybe it's the more pompous-sounding bit later on).'[7]

It is remarkable that these would be classified not as the gripes of nitpicking critics, but of grass-roots fans, the hordes who see the movie, buy the Blu-ray, buy the soundtrack, *then* buy the extended Blu-ray. They are also, seemingly, the groups who cry out for continuity, for a repetition of the aesthetic fix each new volume of the saga will hopefully provide. Professional critics are equally willing to laser in on a composer cribbing from earlier work. Adam Bouyamourn, in a review for *The National*, notes of John Williams's score to *The Force Awakens* (J.J. Abrams, 2015):

'*The March of The Resistance*, an orchestral fugue, is, much like the Resistance itself, a warmed-up version of previous ideas—*The Imperial Motif*, the *Pomp and Circumstance*-inspired *The Throne Room*, and *Episode I: The Phantom Menace's* forgettable *March of The Trade Federation*. It's perfectly satisfactory but it doesn't win many points for distinctiveness.'[8]

And this a scant 17 years from the choral accompaniment 'Kora Ratama' to the climactic battle of *Star Wars: The Phantom Menace* (George Lucas, 1999), a *Carmina Burana*-esque accompaniment to what was ironically a dull film. John Williams, it would appear, does not need to be bounded by repetition, despite his penchant for sequels, and yet the era we are in fosters thematic and compositional conservatism, in turn running parallel to unfocused, overresourced experimentalism.

Seemingly, this concurrent trend indicates scores may become an inherent component of a film's expression of theme—the alienation of *The Social Network*, the 'heroic notes' of *Inception*. It may also be, in an era which has essentially perfected the process, a basic constituent of a franchise's brand. Think of the ongoing reprise of John Williams's Hedwig theme throughout the *Harry Potter* franchise. Patrick Doyle, Nicholas Hooper and Alexandre Desplat, irrespective of their own compositional styles and thematic preoccupations, were all partially subordinate to a theme generated up to a decade before. Where their films dealt with the character's journey through his teen years, this early theme was from an iteration of the character of Harry Potter as a then-child. Equally, the themes for the Shire in Peter Jackson's Tolkien films symbolize the branding of Hobbits, the series' consistent heroes. These themes are, like a jingle, a means of reminding the audience of the brand. What is most striking about the inclusion of these themes is the manner in which they are effectively lifted, wholesale, from previous films' scores. Irrelevant to event, or character, the theme represents a statement, and a reminder: You. Are. Watching. A. Harry. Potter. Film. There are exceptions to this overt branding. Thomas Newman's scores for the Bond films *Skyfall* (Sam Mendes, 2012), and *Spectre* (Sam Mendes, 2015), extrapolate on the traditional, iconic, franchise theme, yet truly do use the source material as a quotation. This is the essence of Bond, we are assured, yet it is an essence buried beneath, and surrounded by, a score whose own identity is never compromised, never schizophrenic. Such choices, though, depend on, perhaps, a more subtle sensibility, wherein a brand may shine through via its musical colours, less so via the musical equivalent of simulacra.

Despite the dominant trends described above, there are other approaches in contemporary film scoring than those found in big-budget superhero, fantasy, and science fiction franchises. The purpose of this book is to explore different aspects of some of these approaches through a combination of interviews with important film composers, and essays about particular features of those composers' work. In the interview portions of the book, six composers discuss their film music from the 1980s to the present day: Carter Burwell (b. 1955), Mychael Danna (b. 1958), Dario Marianelli (b. 1963), Rachel Portman (b. 1960), Zbigniew Preisner (b. 1955), and A.R. Rahman (b. 1967). The focus is on the practical considerations of film composition, the relationships each composer has with the moving image, technical considerations, personal motivations in composing, the relationships composers have with their directors, and their own creative processes.

The essays are written by fellow composers, musicologists and film academics, and explore particular elements of a composer's output. In the first chapter, Felicity Wilcox examines A.R. Rahman's film music through a comparative study of aspects of Indian and Western musical and cinematic conventions, and analyses five of Rahman's scores: two collaborations with Tamil director Mani Ratnam (*Roja*, 1992 and *Bombay*, 1995), one with Indian-Canadian director Deepa Mehta (*Fire*, 1996), and two with Danny Boyle (*Slumdog Millionaire*, 2008 and *127 Hours*, 2010). According to Wilcox, 'these films together represent important aspects of Tamil, Hindi, multinational and Western cinemas, and offer insights into how Rahman's music so successfully bridges the cultural and aesthetic divide between East and West.' In her analysis Wilcox not only discusses the key elements of Rahman's sound, but also highlights the important narrative functions of his music.

Jonathan Godsall's essay explores the network of fictional composers and compositions developed across the collaborations of Zbigniew Preisner and director Krzysztof Kieślowski. Godsall defines fictional music as 'original music, existing within a work of fiction's storyworld, that the work implies has been composed by one or more of its fictional characters'. The most obvious examples in the Kieślowski-Preisner collaboration are the music by Van den Budenmayer, a fictive eighteenth-century composer whose fictive music was composed by Preisner, and the central composer characters, and their work, in *Three Colours: Blue* (1993). Godsall's essay focuses primarily on the fictional compositions, considering their functions and effects within the films, the processes behind their creation by Preisner, and their place in his work more generally. However, as Godsall points out, despite the rich tradition of fictional music, musicology has barely begun to consider this phenomenon. According to Godsall, the essay, then, 'will be of wider interest in investigating a uniquely extensive but nonetheless illustrative filmic system of musical pretence'.

In his essay 'Burwell and Space: Inner, Outer, Environmental and Acoustical', Andrew Waggoner argues that Carter Burwell's film music 'impart[s] an immediate sense of place and of the varied, complex human relationships that unfold within it' through a specific, tripartite approach. As a result, our experience of a Burwell score, 'is one in which varied repetitions of a simple yet strongly *physical* set of musical gestures combine and re-combine with image over time to produce a seemingly limitless range of emotional and dramatic significations.' Waggoner explores this process in a discussion of four films he finds especially illustrative of Burwell's work: *Miller's Crossing* (Coen brothers, 1990), *Fargo* (Coen brothers, 1996), *Gods and Monsters* (Bill Condon, 1998) and *True Grit* (Coen brothers, 2010).

Lindsay Coleman's essay focuses on Rachel Portman's score for *Emma* (Douglas McGrath, 1996), and the manner in which it conforms to Finnish musicologist and semiologist Eero Tarasti's narratological model, as well as to his theories of embodiedness. The films scores of Rachel Portman are noted for their narratological value; the manner in which a given, innate point of view informs the gestural components of the music. Whether it is the duelling masculine embodiments of Homer and Dr Larch in the score for *The Cider House Rules* (Lasse Hallström, 1999), or the innately feminine components of the titular character of *Emma*, Coleman argues that Portman maintains a strong narratological hand in her compositions. Ultimately the essay treats Portman's score for *Emma* as proof of Tarasti's theories on the impact of narrative on music.

Joakim Tillman explores how Dario Marianelli uses solo instruments to represent individual characters, a convention that has a long tradition in opera and programme music. In representing characters, solo instruments most often speak *for*, and not just *about*, those characters, and Marianelli states that, in *Pride & Prejudice* (Joe Wright, 2005), 'the piano is the inner voice of Elizabeth'. In this way, solo instruments are used for what French literary theorist Gérard Genette calls internal focalization; that is, the narrator presents information from the point of view of a character. The essay examines the role different solo instruments play in conveying the inner states of Elizabeth Bennet in *Pride & Prejudice*, and Robbie Turner in *Atonement* (Joe Wright, 2007), but also how the subjective perspective in the latter film is made ambiguous by its denouement.

In 'Mychael Danna: Music as Metaphor', Peter Golub and Katy Jarzebowski use Danna's claim that a good film score asks more questions than it answers as a point of departure. They argue that Danna's approach shows a respect for the audience and functions like a literary metaphor, 'a device which complicates the text in order to facilitate a reader's understanding; each juxtaposition between music and image serves to complete a film's tonal context and deepen the viewer's awareness.' Thus, in contrast to traditional film music, where the audience associates certain musical conventions with an exact genre, emotion, or atmosphere (as a Pavlovian response), Danna creates meaning by suggestive juxtapositions, which activate the audience by offering the unexpected. Golub and Jarzebowski demonstrate how instruments and ensembles from non-Western cultures are interwoven with orchestral elements in *The Ice Storm* (Ang Lee, 1997) and *Life of Pi* (Ang Lee, 2012), enlivening the interplay between music and image in ways that encourage the audience to reflect on the significance of the 'dissonances' between music and picture. But they also discuss *Moneyball* (Bennett Miller, 2011) to show an approach where Danna uses a more traditional ensemble, the orchestra, in a reimagined way.

A common feature that unites all the composers in the first six chapters is that neither of them is part of the mainstream Hollywood tradition. On the contrary, many of them explicitly distance themselves from the conventions of Hollywood film music. The last chapter of the book, though, considers one of the giants of that tradition, John Williams. Born in 1932, Williams has had a long career, but is amazingly, as the last survivor of his generation, still active as a film composer. Instead of an interview,[9] this chapter begins with an introductory essay by Williams expert Emilio Audissino, who argues that it is Williams's versatility, and his talent for absorbing different musical idioms, that have allowed his career to successfully span over six decades of Hollywood history. As Audissino demonstrates, 'Williams can write full-orchestra romantic symphonic music, atonal avant-garde, ear-catching songs, hummable marches, jazz from different ages, and even tackle the pop idioms of the day.' Audissino also shows how Williams has made stylistic changes as a result of new circumstances in the film industry since the new millennium, with music now having to cope with a thicker and louder texture of sound effects, and be easily adaptable to last-minute changes in the editing of the film.

Audissino underlines that one of the most outstanding traits of Williams' film music is his talent for writing striking and memorable themes. As Konstantinos Zacharopoulos points out in the last essay, 'Musical Syntax in John Williams's Film Music Themes', film music themes have most often been discussed in terms of their narrative functions. Zacharopoulos, though, presents an analysis of the syntactic structure of Williams's themes between 1975 and 2013. He demonstrates how the main two theme types of the Classical era, the period and the sentence, have a prominent position in the composer's film music. Given Williams' admiration for Haydn, Mozart and Beethoven, Zacharopoulos finds this hardly surprising, and states that 'these forms contain and are characterized by all those elements that … contribute to a transparent and intelligible presentation of the musical idea, which leads inevitably to memorability'.

The first part of this introduction highlights some of the most important changes and trends in contemporary filmmaking and film scoring. Many film music critics, fans and composers strongly dislike those trends, and the quoted reviews are representative samples of opinions in film music criticism today. However, complaints about the present state of film music have been voiced before, for instance in the first half of the 1970s by film composers Elmer Bernstein and David Raksin in their respective articles, 'What Ever Happened to Great Movie Music' and 'Whatever Became of Movie Music?'[10] Both criticized the increasing use of pre-existing pop songs, which in their view just played on, quite unrelated to the events in the movie, instead of original scores tailored to suit the needs of the film. Raksin blamed this trend on changes in the film industry, where the appropriateness of the music to the film was secondary to selling records, garnering publicity for the film, and reaching demographically defined audiences.[11] However, during the second half of the 1970s, John Williams and others composers demonstrated that the orchestral and symphonic score was far from dead, and the composers included in this book prove that great movie music continues to thrive today.

Notes

1. David Fincher, 'Commentaries', Disc 1, *The Social Network*, Collector's Edition DVD, directed by David Fincher (Culver City, CA: Sony Pictures Home Entertainment, 2011).
2. HardTalk BBC podcast, 8 July 2016, http://open.live.bbc.co.uk/mediaselector/5/redir/version/2.0/mediaset/audio-nondrm-download-low/proto/http/vpid/p040tf93.mp3, accessed 15 July 2016.
3. Marc Ciafardini, 'Exclusive: Video Interview … Film Composer James Newton Howard', *Go, See, Talk*, 20 January 2012, http://goseetalk.com/interview-james-newton-howard/, accessed 15 July 2016.
4. Rick Florino, 'Interview: Hans Zimmer talks 'Inception' Score', *ARTIST direct*, 12 July 2010, http://www.artistdirect.com/entertainment-news/article/interview-hans-zimmer-talks-inception-score/7323382, accessed 15 July 2016.
5. James Southall, 'The Man of Steel', *Movie Wave*, 15 June 2013, http://www.movie-wave.net/man-of-steel/, accessed 15 July 2016.
6. Quoted after Matt Bromley, 'Essay: Invisible and inaudible? A Comparison of Post–Classical and Classical Hollywood Scoring', *mattbramley.com/journal*, 2 March 2015, http://mattbrombley.com/journal/2015/3/2/essay-invisible-and-inaudible-a-comparison-of-postclassical-and-classical-hollywood-scoring, accessed 15 July 2016.
7. Anon. (2013), 'First review: Howard Shore's soundtrack for The Hobbit: The Desolation of Smaug,' *TheOneRing.net*, 25 November 2013, http://www.theonering.net/torwp/2013/11/25/83271-first-review-howard-shores-soundtrack-for-the-hobbit-the-desolation-of-smaug/, accessed 15 July 2016.
8. Adam Bouyamourn, 'Album Review: With The Force Awakens, John Williams Finds His Majestic Music Playing Second Fiddle to Frenetic Pacing', *The National*, 22 December 2015, http://www.

thenational.ae/arts-life/music/album-review-with-the-force-awakens-john-williams-finds-his-majestic-music-playing-second-fiddle-to-frenetic-pacing, accessed 15 July 2016.
9. Regrettably, John Williams's busy schedule made it impossible to arrange an interview. Because of his tremendous importance, though, we considered this an insufficient reason not to include him.
10. Elmer Bernstein, 'What Ever Happened to Great Movie Music', *High Fidelity* (July 1972), and David Raksin, 'Whatever Became of Movie Music?', *Film Music Notebook* 1, No. 1 (Autumn 1974).
11. For a critical discussion of Bernstein's and Raksin's claims, see James Wierzbicki, *Film Music: A History* (New York: Routledge, 2009), 189–202.

Bibliography

Anon. 2013. First Review: Howard Shore's Soundtrack for the Hobbit: The Desolation of Smaug. *TheOneRing.net*, 25 November. http://www.theonering.net/torwp/2013/11/25/83271-first-review-howard-shores-soundtrack-for-the-hobbit-the-desolation-of-smaug/. Accessed 15 July 2016.

Bernstein, Elmer. 1972. What Ever Happened to Great Movie Music. *High Fidelity* 7: 55–58.

Bouyamourn, Adam. 2015. Album Review: With the Force Awakens, John Williams Finds His Majestic Music Playing Second Fiddle to Frenetic Pacing. *The National*, 22 December. http://www.thenational.ae/arts-life/music/album-review-with-the-force-awakens-john-williams-finds-his-majestic-music-playing-second-fiddle-to-frenetic-pacing. Accessed 15 July 2016.

Bromley, Matt. 2015. Essay: Invisible and Inaudible? A Comparison of Post-Classical and Classical Hollywood Scoring. *mattbramley.com/journal*, 2 March. http://mattbrombley.com/journal/2015/3/2/essay-invisible-and-inaudible-a-comparison-of-postclassical-and-classical-hollywood-scoring. Accessed 15 July 2016.

Ciafardini, Marc. 2012. Exclusive: Video Interview … Film Composer James Newton Howard. *Go, See, Talk*, 20 January. http://goseetalk.com/interview-james-newton-howard/. Accessed 15 July 2016.

Fincher, David. 2011. Commentaries. Disc 1. *The Social Network*, Collector's Edition DVD. Directed by David Fincher. Culver City, CA: Sony Pictures Home Entertainment.

Florino, Rick. 2010. Interview: Hans Zimmer Talks 'Inception' Score. *ARTIST direct*, 12 July. http://www.artistdirect.com/entertainment-news/article/

interview-hans-zimmer-talks-inception-score/7323382. Accessed 15 July 2016.
Raksin, David. 1974. Whatever Became of Movie Music? *Film Music Notebook* 1(1): 24–28.
Southall, James. 2013. The Man of Steel. *Movie Wave*, 15 June. http://www.movie-wave.net/man-of-steel/. Accessed 15 July 2016.
Wierzbicki, James. 2009. *Film Music: A History*. New York: Routledge.

CHAPTER 2

A.R. Rahman Interview

Lindsay Coleman

A.R. Rahman is probably the most widely recognized and popular film composer in the world, and also one of the most successful recording artists. He has 154 listed credits as composer. He has collaborated with celebrated Indian directors, such as Mani Ratnam, on films like *Roja* (1992), *Bombay* (1995) and *Dil Se* (1998), and Deepa Mehta, on *Fire* (1996), *Earth* (1998) and *Water* (2005). To Western audiences he is most familiar through his two collaborations with Danny Boyle, *Slumdog Millionaire* (2008) and *127 Hours* (2010).

The following interview was conducted, via Skype, in late 2014. Lindsay Coleman conducted the interview

Q: The 'Bombay Theme' is quite unusual. It is a lullaby.
A: A beautiful society, Bombay, had reached a point where there were groups caught in a serious conflict with one another, Hindus and Muslims. *Bombay*, the film, was created as a healing film experience, or at least it was pretending to be that for people. It was important for me to follow that, to create music about humanity, rather than about taking sides. It's about India, it's about what we stand for. It's

---

L. Coleman (✉)
Nunawading, Australia

© The Author(s) 2017
L. Coleman, J. Tillman (eds.), *Contemporary Film Music*,
DOI 10.1057/978-1-137-57375-9_2

got the raag of many national tunes actually. I don't know how it came in. Maybe subliminally.
Q: When the same music is used in *Lord of War* (Andrew Niccol, 2005), the focus is more on the pulse you have going through the piece.
A: Yes, that's right.
Q: How do you feel about how the piece can be used in many different ways, based on your orchestration?
A: Yeah, I never really thought about that. I wanted something simple, but also not too Indian. That is why the strings came in, the John Williams-ish strings. It integrates into this kind of music very well. It was a very long piece, but then I decided to shorten it. There were many phrases, but then I decided to cut them down.
Q: Did you decide to use it again in *Fire*, which you also scored, or was that decision made by the director?
A: I think in *Fire* it was the temp music, and people fell in love with it again. I tried to do something else, but then it was too late [laughs].
Q: You used autotune on your singing on *127 Hours*. On your singing for the song 'Tere Bina' in Mani Ratnam's *Guru* (2007) your voice is very beautiful, and technically good, so I was surprised you opted for that choice.
A: It's more like an effect. Also, the way I use autotune is not to correct my singing. It is more for the effect, and then we don't just leave it on, we bring it in and out. For some phrases I have it, for others not. It's a blessing and a curse.
Q: Do you think it makes your music in the film more accessible to a Western audience?
A: No, not really. I think when you're a keyboard player you get very finicky about tuning. You keep hearing perfect tuning constantly, then your voice doesn't match your expectations.
Q: People have credited your voice as getting better and better.
A: [laughs] Oh, that's sweet. Who said that?
Q: The Sigur Ros track 'Festival' is a major part of the music of *127 Hours*. It features as the main character finally escapes from the canyon. However, your music features as he is amputating his own arm in order to escape. Then Sigur Ros takes over immediately following.
A: The scoring finished. I was replacing temp music with my cues. For that sequence, 'Festival' was the temp music. When the sequence came back the mix was already done on it. Everybody really loved

'Festival' with that sequence, so we just decided to stick with it. I love that track! Sigur Ros!

Q: Your decision to go with guitar as one of the main instruments on *127 Hours*, what was that decision based off?

A: Whenever you have a guitar there is an independent feel. There's no strings attached. The character in the film was also very independent. He'd just put a pack on his back and head off on an adventure. So I felt the sound of the guitar really went with that.

Q: When he's amputating his arm the music is there to express pain. How does one go about orchestrating for pain?

A: The temp we had was very, very different. In Detroit, during my Jai Ho Tour in 2010, there was an accident and the stage collapsed. After that incident I said to my guitarist, Joel Shearer, 'let's go and write the track for the scene'. So it was produced in a similar state of mind. The piece is more agony, coming in a very different way. It's not literally 'pain'. Danny liked the piece a lot, and then we added strings on top of it. On top of that the sound design features this really annoying sound.

Q: So it's not physical pain which is being described by the music?

A: No. It's more of a struggle for redemption, a struggle for freedom. He's trying to get away from the boulder, and what it represents. I think the piece conveys that. He wants to free himself from his captured state.

Q: *127 Hours* is a tough story. Would you say your duet with Dido in the film was designed to make the tough story a little bit easier for the audience?

A: Yes. I come from a very different sensibility. I come from India. Some of the stuff is very focused, some of the stuff is all over the place. So I let the director, Danny, hear different ideas. In this particular case he started hearing the melody, and loved it so much that it became the theme for the canyon. Then it became the song. Then it was repeated at the end. One thing I believe is that the reason why the amputation scene was so effective, so devastating, was that this particular song makes the audience feel so vulnerable, so tender. It was too hard-hitting for the audience, the sequence.

Q: With Dido, did you request her?

A: I had a call from Dido's people to meet. So we started writing songs together. Then this opportunity developed on the film. She saw

the film, then agreed. She's never sung anybody else's composition before. And Rollo, her bother, also.
Q: What do you feel she brought to the track?
A: Her voice is very hypnotic. It is a very meditative voice. I liked the personality in her voice on 'Thank You', her hit from the early 2000s.
Q: Tan Dun referred to how he establishes a counterpoint relative to the image, and in turn to the editing. It is a sort of double counterpoint. Is your approach similar?
A: [laughs] I am not that intelligent. I tend to go by instinct. I just go with what works, what doesn't work. Sometimes I don't know how to explain it, but it tends to work, it falls into place. If I start analysing everything, which people do, amazingly, I don't think I'd do so much work [laughs]. Also, I need to coexist with the director's vision. Sometimes, they don't allow the approach we take, other times they will totally allow for the new approach we might take to the material. The graph of the movie which Danny constructs is for today's people. It's almost a disco feel. Even in the toughest stories it can have that 'four to the floor' feel. It's a style that really works.
Q: The first few bars of 'Jai Ho' feature a phrase universal to Bollywood music. Was this meant as a quote?
A: It is very formulaic. When you have a song like that you need an instantly recognizable hook.
Q: I grew up in Tamil Nadu and, in Tamil Cinema, violins are always used to open every song. You did not open songs with strings on your first major score, *Roja*. Why did you choose to forgo that convention of the time?
A: At that point my state of mind was, 'this is my last movie. I don't want to do anything from any other movies because Mani Ratnam, a great director who I really respect, has approached me for the movie.' Everything was about trying to find an alternative space. When I put this to the director, he helped me a great deal to try to find that spot. He was always trying to force himself to think differently from other people. We matched.
Q: 'Kehna Hi Kya', which you wrote for your next collaboration with Ratnam, *Bombay*, is a very beautiful song, a very vulnerable song, and was written in a minor key. It seems like an unusual choice.
A: In India, I think a minor key is not sad. Raags are much more than 'happy' and 'sad'. You have a raag for the morning, one for the night, one for romance, one for sadness, one for anger, one to make the

rain come down [laughs]. So it's not as simple as a happy tune is major, and a sad tune is minor. And this is something I face when I play for filmmakers in the West. I play in a minor key and they say, 'why are you playing in a minor key, this scene is a happy situation!' Hollywood! [laughs]

Q: In 'Tu Hi Re', of the same film, the editing of the film suggests the hero is contemplating suicide. Yet the song is optimistic, and tender, throughout. Are you consciously setting a different emotional tone for the music, in comparison with the images?

A: In those days I never used to think very hard. I always asked, 'what is the soul of the song? How can the song work for me?' I think Mani Ratnam cut it, then, in a way I didn't expect. Also, there was the magic of how the cast came together on the screen, Arvind Swami and Manisha Koirala, the cinematography, the ambience. In this particular case there was a lot of doubt, because there was no rhythm in the song. The emotion of love which came out of that song saved the day, though.

Q: You could also be quite conventional at that period in your career. When Arvind Swami peeks under Koirala's veil you are playing typical comedy music, for a Tamil film.

A: [laughs] True! I feel very bad when I listen to it now.

Q: Would you take it out if you could?

A: Yes, maybe.

Q: With 'Latika's Theme', used in *Slumdog Millionaire*, the interesting choice is to put it at the end of the film, rather than just using a fragment of it for the track 'Mausaam', when Dev Patel sees his love at Victoria Station. Why was that decision made?

A: 'Latika's Theme', because Danny liked it, he started using it in reverse, pasting part of it in previous scenes, like when he sees her at Victoria Station. It was a good choice on Danny's part. At that point in the film, at the station, it was really too busy a point to play something so soft, I would say. That was why we made the choice to make it more orchestral than vocal at that point.

Q: It's frustrating to me, the version of it in the film, because the entire piece is very beautiful, but it's only featured in the last 30 seconds of the film!

A: That's true. If it was a Hindi movie it would have been all over the place. The movie is partly a love story, but it's got so many other layers. Maybe Danny didn't want to take it *too* much in that direction, he just wanted to touch, and go.

Q: Latika doesn't speak very much. Jamal—Dev Patel—doesn't see her very much in the film. Technically, the romance is entirely in the mind of the audience. Did you feel the music was tying together the characters in a way which was difficult to achieve for the film itself? The theme makes it possible for the audience to think, 'oh, Latika is *this* type of person.'

A: True. You know I never thought about that. You know, actually, it wasn't even meant as a theme, it was meant to be a song. When I did the song the lyrics were describing too much of the situation, so that is why we made it more of a humming thing. Then the song version on the soundtrack was really more of an afterthought.

Q: On 'Pi's Lullaby' by Mychael Danna, for the film *Life of Pi* (Ang Lee, 2012), I noted that there is technically something of an absence of quarter tones, and he explained that, for a very big film such as that, you could not have music that would be too foreign to the ear of a very broad audience. Can you relate to that situation?

A: The more I work in Hollywood, the more I learn about how they crack the code of producing something which is loved all over the world. I think what they prefer is to have the main themes more mainstream, and subtle filler more regional. It passes as the regional character, but it is not forced on a mainstream audience so they say 'what the hell is that!' It is really about creating a balance. You can put a Karnatak burst in [singing], in one of those interstitial spots. I just did that on a film I am working on with Lasse Hallström and Oprah Winfrey.

Q: Do you think people are using Indian music just as an exotic touch?

A: Yes, it is just used as a palette. Absolutely, it is just being used as something which is exotic. When you go to a South Indian film, and you hear a raag ... Imagine you have a scenario and you have a teacher and student looking at one another, and you would have a specific raag [sings]. Here in the West people would hear that and would say 'what the hell is that?' But for us it immediately brings the smell of sandlewood, a sense of sanctity, all of this comes in as soon as the raag is sung. There is so much history behind each nuance of a raag.

Q: But Danny Boyle is very liberated in his outlook on human nature.

A: Absolutely. I'm not talking about Danny Boyle, more Western sensibilities in general. I thought Mychael Danna's score for *Pi* was amazing, and the whole movie is about what is in the Lullaby.

Q: He also believes that there is a strong interpretative element in his scores, where his view is different from the director's, and so in turn from the audience. Do you hope to enter such an interpretive realm, in your scores?

A: I want to do more of that. I want to do more on the classical side, once I have paid off the loans for the school I have founded. I want to write more piano pieces. I have opened a huge music centre, and to fund this I am doing, left, right and centre, things I normally wouldn't do.

Q: You want to do something completely new?

A: I want to, God willing. The more you get older the more you want to go into the things you really wanted to do. In the past four years I have developed a greater desire to study the history of music. The possibility of using any orchestra I choose is now a reality.

Q: When you are characterized as the Mozart of Madras, how do you feel about that name?

A: I hate it. It's not fair being compared to Mozart. Mozart is great. I write film music. People get offended at the comparison.

Q: Elliot Goldenthal feels he is having a conversation with Mozart, and Beethoven, and all the greats when he composes. Do you feel similar?

A: No, for me the more I came into the Sufi spirituality, it is more cleansing, and every thought and feeling I have in my mind, I try to get a pure feeling for whatever notes I play. That is on the softer songs. For the others I go off my energy for how the sounds will play. The sound of the orchestra inspires me to write more stuff. The brass! Staccato! Whatever. What Elliot's talking about is human; what I'm talking about is the highest possible perspective. For me everything comes from the Creator. Everything painful, and wonderful, comes from the same source. When you tune into that source, which doesn't happen very often, He becomes you. That is a state you always want to achieve; when you become nothing, only pureness exists. That's something people ask me: 'why am I having a spiritual feeling when I listen to your love songs?' Well, that is a long story.

Q: Do you feel 'Tere Bina' is a very personal song for you?

A: Yes, I do. I am such a fan of Nusrat Fateh Ali Khan. Most of the vocabulary came from him, from 'Tore Bina'. Of course it had been in Hindi movies before, but I heard 'Tore Bina', his version. 'Tere Bina' is totally different, but when I did it I did it as a dedication to him.

Q: The quality of your voice has great clarity on 'Tere Bina'. What do you credit that to?
A: We had another singer. But Mani Ratnam said to me, 'I don't want that song if you don't sing it.' I was fasting for Ramadan at the time. He said he wouldn't shoot the scene in the film, where the music and song plays, on the following day, if I didn't record it for him. So, I literally sang it an hour before I broke my fast. Maybe that was something which made it very soft and nice, I would say.
Q: You described feeling troubled about receiving your Oscars.
A: The after-effect of winning, for the year which followed ... how much can you shake hands? How much can you be diplomatic, and say 'God is great'? After a while you feel like throwing up. Leave me alone. I had that feeling for a couple of years. But, it is a huge achievement. When I brought my Oscars through customs in the US, the officials noted I had an Oscar. The minute the Oscars came out almost 100 people started to rush over to have a look! I realized how huge it was.
Q: You are beloved by many millions of people in India. How is winning the Oscars different from that?
A: It's a strange thing in my life. I wonder 'do I really deserve it?' When I did my first movie, usually a national award comes for someone who does one hundred movies. Straight away, I won! Like many things in my life. This, again, was probably only my third film in English, then 'boom'! I never thought when writing, or even mixing it, that it would have that effect. It was only 18 cues. Normally for a film it will be 153 cues, 93 cues.
Q: Speaking of cues, one of your first hits was 'Choti Si Aasha' in *Roja*. The last portion of 'Choti Si Aasha', is that segment of the music derived from an improvisation?
A: Yes, in a way. I wanted that to be a fisherman's voice, but not a typical South Indian sound. That's why I used a lot of reverb in it. Reverb was the 'in' thing at that time.
Q: Do you feel a slave to fashion? The guitar on 'Chaiya Chaiya' is very '90s'.
A: I don't really see that. Sometimes I do something very retro; I like it. Unless it's a dance song I'm not very religious about it. I draw from all over the place. Even in our lives we might listen to an 80s song, feel good about it, a 90s song, feel good about it, listen to something now, and we might like it. If I like something, I use it.

Q: What about musical purists?
A: In India nobody used to care. In the West I think people can be very, very particular. People will say 'oh, that's a reggae sound' or whatever. But they are open too.
Q: You speak about needing to stop composing sometimes, to give your brain a rest.
A: True. When I'm on the plane I don't want to even listen to the soundtrack of films. I just listen to them without sound, activate the subtitles, don't put headphones on. Disconnecting, then coming back, can work really well. Also prayer. I pray five times a day. That process of disconnecting helps give you perspective. You come back and listen again, and say, 'oh, why is this sounding like this?' When you are in it you don't realize where the flaws are. When you come back you actually listen like a listener. Then you can shape the music much better.
Q: You are your first audience.
A: Absolutely. If you are in this process, then you can understand what is going on. Apart from that, people, most of them, are happy about it.

CHAPTER 3

The 'Alternate Space' of A.R. Rahman's Film Music

Felicity Wilcox

Introduction

S. Dileep Kumar was born on 6 January 1967 in Madras (now Chennai), Tamil Nadu, India. His father, R. K. Shekhar, a film composer and conductor, died when his son was nine years old. Rahman went to work as an arranger for local recording artists to help his mother, Kareema, support the family, and played keyboards for several music directors, including Malayalam composer M. K. Arjunan, and star Tamil composer Ilayaraja. He received a scholarship to learn Western classical music at the Trinity College of Music, London. As a young man he converted from Hinduism to Sufi Islam, changing his name to Allah Rakha Rahman. After successfully composing for advertisements for several years, he made his film music debut in 1992, with the score for Tamil director Mani Ratnam's film *Roja*, which won many awards in India, and paved the way for Rahman's success at the international level. His music became well known to audiences outside India after British director Danny Boyle's *Slumdog Millionaire* was released in 2008. In 2009 the film won Academy Awards for Best Original Score and Best Original Song, for 'Jai Ho'. Rahman went on to score

---

F. Wilcox (✉)
Lecturer in Music and Sound, School of Communication, Faculty of Arts and Social Sciences, University of Technology Sydney, Australia

© The Author(s) 2017
L. Coleman, J. Tillman (eds.), *Contemporary Film Music*,
DOI 10.1057/978-1-137-57375-9_3

Boyle's next film, *127 Hours* (2010), and was again nominated for an Oscar. Rahman has been embraced by popular music royalty in the West, counting among his collaborators icons such as Dave Stewart, Mick Jagger and Andrew Lloyd Webber.

A.R. Rahman was steeped in the natural syncretism of Indian film music from birth through his father's work as a composer and conductor, and his own early entry into professional music. Rahman's official website acknowledges the legacy of 'past and contemporary Chennai film composers' in influencing his ability to successfully blend musical genres in a way that 'cuts across the spectrum of classes and cultures within Indian society'.[1] Yet, Rahman's music is remarkable because it speaks to Western audiences as well, despite drawing consistently on Eastern (and often specifically Islamic) aesthetics. He offers this insight into the way he successfully manages different cultural references within his scores:

> The more I work in Hollywood, the more I learn about how they crack the code of producing something which is loved all over the world. I think what they prefer is to have the main themes more mainstream, and subtle filler more regional.[2]

Artful mixing of mainstream and regional cultural reference points is a large part of the appeal of films like *Fire* and *Slumdog Millionaire*: films made about Indian families, with English dialogue, whose stories and characters resonate with both Indian and Western audiences. A strong cinematic framework couches elements that may feel foreign, depending on the cultural orientation of the viewer, but that pass easily into meaning when supported by the familiarity of the movie format. Rahman's approach to his craft is similar, with musical influences on the one hand drawn from a wide spectrum of global cultures to specifically represent the characters and situations in his films, while a standard approach to instrumentation and scoring often dovetails with these.

This chapter examines Rahman's film music through a comparative discussion of aspects of Indian and Western musical and cinematic conventions, and analyses of five of Rahman's scores: two collaborations with Tamil director Mani Ratnam (*Roja*, 1992 and *Bombay*, 1995), one collaboration with Indian-Canadian director Deepa Mehta (*Fire*, 1996), and two collaborations with Danny Boyle (*Slumdog Millionaire*, 2008 and *127 Hours*, 2010). These films together represent important aspects of Tamil, Hindi, multinational and Western cinemas, and offer insights into how

Rahman's music so successfully bridges the cultural and aesthetic divide between East and West.

Comparative Conventions in Indian and Western Film Music

Indian cinema is loved the world over for its larger-than-life film song performances. Ethnomusicologists Joseph Getter and B. Balasubrahmaniyan state, 'Film songs are essential to the creation and reception of movies in India, and they play a key role in the expressive nature of the cinema ... Of all the music genres in India, film songs of any language possess the largest audience, and are the most geographically and culturally widespread.'[3] These original songs are specifically composed to broadcast the characters' internal thoughts and discourse through lyrics that relate to the plot of the film and also to broader contexts that allow a song to translate as a piece of popular music.

The film song phenomenon in mainstream Indian cinema separates it from its contemporary Western equivalent. While Indian films have correspondences with Hollywood filmed musicals, the distinct structural and aesthetic features of the latter genre are not necessarily present in Indian films, where singing and dancing are rarely central to the story. Film music scholar Guido Heldt argues that the characteristic feature of Hollywood musicals is 'the form of musical numbers that showcase the stars and their talents',[4] a characteristic which applied to Indian films before playback technology was adopted mid-last-century in India, but which is no longer the case, as most Indian actors do not sing but instead lip-sync their song performances to the voices of well-known recording stars. Likewise, while the actors are generally present in the montage of film song set-pieces, professional dancers are often cast to represent them in intricately choreographed and technically demanding dance sequences. In most Indian films 'the number ... is a function of the plot', where in Hollywood musicals, 'the plot ... is a function of the numbers: the scaffolding for the numbers it has to frame and motivate, however flimsily'.[5] Originally composed film songs are a staple in most genres of Indian cinema; an integral component of the nation's film music practice unparalleled in Western cinema.

In the West, from the late 1950s, through the 60s and into the 70s, songs were composed primarily for the title sequences to feature films, and often themed in instrumental versions that underscored the dramatic action.[6] The 1960s saw the emergence of the 'compilation soundtrack' as a way of scoring films that continues to the present, the score consisting of a collection of popular songs, with no thematic links, often drawn from a variety of genres, which support narrative through a 'system of extramusical allusions and associations activated by the score's referentiality'.[7] In this treatment, as noted by film music theorist Anahid Kassabian, 'perceivers bring external associations with the songs into their engagements with the film',[8] which are personal and historical, and operate quite differently from the way in which original film songs affect their audience. Songs in Western cinema today, with few exceptions, differ from film songs in mainstream Indian cinema in that they generally pre-exist the film, are sourced from a variety of artists, and have already had their moment in time, which the film attempts to exploit.[9] According to musicologist Jeff Smith, the two main ways in which popular songs are incorporated into Western films are, first, 'as a kind of referential intertext capable of commenting on or satirizing the image track', or second, as music for montage sequences, where rapid and rhythmic editing of images is accompanied by a song which dominates the soundtrack, creating the 'aural-visual set piece that ... became a staple of rock scoring', in a style that predated and later reflected the music video.[10] These techniques for using songs as film music are prevalent in Indian cinema as well, in addition to the ubiquitous presentation of songs as musical performances that sit somewhere at the boundaries of the diegesis. Heldt elaborates on Rick Altman's term 'supra-diegetic' to describe song performances in filmed musicals, describing them as 'transcendent spaces where normal diegetic logic is suspended, music takes over, and the genre reaches its purpose in displays of pure performative bliss'.[11]

Another point of difference between Indian and Western cinemas is that Indian film composers, or 'music directors' as they are known at home, are first and foremost songwriters, and the underscore, or 'background music', is considered ancillary to the songs, which are characteristically presented via six to eight highly choreographed and dramatically edited music scenes per film.[12] Rahman's Tamil film songs with lyricist Vairamuthu, including 'Chinna Chinna' from *Roja*,[13] and 'Uyire' from *Bombay*,[14] met with critical and commercial success in India, contributing enormously to the success of these films. This reflects what Greg Booth, a scholar of South Asian music, refers to as 'the ambiguous identity of film songs as popular music and as components of popular films'.[15] 'Jai Ho' achieved similar goals for *Slumdog Millionaire* both in India and in the West, and was incorporated at the end of Boyle's film as a set-piece homage to Hindi film song tradition. More often, Rahman's original songs for Hollywood films conform to Western aesthetics through providing a non-diegetic accompaniment to images; yet, as original songs composed specifically to speak to the films' characters and situations, and often featuring the composer's own vocals, they remain somewhat unconventional by Western standards.

Aside from the 'compilation score' model mentioned above, which capitalizes on the synergy between contemporary film and popular music, Western film music aesthetics are largely dominated by the model of the 'classical film score'. Film music theorist Kathryn Kalinak cites the latter's conventions as: 'selective use of non-diegetic music; correspondence between that music and the implied content of the narrative; a high degree of synchronization between music and narrative action; and the use of leitmotiv as a structural framework'.[16] Leitmotif is 'a theme, or other coherent musical idea, clearly defined so as to retain its identity if modified on subsequent appearances, whose purpose is to represent or symbolize a person, object, place, idea, state of mind, supernatural force or any other ingredient in a dramatic work'.[17]

Directly translated from the German, a leitmotif is a 'lead' or 'guide' motif that serves to guide the listener through the narrative.[18] The term was first coined in the late nineteenth century to refer to Richard Wagner's use of recurrent musical motifs in his operas, which forged powerful links between text, drama and music. Wagner's leitmotifs were remarkable for the way in which they were able to 'embody such a power and directness of expression that the emotion concerned would be recalled when the motif itself returned, even if action or text no longer alluded directly to its original associations'.[19] Leitmotifs are important signifiers in music for films, and has now been assimilated as a scoring convention in many world cinemas, following its adaptation after opera to early Western multimedia forms such as ballet, pantomime and musicals, leading to its rapid take-up in film music in the early twentieth century. Film music scholar James Wierzbicki cites musicological discourse that problematizes the appropriation of the term leitmotif when referring to 'film-score themes', arguing that 'Wagner's technique (which involved fragmentary motifs capable of being not just developed but also intermixed) differs substantially from the basic Hollywood approach (which involved tune-like musical ideas that were for the most part simply reiterated whenever their associated filmic entities entered the narrative)'.[20] No doubt these commentators seek to differentiate hack film composition from Wagner's approach where motifs 'move beyond their exact or varied repetition at textually appropriate moments into the kind of transformation that creates deeper dramatic resonances and larger-scale musical continuities',[21] yet to deny that sophisticated film scores such as Bernard Herrmann's *Vertigo* (Hitchcock, 1958) apply leitmotifs in complex ways is to do a disservice to the best exemplars of the 'classical' score. Indeed, the ability to skilfully weave leitmotif into the overall text of a film score is an aspect of compositional technique that sits at the very core of the accomplished screen composer's craft.

In India, the association of characters with musical themes has correspondences in traditional forms of theatre, codified in the *Nātya Śastra*, the first or second century C. E. Sanskrit treatise on drama. Music is organized selectively 'so that audiences may identify a particular character by hearing a composition'.[22] While it is tempting to speculate that Wagner may have South Asian influences to thank for the leitmotif it is at least clear that Indian music directors, whether influenced by Indian or Western precedents, draw on leitmotif to define character in their scores. A.R. Rahman's use of leitmotif has developed from a simplistic approach in his early films to a certain level of complexity in his later films. In *Slumdog Millionaire*, echoes of 'Latika's Theme' sprinkle other cues as a way of bringing the girl's character to mind during her long absences from the narrative; in *127 Hours*, the ethereal melody of the signature song 'If I Rise' is rearranged to underscore the canyon landscape, and also turns up in the gruelling amputation scene layered with electric guitars and drums.

Unlike in the West, where instrumental themes to films often become part of a shared musical and cultural lexicon,[23] in India themes are 'occasionally a topic for discussion among fans and filmgoers, but … usually do not circulate outside of the film itself as do the songs'.[24] Rahman himself provides a notable exception to this rule with his theme for *Bombay*, which is so well loved that it has been reappropriated into many other contexts.[25] Indian films that omit songs entirely and include only background music tend to belong to the Parallel Cinema[26] genre, which has appeal among urban audiences, without enjoying the box-office success of Bollywood films with their quota of film songs.

Due to the coexistence of diverse ethnicities, religions, cultural practices and languages in twentieth-century India, its film music became a melting pot of styles. From the 1930s onwards, background music began to integrate a steadily growing range of foreign influences such as large orchestras, Latin music, colonial-era jazz and dance band styles, Western classical and popular music genres, traditional Indian instruments and folk music, Hindustani and Carnatic classical music, Bharata Natyam dance music, urban Indipop, and many genres of religious music.[27] The classical Hollywood score, central to 'compelling yet absolutely unambiguous storytelling'[28] in the West, was far from standard fare in Eastern cinema's musical diet. Film audiences in India were interested in different kinds of stories, and Indian filmmakers and music directors had different ways to tell them.

Many cultural and socio-economic factors were driving the gradual standardization of Indian film music as a broadly multicultural practice by the end of the twentieth century, when Rahman was approached by Ratnam to write his first film score. This set the foundations for the 'alternate space' his music inhabits. His compositional eclecticism cannot be discussed without making reference to his predecessor, the Tamil music director Ilayaraja, whose 'music is distinctive for its complex arrangements and unique blend of Tamil folk, Indian classical, and Western classical and pop music genres'.[29] Rahman's *Bombay* theme contains similar influences, opening with a melody based on a Tamil lullaby,[30] played on the traditional Indian bamboo flute (bansuri) and later developed in a more 'classical' Hollywood rendering by the orchestra's string section. This theme functions as a microcosm for the whole score, which alternates consistently between Indian and global elements. In this respect, Rahman's music exemplifies the Indian film music aesthetic of a natural 'world music' that is evolved and unselfconscious, reflecting the diverse cultures assimilated over centuries into contemporary India.

Aspects of Tonality and Extra-Musical Meaning in Indian and Western Music

If one accepts that in Western cinema the 'classical' score 'remains the standard with which film music in general continues to be compared',[31] a brief analysis of the key musical conventions embodied in that standard is helpful in understanding how an alternate sound might be constructed. Musicologist Ronald Rodman cites the scores of leading mid-twentieth-century composers Max Steiner and Erich Wolfgang Korngold as exemplars of the classic Hollywood score, with their 'traits of nineteenth-century concert and operatic music. These traits include: the use of symphony orchestras ... (and) an adherence to functional tonality with highly conventional Germanic-style chromaticism.'[32] Western film music's basis in nineteenth-century tonality and functional harmony has important ramifications for how narrative and music interact within a film, which, as proposed by Royal S. Brown, have to do with expectation and resolution.[33] The dialogue between what is musically 'expected' and what is expected from the drama within a scene is vital to filmic narrative.

Ethnomusicologist John Blacking's extensive field research in Africa last century supported the idea that extra-musical communication only occurs within frameworks of culture where associations that pertain to tonality, rhythm, performance style and the like are shared, and that sounds that are divorced from their cultural environment are unlikely to communicate with any consistency.[34] Shared understanding of its tonal language is key to the longevity of the 'classical score' in the West, yet Rahman positions himself both within and outside its tonal framework. For example, he makes the observation that 'a minor key is not sad'[35] a view that, to Western ears, would appear to be anathema, and which reflects the extent to which Rahman's Indian musical heritage shapes his perception of modality. Royal S. Brown asserts that an 'extraordinarily important element of tonality constantly exploited by film music is the major mode-minor mode dialectic ... To this day, composers of film music continue to exploit the emotional implications of the major/minor dialectic, no matter how modern their style, as long as it is based in tonality.'[36] If this is so, how does Rahman communicate so effectively with his global audience?

Musicologists Phillip Tagg and Bob Clarida arrive at the same position as Rahman in their survey of music for the mass media, *Ten Little Tunes*, dismissing binary interpretations of modality such as 'major is happy and minor is sad' as 'culturally restricted assumptions about links between the musical and paramusical'.[37] They explain:

> The unimodal development of the nineteenth-century Central European tonal system put minor modes de facto into the cultural position of archaisms. Ousted by the then 'more modern' major key, minor could acquire general connotations of oldness and the past and, by further connotation resident in the European bourgeois symbolic universe, lead associations ... into nostalgia, quietude and sadness.[38]

Tagg and Clarida further assert that, outside the Central European canon on which most Hollywood film music is based, associations between modality and affect are less codified: 'There has never been anything intrinsically sad in most of Europe about minor modes, as anyone will testify who has sung, played or danced to songs like *What Shall We Do With The Drunken Sailor*.'[39] Rather, they cite research that establishes that sounds that are quiet, slow, of long duration, limited range, more legato than staccato, low in pitch, whose timbres comprise lower, rather than higher, frequency content, and that incorporate downwards-sliding tones, are most universally associated with 'sad' affect. By way of illustration, these parameters, rather than any clear minor modality, can be heard in Rahman's cues for the night scenes in *127 Hours*, where the main protagonist experiences his most acute moments of despair and disorientation. Here is music that broadcasts a depressed emotional state in any language: unidentifiable timbres, guitar harmonics of indeterminate pitch, sustained bass drones, low-register pads sliding through downwards portamento gestures, dissonant chords on guitar muffled by heavy reverb, and the absence of a rhythmic pulse.

Rahman's response to modality relies on his own set of influencing cultural factors. He refers to the Hindustani and Carnatic traditions of Indian classical music, where there is a raga 'for the evening, there's one for the morning, there's one for the afternoon, one for the night, one for romance, one for sadness, one for anger, one to make the rain come down'.[40] This points to the complexities of a musical tradition founded on the ancient Vedic aesthetic theory of *rasa*: 'initially associated with theatre and poetry; it referred both to the state of bliss induced by artistic creation, and to the transitory states of being such creation induced in an audience. Traditionally there were eight *rasa*, linked with deities, colours, and the eight permanent emotions: love, laughter, sorrow, anger, energy, fear, disgust, and surprise'.[41]

Music was used in theatre to coordinate aspects of a performance and to induce specific emotional responses from an audience. Today, the performance of a certain raga is still calculated to induce a particular emotion, or *rasa*, in the listener. The ways in which this is done are complex. While ragas are identified in part by their mode, other factors come into play in their classification, such as intervallic organisation of modes, which can vary depending upon the direction of the melody, and the manner in which ornamentation is applied, which can often be the discriminator between two different ragas:

> Ornamentation can be defined as the connection between two given notes to enhance the beauty and aesthetic value of the raga. Thus many microtonal variations are seen in the frequency of any given note from one raga to another.[42]

Aside from modality, microtonality, varying scales in ascent and descent, and the execution of ornamentation, ragas can also be identified based on their position in a concert programme, the time of day they are performed, and subtle variations of phrasing in performance.[43] For Indians to draw extra-musical meaning from modality, there is clearly a more extensive vocabulary to consider than that of major and minor intervals.

Indian classical music is based on three core components: drone, melody and rhythm. Drone, by its nature as a static harmonic entity, precludes any possibility of progression along the lines of functional Western harmony, which moves in vertical pitch organization that adheres to strict rules as to chord progression, voice-leading and intervallic layering. Rather, in the complex modal system that characterizes the ragas of Indian classical music, intervals may vary between major and minor versions according to the expressive choices of the performer, and factors such as melodic direction and ornamental style. The drone provides a non-reactive harmonic support for the flexible melodic extemporization essential to performance of a raga. The most important instruments in both north and south Indian classical music have sets of strings for melodic and drone performance, including the long-necked lutes (the sitar and vina), the sarod, a smaller lute, and the bowed lutes (sarangi and dilruba). The four-string tambura (or its electronic equivalent) provides the continuous drone that underpins every raga performance.

Drones feature in all Rahman's scores for Indian and Western films, often underpinning ornamented, agile and microtonal melodic lines rich with shakes, vibratos, trills, grace notes, turns, portamenti and glissandi. He explores the full range of modes, sometimes shifting from one to another within a single tune or even within a phrase. Here is a composer who could not be less interested in limiting himself to the Western standards of Ionian major and harmonic minor modes. Consider, for example, the opening melody of the *Bombay* theme. Based on a Tamil lullaby, it is 'music about humanity',[44] chosen to represent a united India to support Ratnam's aspiration to heal a wounded nation in the wake of the Bombay riots of the early 1990s. Although its mode is the Aeolian (natural minor), the high-frequency timbres and high-register pitches of bell and bansuri, the melody's quick tempo, agile ornamentation, repeated staccato notes, and the lullaby genre's warm associations with childhood, family and security combine to give this tune an appealing and reassuring presence. The only element that adds ambiguity to the theme is the bass synthesizer drone, suggestive of a brewing darkness. When the bansuri motif gives way to a raw male vocal that articulates a note somewhere between yelling and singing, and a slow, low percussion groove sets in, we begin to fear the worst. Here, clear emotional signifying is achieved without the formulaic use of major modality as a trope for 'goodness', and minor for 'sadness or badness'.[45]

ROJA, 1992 AND *BOMBAY*, 1995

The collaboration between A.R. Rahman and Tamil director Mani Ratnam has changed the way films are scored in India. Working in collaboration with Ratnam, Rahman introduced an expansive sound to Tamil films that incorporated orchestral instruments, samplers, synthesizers, voices and traditional Indian instruments in a way that challenged established treatments at that time, and brought a new element to the mix: the voice of music technology. Rather than putting the studio at the service of the orchestra to produce the most transparent sound possible, the sound of digital technology became a presence in its own right. Getter and Balasubrahmaniyan claim that Rahman's success 'has shifted musical tastes and production strategies so much that now all of Tamil film music seems to bear a resemblance to his sounds and methods'.[46] The sound of technology characterizes all of Rahman's film scores, from *Roja*, which somewhat self-consciously featured sci-fi synth effects, synth brass leads and oscillating pads as underscore for Rishi's cryptology work in a high-tech computer lab; to later scores for *Slumdog Millionaire* and *127 Hours*, where Rahman selectively applied autotune and other signal processing for specific colouristic effect.[47] When he was approached by Ratnam to compose for *Roja* in 1992, Rahman was a tech-savvy composer in his twenties, with a background in the advertising industry, running the latest musical equipment, and indoctrinated with the focus on high production values central to the commercial music industries. From early on, his Chennai studio, Panchathan Record Inn, was widely regarded as one of the most modern in the whole of India. His generation of composers in the West were exploiting the power of samplers, a revolution in digital audio at the time, which allowed pre-recorded, bite-size performances (samples) to be layered with other sounds via MIDI sequencing software. The sound of Rahman that so changed Indian cinema is very much the sound of a young studio musician with a good head for the latest gear.

Rahman's incidental music in his early Tamil films at times displays a compositional inconsistency that sits at odds with his refined approach to film song in these films, and perhaps reflects the broader aesthetic in Indian cinema that prioritizes songs over 'background' music. His overuse of pastiche and clumsily rendered comic cues in *Roja* and *Bombay* contrasts with his later scores, which maintain the high level of song craft evident from the outset of his career, as well as offering a more nuanced and integrated compositional approach towards underscore. At its most successful, Rahman's underscore for *Roja* and *Bombay* incorporates leitmotifs to contribute to narrative development in line with the most important function of the classical Hollywood score, blending instruments and voices in an evocative manner that would come to define the Indian composer's individual style.

Rahman's preference for the human voice as a timbre to communicate the feelings and identity of characters was established with his first score for *Roja*. During various conversations about marriage, a non-diegetic female sings in a sweet tone, conveying the yearning for romantic love that drives the plot at these points. The Islamic identity of the rebel gang and boss is frequently heralded by a 'call-to-prayer'-style vocal melody; a Bulgarian female chorus signals the sound of 'otherness' in Kashmir, where Rishi is being held hostage, and Rahman makes use of a multitude of wordless vocal samples in this film to evoke aggression and hostility during the scenes when Rishi tussles with his captors. For the film song 'Rukkumani, Rakkumani' Rahman recorded a variety of singers, from professionals such as S. P. Balasubrahmanyam and K. S. Chithra, who feature as soloists, through choruses of children, to solos by vocally untrained Tamil women. The range of voices engaged in the singalong-style melody evokes the strong community spirit of Roja's village, with contrast and interaction set up through conversational question-answer melodic phrasing.

Again, in *Bombay*, Rahman uses voices to signal the incompatible religious affiliations of his two main characters, Shekhar, a Hindu, and Shaila Bano, a Muslim, who fall desperately in love. Early in the film, when the wind blows the beautiful young woman's veil off her face, we hear a high-register female voice articulating an ornamented natural minor melody, leaning at times into an augmented fourth. The wordless and irregular contour of this vocal line does not fit within Shekhar's modern mainstream world. Yet Bano's alluring exoticism is repeatedly reinforced through musical signifiers: when she runs away to avoid an arranged marriage after a violent confrontation with her strict Muslim father, her religious identity is signalled by a male voice singing in a style resembling the 'call-to-prayer'; when she first meets Shekhar's disapproving Hindu landlords, there is an accompanying melodic line in the Phrygian minor mode so characteristic of Arabic music. When Bano watches a demonstration in the street, male singers are heard very distantly in the score; voices that steadily grow in volume through the underscore as the conflict between Muslims and Hindus increasingly dominates the narrative. To newspaper headlines announcing the 1992 Ayodhya riots, a Qawwali[48] singer's melody comes to rest on the fifth above a bass drone, clashing with the tritone sung by another male voice, in a dissonance that works as a metaphor for the disharmony unfolding in the plot. At the start of the film's second half the Islamic Qawwali vocal rises high above the tambura drone, a feature of classical Hindustani music; we hear raw, screaming vocals when the murders that spark the second riots occur, Qawwali singing when a family's house is set on fire, as Bano and Shekhar race to the hospital in search of their missing sons, and again in a later scene when an Imam visits Muslims wounded in street violence. The raw beauty of the ornamented high-register Qawwali vocal, sung loud and without words, evokes a strong emotion every time it is heard as counterpoint to images of violence and suffering, becoming in effect the voice of India's pain. In *Bombay*, strategic use of vocals that reference religious identity is an important device that promotes both musical and narrative cohesion across this long film.

Although Rahman's widespread use of vocal performances in his underscore to communicate subtext is unusual by Western standards, it is perhaps a natural extension of the many vocal performances featured in Indian film songs, whose role is as much functional as commercial and aesthetic. Until very recently Indian films portrayed a society in which marriages were arranged by parents, and where young men and women were not permitted to speak to each other beforehand, so opportunities for dialogue that revealed the true feelings of young lovers and at the same time adhered to basic standards of 'real' storytelling were limited. The film song as a surreal set-piece, where disbelief is momentarily suspended, and metaphors for love and lust abound, is a necessary device that allows singers to articulate the 'unsayable' thoughts of the film's characters. This is particularly the case in the songs 'Kannalanae', 'Uyire Uyire' and 'Hamma Hamma' in *Bombay*, and for 'Rukkumani Rukkumani' and 'Pudhu Vellai Mazhai' in *Roja*, which convey the passionate and suggestive words the protagonists *would* share if young men and women were able to speak to each other of such things. Film songs in India are an outlet for the suppressed sexuality of its society, with the sensual quality of the singing voice in the Indian tradition perfectly suited to obliquely convey love's emotions, and the standard musical arrangements and choreography for large groups of performers in effect making intimate lyrics more palatable for a public audience.

The film song 'Hamma Hamma' in *Bombay* provides a clear example of not-so-oblique sexual referencing and illustrates how Rahman's Tamil film scores 'responded to the global influences of MTV'.[49] The moves and costumes of the dancers in the song's choreographed sequences reference the music videos of Michael Jackson, while Western popular music elements such as sampled beats, shouts and rhythmic vocal hooks, a contemporary lead vocal, funk bass line, horn stabs and sampled instrumental licks draw heavily on 80s and 90s African-American popular music artists including Jackson, Prince and Cameo. These blend with traditional Indian elements such as the pungi (a reed instrument associated with snake-charmers), which plays a riff in the Phrygian mode, and the exotic female voice that first introduced Bano, entwining with a blues-inflected lead male vocal in a metaphor for the sexual union of a traditional Muslim woman and contemporary Hindu man.

Once a film song has been presented as a supra-diegetic musical performance, it may recur non-diegetically, as with instrumental reprises of 'Uyire Uyire' in *Bombay* to evoke the memory of Shekhar and Bano's mutual declaration of love, and of 'Chinna Chinna Aasai' in *Roja* to evoke Roja's desire for Rishi. Interestingly, both of these songs have signature melodies in the Mixolydian mode (a major scale variant with a minor seventh), and both are about tenderness and desire. The Mixolydian mode is used in the Raga Kamboji (or Khamaj) of classical Indian music:[50] a raga classified as female, suitable for conveying sentiments of tenderness, love and eroticism, and recommended to be played at dusk or dawn.[51] The image sequences that accompany these songs set 'Chinna Chinna Aasai' at dawn and 'Uyire Uyire' in the early evening. The affective associations embedded through Rahman's music via film songs might not be fully apparent to Western listeners but are an integral part of the way these songs communicate with his Indian audience.

When Rahman and Ratnam began to look for alternative approaches to film scoring, songs that were not set-pieces were unusual in Indian films, and, indeed, the songs in *Roja* are all initially presented in this manner; yet when *Bombay* was made only three years later, they presented some songs as set-pieces, while others were presented exclusively non-diegetically, in the approach more common to mainstream Western cinema.

For example, the lyrics of 'Gulla Gulla, Halla Gulla', while describing the thoughts and words of the main characters, are not lip-synched by the actors, and there is no surreal chorus of supporting singers and dancers. In its first iteration, this song compresses narrative to cover Bano's entire pregnancy; in its second, the birth of the twins and their early childhood. In a further reflection of Western aesthetics, songs are incorporated into *Bombay* as a commentary device, as occurs towards the end of the film, where lyrics translated as 'Stop it, stop it!' are heard repeatedly over a montage of images depicting violence. Through its non-diegetic presentation, this song comments directly on the atrocities on-screen, conveying the thoughts of the main protagonists and the omniscient point of view of the filmmaker.

These early scores are peppered throughout with the 'regional filler' Rahman alluded to much later in interview. Traditional characters living old-fashioned lives in remote villages, such as Bano and Shekhar's parents and members of Roja's village, are frequently accompanied by traditional instruments such as the bansuri, pungi, tablas, dholak, bells and other percussion, without the intrusion of electronic or Western instrumental timbres. In contrast, Rahman's main motifs in these films reflect the influence of the classical Hollywood score. The *Bombay* theme evokes regional associations specific to its Tamil audience, through the bansuri lullaby, which connects to narrative themes around innocence, childhood, nostalgia, and Indian solidarity. An example is when Shekhar berates a Muslim and a Hindu for fighting in the street; a tense scene somewhat unexpectedly juxtaposed with the delicate bansuri melody to convey the central message of the film: 'It's about India, it's about what we stand for.'[52] The more universal sound of the theme's string melody expresses a yearning for reconciliation, evoked through repeated descending parallel phrases, articulated in a sobbing rhythm, as though the string section were catching its breath after each one. These strings weave their way through the moments of hurt experienced by Bano and Shekhar's fathers when they learn of their children's love, and narrowly escape death at the hands of a Muslim gang, to scenes of heartbreaking destruction of the city and its people. The orchestration for strings deliberately references Hollywood, connecting this story to the global context of tragic conflict. In this way, the main theme pulls in all listeners, Western and Indian alike, and functions as a musical and ideological unifier throughout the film.

Fire, 1996

Fire is the first film of the 'Elements Trilogy' by Indian-Canadian filmmaker Deepa Mehta. It is the story of sisters-in-law Radha and Sita, their struggle with traditional values and expectations, their evolution as women, and their passionate love affair. A key theme throughout the film is desire: the desire of Sita's unfaithful husband, Jatin, for his Chinese mistress; the suppressed desire of Ashok, celibate husband of Radha; the dysfunctional desire of Mundu, the family's manservant who masturbates to pornographic films; the dormant desire of the infertile Radha; and the nascent desire of Sita, who eventually reignites Radha's desire, resulting in the affair that liberates the women and destroys their family.

Carefully selected vocal treatments once again speak through *Fire*, and in accordance with the social issues at the core of the narrative, the voices heard are predominantly female. As Radha reveals her pain to her husband over not having a child, a solo female voice emerges: close, wordless, soft, breathy, with pitch bends, vibrato and ornamentation that emulates sobbing. The solo voice symbolizes Radha's isolation after her husband's sexual rejection of her, and the strongly Eastern aesthetic of Phrygian mode, microtonal ornamentation and drone point to her role of traditional Indian wife. The same cue is heard again nearly an hour later in the film, when Radha is struggling with the moral dilemma presented by her feelings of desire for Sita.

A variation of these vocal cues, the 'Passion' theme, is first heard when Radha is awakened in the night by her emerging desire. The female voice again wordlessly articulates microtonal ornamentation around a rising melody in Phrygian mode, but here it is lower, louder and raw. Underpinned by a dissonant drone, the voice is joined by bells playing an irregular rhythm (echoing the bell rung by the mute matriarch, Biji, every time something is wrong), and a heavy percussion loop that hints at a growing danger. The 'Passion' theme recurs towards the end of the film where Radha confesses her desire for Sita to her husband. Ushered in by the same drone and percussion loop, the female vocal is heard in a higher register, at its most defiant, wild and raw, in response to Ashok's command, 'Touch my feet!' The moment Radha's sari catches fire a solo violin is heard in a strident countermelody to the voice. Both voice and violin are heavily reverberant, with portamento and vibrato providing a musical 'screaming' to accompany this climactic scene, which ends before the audience knows whether Radha has survived or has been burnt alive.

Another theme incorporating the voice to extend character is the 'Bangles theme', first heard during the courtship between the two women, as they oil each other's hair, and in a later scene when they cook and exchange lovers' looks in the kitchen. Two sensual and provocative female voices interweave, wordlessly suggesting the emotions the two protagonists are feeling. They are accompanied by a combination of timbres: traditional drums, tambura, bells, and a pulsing electronic pad. Modality is major and the mood evoked is joyful, signifying the loving female bonding that is occurring.

While there are no film songs in *Fire*, recycled popular music is used for its referential and associative value, as in Western cinema. In a scene that alludes to the film song genre, Sita (in drag) and Radha lip-synch coquettishly to a recording of the 1957 Hindi love song 'Aaja Zara Mere Dil Ke Sahare'.[53] Here, a well-known film song is recycled in a diegetic parody of the original to convey the romantic love between the women. Popular music is also referenced to convey the narrative of modernity and freedom that the younger characters, Sita and Jatin, seek to embrace. Jatin rides his motorbike across the city to an excerpt from 'Hamma Hamma' from *Bombay*, already a popular hit at the time of the release of *Fire*. Hindi pop is used diegetically during scenes where he is working in his shop, to reflect the fast-paced and commercial world he inhabits. By contrast, the religious values of old India are evoked by the devotional song 'Om Jai Jagdish Hare',[54] sung accapella by male voices, which follows a scene where Jatin flaunts his infidelity with his mistress, Julie, who aspires to materialistic and moral values that reflect modern Western society.

Rahman attributes the choice to reuse the *Bombay* theme in *Fire* to the influence of the temp track,[55] a choice that somewhat compromised the film's individual imprint. Despite giving Mehta his permission to reuse it, Ratnam had commissioned and developed this theme as a signature to his own film, released only one year earlier. Its inclusion in *Fire* was perhaps accommodated by the different contexts into which the two films were initially released: the former as a Tamil film to an Indian audience, and the second as an English-language film to a North American audience. The subsequent international success of both films made their shared musical theme more obvious. Despite this, the *Bombay* theme connects strongly with the narrative in *Fire*, and Rahman incorporates its tonality, timbres and instrumentation into the original score, to ensure its integration. The film opens with the solo bansuri theme accompanying a scene of Radha as a girl sitting with her parents in a green field strewn with yellow daisies, and throughout the film each restatement of the bansuri theme accompanies a reprise of this scene, establishing a strong audiovisual motif. As we have explored in the *Bombay* analysis, the evocation of a lullaby generates associations with childhood, and in *Fire*, it evokes the young Radha's dreams and innocence.

Breath instruments work throughout *Fire* as a sonification of innocence, and of its counterpart, desire. When Radha and Sita sleep together for the first time, the bansuri returns with a maturity and sensuousness not heard before, playing a low-register, repetitive, ornamented melodic figure in the Phrygian mode, to symbolize the mature Radha's innocence transformed into sexuality. The instrumentation in this cue is virtually the same as in the opening theme: the same bass drone underlies the flute melody, and the bell's regular rhythmic figure has been replaced by an erratic rhythm that reflects the scene's tension and desire. The bansuri melody emphasizes the minor second; dissonance that is further extended by a very long reverb, to recall the guru Swamiji's warning of the evils of 'desire night'. When Ashok succumbs to desire, remembering his wife and Sita making love, an ocarina squeals a repeated high-pitched note,[56] in a cue also borrowed from the *Bombay* score. As in his Tamil films, in *Fire*, Rahman harnesses Eastern and Western musical influences to present themes signifying the duality of traditional and modern India, clashing values, and the characters' internal conflicts as they straddle the contradictions present within their society to confront their deepest desires.

Slumdog Millionaire, 2008 and *127 Hours*, 2010

Rahman, with his background in film song, and British director Danny Boyle share an understanding of popular music's ability to drive and influence narrative. Both bring a history of successfully incorporating popular songs into their storytelling language. In his cult classic *Trainspotting* (1996), Boyle harnessed the celebrity of pop icons such as Brian Eno, Iggy Pop and Lou Reed, along with newer 'Britpop' bands Underworld, Primal Scream and Blur, incorporating their songs into his film to add depth to narrative and characters. Boyle makes films 'for today's people', constantly referencing popular culture and pre-existing popular music to create a focus away from 'the musical artifact itself to musical styles, and the social discourse about music and beyond'.[57] He uses the hit international TV show 'Who Wants to Be a Millionaire' to underpin the plot of *Slumdog Millionaire*, incorporating its musical theme within Rahman's original soundtrack. Sri-Lankan/British singer M.I.A.'s hit song 'Paper Planes' is used in *Slumdog* to score the montage sequence where the two central characters, Jamal and Salim, work the trains as child pickpockets, with Boyle trading on M.I.A.'s celebrity and 'street cred' to convey messages about his story world, with lyrics such as 'third-world democracy' describing early 90s India. An original song co-authored by Rahman and M.I.A. for *Slumdog*, 'O Saya', opens with Rahman's soaring solo vocal ushering in a storm of percussion, pulsing synth pads, and children's rhythmic chanting, layered with heightened sound design that complements the music. M.I.A.'s distinctive vocal tells us, 'They can't touch me, we break off, run so fast they can't even touch me'; lyrics that underscore images of the boys dodging cops and gangsters in the alleyways of the slum. Here, M.I.A.'s identity, her rap singing style and London accent hold strong associative value for Western listeners familiar with her music. These associations are recalled towards the end of the film, when 'O Saya' returns in isolated fragments as backdrop to a private conversation between Jamal and the 'Millionaire' show host, who reveals he shares Jamal's past as 'a guy from the slums (who) becomes a millionaire overnight'.

Rahman's collaboration with British singer Dido[58] on *127 Hours* also harnessed the identity of a pop icon known to Boyle's audience. The song 'If I Rise' was co-composed for the film, with lyric content reflecting the thoughts of the central character, Aron Ralston, as he endures one hundred and twenty-seven hours pinned under a boulder in a remote canyon. The first time we hear the song's lyric, 'If I rise, have one more try, if I believe, there's more than this', Dido's ethereal voice is foregrounded; a transcendent companion to the dying Ralston's vision of his future child. Rahman's voice joins Dido's, high and gentle, with autotune added to create an abstracted effect, and is synchronized with Ralston's premonition of himself as a father playing with his young son. The delicate timbres suggest a vulnerability that affirms the more 'feminine' qualities of relationship, family and love; values that play a central role in Ralston's choice to survive. In the full arrangement of 'If I Rise' that accompanies the closing credits, Dido's already breathy vocal is couched in delicate chorus and delay effects to make it even smoother. She is accompanied by clean electric guitar, fretless bass, soft brushes and airy synth pads, Rahman's high, breathy voice, harp glissandi, strings, and a children's choir; elements that embody the message of spiritual transcendence at the core this film. The placement of 'If I Rise' over the closing credits represents a paradigm shift from the mood established with the opening title track, 'Never Hear Surf Music Again', performed by Free Blood.[59] This track has a dance music aesthetic conveyed by breathy rhythms, groans and shouts, heavy grinding electronic bass, guitars and sampled drum loops. With its provocative lyrics ('Take it if it makes you come'), this track is more typical of Boyle's musical aesthetic as heard in *Trainspotting*, depicting a hyper-energetic music of youth, addiction and escapism that establishes Ralston as a Gen-X, extreme-sports adventurer, confident, masculine and invincible. The stark contrast between the songs for the opening and closing credits represents the radical personal evolution Ralston undergoes through the course of his ordeal.

Boyle has said of his films: 'There's a theme running through all of them ... They're all about someone facing impossible odds and overcoming them.'[60] This narrative arc is the classic 'hero's journey' trope and, as Boyle suggests, is presented in both *127 Hours* and in *Slumdog*. In *127 Hours* Rahman identifies his hero with an instrument that represents the young male archetype: the guitar. The guitar sounds of Joel Shearer and Sanjay Divecha range from distorted electric guitar accompanying Ralston on his extreme mountain-bike ride at the start of the film; through pulsing electric guitar driving his desperate bid for survival in the 'Liberation' theme; to the abstract, digitally treated guitar timbres of his nightly hallucinations; to the gentle electric guitar melody in the 'Touch of the Sun' theme, which is introduced roughly thirty minutes into the film, when sunlight floods the canyon for the first time. Here, the electric guitar, the instrument for Ralston's character, is placed front and centre in the mix, clean and warm, playing in its lower register, reflecting a soft male essence that underscores the warm memory of his father bringing him to the canyon as a child to watch the sunrise. This theme recurs when Ralston walks into the sunlight at the end of his ordeal, and again in the epilogue to the film, when the real Aron Ralston appears on-screen with his wife and baby son. Through this motif, Rahman indicates that the father/son relationships that underpin the 'hero's journey' have come full circle.

Delineating the tale's two extremes of entrapment and transcendence are two contrasting musical themes: 'Liberation' and 'The Canyon'. The Canyon theme contains the main melodic idea from 'If I Rise', in a rendition that resembles a hymn setting. It conveys the peace of the environment to which Ralston is drawn, and hints at his unexplored spirituality. In the scene where Ralston recalls lying in bed talking to his girlfriend, the theme signals Ralston's potential for love; that this vision is abruptly cut short by a clap of thunder signals that he is not there yet. The third time we hear the Canyon theme is over an hour into the film, when Blue John, the explorer after whom the canyon is named, visits Ralston in an hallucination. As Ralston teeters in and out of consciousness, the return of the Canyon theme is like a spiritual reckoning in preparation for his death. Later, the theme briefly returns towards the end of the film when the image presents a boy standing witness to the amputation. The Canyon theme's melody is louder and lower than before, a single phrase mixing with the driving rhythms of the Liberation theme in an unexpected, yet significant layering of leitmotif that, with the image, clarifies Ralston's motivation to continue with his improbable bid for redemption. Throughout the film, the melodic connection between the Canyon theme and 'If I Rise' ties together narrative threads relating to the spiritual path of the central character—his evolution from boy to man, from outer strength to inner strength, and his acceptance of love—to underscore the hero's journey narrative at the deeper level.

The Liberation theme draws on Eastern musical structures, while its instrumentation stays within a Western framework for this all-American tale. The different versions of this theme gradually build in intensity from the scene where Ralston initially tries to free his arm, through the scene where water rushes into the canyon, spurring fantasies of escape, to the climactic amputation scene. Rahman layers electric guitar (subjected to different EQ treatments), pulsing electric bass, glitch effects, distorted resonant pads, high piano tones, strings, drum kit, synth bass drones, and sampled percussion grooves, within a largely Eastern approach to modality. Drones underpin each of the theme's three iterations, and the prevailing guitar melodic figure is in the Phrygian mode. The darkness of the low drone and the minor seconds and sixths of the Phrygian guitar melody, while distinctly 'Rahmanesque', also tie in with the Western rock stylistic references in the soundtrack, and express the urgency and desperation of Ralston's struggle. Piercing high-frequency noises, designed to represent the breaking of Ralston's nerves (which Rahman indicates were created by the sound design team),[61] blend with the musical content to create a visceral experience of Ralston's physical pain. Rhythm, repetition and harmonic stasis are important constants in this theme that allow the drama to continue to build through this long and taxing scene.

In *Slumdog Millionaire*, it is 'Latika's Theme', with its humming female vocal (performed by Indian singer Suzanne D'Mello),[62] airy pads, pure electric piano tones, softly pulsing bass line, delicate guitar arpeggios, string section and sitar, that most closely resembles the transcendental sound of 'If I Rise' in *127 Hours*. These two themes share warm and airy timbres, rich reverbs, melodies in the major mode, and minimal rhythmic content. As with 'If I Rise', love and redemption are implicit in the message of 'Latika's Theme', which reflects her purity, gentleness and femininity. It underscores scenes where Latika's presence is either actual or sensed by Jamal, such as her first appearance in the rain after the children lose their mother, her separation from the boys as they jump the train, her memory when the brothers return to Mumbai, her reappearance at Jarvin's house, when Jamal sees her at the station during their attempted escape, and in their final reunion at the station. The elusiveness of the theme, which is teased out slowly in fragments throughout the film before its final full statement in the last ten minutes, reflects the girl's elusive presence in the narrative. Here again, the hero will only taste her love and achieve his own redemption once his tortuous journey is complete.

In Coleman's interview, Rahman alludes to the role his Sufi faith plays in his composition, and cites it as an important influence in his 'softer' compositions, speaking of his efforts to strive for 'a pure feeling'.[63] If such a state can be translated into sound, the breathy timbres of his own and his female singers' vocals, the gentle instrumental gestures and suspended temporal quality of 'Latika's Theme', the Canyon theme, and 'If I Rise', are surely manifestations of Rahman's spirituality connecting with the underlying narrative of both films. At the other end of the sonic spectrum, Rahman channels the energy of an orchestra and his suite of electronic instruments to underscore the visceral human predicaments that Boyle so loves to present on-screen. Dramatic, high-action scenes feature percussion of various kinds, from Indian skin drums to thumping taiko and timpani, processed electronic percussion, and sampled breakbeats. In the riots scene from *Slumdog*, Rahman blends Eastern and Western instruments in his trademark approach, incorporating a dholak loop, the swaramandal (Indian harp), pulsing electronic timbres, low piano notes, warped synth bass tones, glitch effects, and a drone; music that feels contemporary and urgent even as it references the ancient culture torn apart by the events unfolding on-screen.

In *127 Hours*, the cue called 'R.I.P' is perhaps most representative of the typical Rahman sound, with a low drone, steadily building percussion groove, layers of smooth, airy pads, female and male voices dripping with reverb, entwining in blended Western and Eastern styles of singing. This cue recalls the 'Passion Theme' in *Fire*, and the various vocal motifs in *Bombay*.

It fades out over a close-up of ants crawling over Ralston's face, leaving us with the expectation that at this point in the story he dies. With its eerie grace, it signals both the low-point and the pivot-point of the narrative, for it is in the following scene that Ralston makes his decision to survive. Multiple voices also signal the high-point and end-point of the narrative, although this time neither the voice nor the composition are Rahman's; rather the ambient rock track is 'Festival' by Icelandic band Sigur Ros.[64] As Ralston stumbles away from his ordeal, people appear through the haze, while at the musical level, drums build through thirty-second-note runs, and we hear a falling string gesture, a throbbing bass pedal tone, and a messy falsetto chorus in an example of one of the many spellbinding 'sonic dominant' moments across Boyle's oeuvre. Here, the wild collectivity of the voices and driving rock rhythms evoke an almost tribal, unconditional, human solidarity. This moment of communion and release is moving, and the particular alchemy forged between music and image justifies Boyle's choice to go with a pre-existing composition at his film's climax. That it sits so comfortably alongside the original score is a tribute to both Boyle's and Rahman's intuitive approach to overall musical design. This particular skill is also very much in evidence in *Slumdog*, through the way Rahman's original score consistently works in interplay with the theme from 'Who Wants to Be a Millionaire', which weaves across diegetic boundaries, at times heard as source music accompanying the show, and at others extending beyond the show's parameters into non-diegetic music to underscore dramatic action.

Although the product of a British production team, *Slumdog Millionaire* is in many ways a Hindi film. Its five original songs were sung primarily by well-known Indian singers, including the legendary Alka Yagnik and Ila Arun, who perform on 'Ringa Ringa'. This track embodies the sound of Hindi pop, with a high, piercing, lead female vocal, rhythmic and sensual backing vocals, shifting modality, which oscillates from minor to major and back, a catchy groove played on tambourine and dholak, counter-melodies played on bansuri and pungi, and a lush string section. While working as underscore to montage rather than as the supra-diegetic set-piece of a Hindi film song, there is nonetheless an ambiguity to the way in which 'Ringa Ringa' is used; it dominates the sound space, and stylized shots of Latika dancing for a client are cut to synchronize rhythmically with the track, in a manner that alludes to a choreographed film song performance. Another example of cultural ambiguity is the song 'Jai Ho', whose presentation takes the traditional form of a film song through its choreography, yet feels more like an homage to the genre, occurring at the end of the film to neatly connect the resolving narrative with the closing credits. The song features several well-known Indian singers (Sukhvinder Singh, Tanvi Shah and Mahalaxmi Iyer), as well as Rahman, who sings the chorus chant. The instrumentation blends cultural influences: a string section articulating classic Bollywood riffs[65] and countermelodies as well as a lyrical coda in the 'classical' Hollywood style; there are sampled beats, a santur ostinato, dholak rhythms, hand claps, and a tambura drone. A chorus of voices rapping in Spanish further extends this song's cultural reach and appeal. Here, Rahman's typically eclectic blend of instruments and styles celebrates modern India as a global melting pot, where money and love rain down.

Conclusion

> The composer was expected to be a competent performer ... was expected to know his audience ... rising above his own likes and dislikes, in order to bring delight to everyone. This exemplified the traditional doctrine of non-attachment, propounded in the *Bhagavadgītā*.[66]

This might sum up A.R. Rahman, a respected singer and keyboardist, who performs on his own scores, and composes music that is technically well crafted and aesthetically pleasing. He cites his Sufi spirituality as an important influence for his music, whose inspiration is derived from a non-attached state 'when you become nothing, only pureness exists.'[67] His ability to blend Eastern and Western musical elements to create strong associations for audiences from both contexts while supporting receptivity to sounds that might sit outside the listener's cultural context is notable, even remarkable, and enriches every film he works on. His sound captures a multicultural aesthetic, drawn from his roots as a Tamil musician, that speaks to global audiences.

In summarizing his success, one must acknowledge the long tradition of eclecticism in the work of his musical predecessors in Tamil and Bollywood films. One must equally acknowledge the expertise of the directors with whom he chooses to work, who are respected as some of the leading film-makers in the world, and who understand that the best films find common elements of human experience, create narrative around these, and employ music and other modalities to embellish and deepen emotional response to their stories. In music for cinema, as distinct from music by itself, it is the *film* that provides context for the audience, often transcending cultural specificity to communicate emotions and ideas through narrative drawn from shared human experience.

Notwithstanding the enormous contribution of his predecessors and collaborators, the 'alternate space' Rahman's music inhabits is one of his own making, polished over years of practice in several cinematic contexts, and characterized by a flexibility that allows his talent to translate across boundaries of culture and style. His songs reference a multitude of traditional and contemporary genres and work as both supra-diegetic set-pieces and non-diegetic music for montage. His leitmotifs layer regional and global musical references, and are embedded with triggers that touch Indian and Western audiences in different ways to draw the intended overall response. The prevalence in his music of drones, of microtonal melodic ornamentation, and of modes that sit outside the regular Western lexicon are strong trademarks of his sound. The way he uses the human voice (the instrument shared by all cultures) as a primary agent to communicate character identity and emotional subtext is exceptional, and key to his scores' success in traversing cultural boundaries. His well-produced sound includes the voice of technology so important to twenty-first-century people. Yet, for all the 'multis' it encapsulates—multicultural, multiplatform, multimodal, multi-instrumental, multi-referential—the sound of Rahman unifies its many polarities into a singular aesthetic, an 'alternate space' that speaks clearly to our common humanity.

Notes

1. *A.R. Rahman—The Official Site*, http://www.arrahman.com/biography.aspx, accessed 8 July 2016.
2. Lindsay Coleman, A.R. Rahman Interview, this book, Chapter 2, 22.
3. Joseph Getter and B. Balasubrahmaniyan, 'Tamil Film Music: Sound and Significance', in Mark Slobin (ed.), *Global Soundtracks: Worlds of Film* (Middletown, CT: Wesleyan University Press, 2008), 116.
4. Guido Heldt, *Music and Levels of Narration in Film: Steps Across the Border* (Intellect: Bristol, 2013), 137.
5. Heldt, *Steps Across the Border*, 138.
6. Jeff Smith, *The Sounds of Commerce: Marketing Popular Film Music* (Columbia University Press: NY, 1998), 45–68.
7. Smith, *The Sounds of Commerce*, 155.

8. Anahid Kassabian, *Hearing Film: Tracking Identifications in Contemporary Hollywood Film Music* (Routledge: New York, 2001), 3.
9. This statement refers to current norms in conventional Western narrative cinema, rather than early examples of song in Hollywood films, or filmed musicals.
10. Smith, *The Sounds of Commerce*, 159.
11. Heldt, *Steps Across the Border*, 106–7.
12. Greg Booth, 'That Bollywood Sound', in Mark Slobin (ed.), *Global Soundtracks: Worlds of Film Music* (Middletown, CT: Wesleyan University Press, 2008), 110.
13. 'Chinna Chinna', 1992, featured vocals by Minmini and A.R. Rahman.
14. 'Uyire', 1996, featured celebrated ghazal singer Hariharan: http://www.singerhariharan.com, accessed 26 November 2015.
15. Booth, 'That Bollywood Sound', 111.
16. Kathryn Kalinak, *Settling the Score: Music and the Classical Hollywood Film* (Madison: University of Wisconsin Press, 1992), 113.
17. Arnold Whittall, 'Leitmotif', *The New Grove Dictionary of Music and Musicians*, 2nd ed. Vol. 14 (Macmillan, 2001), 527.
18. James Wierzbicki, *Film Music: A History* (New York: Routledge, 2009), 144.
19. Whittall, 'Leitmotif', 527.
20. Wierzbicki, *Film Music*, 144.
21. Whittall, 'Leitmotif', 528.
22. Getter and Balasubrahmaniyan, 'Tamil Film Music', 131.
23. For example, Ennio Morricone's theme for *The Good, the Bad and the Ugly* (Sergio Leone, 1966), and John Williams's theme for *Star Wars* (George Lucas, 1977).
24. Getter and Balasubrahmaniyan, 'Tamil Film Music', 131.
25. The *Bombay* soundtrack has sold some 15 million units, while its main theme has been appropriated for use in international releases (*Fire*, 1996, *Divine Intervention*, 2002, *Lord of War*, 2005, *Miral*, 2010), as advertising music, and in many compilation albums.
26. A movement in Indian cinema that originated in the 1950s as an alternative to mainstream Indian cinema, and was a precursor to the Indian 'New Wave' of the 1960s.

27. Booth, 'That Bollywood Sound', 86, and Getter and Balasubrahmaniyan, 'Tamil Film Music', 121.
28. Wierzbicki, *Film Music*, 138.
29. Getter and Balasubrahmaniyan, 'Tamil Film Music', 124.
30. As explained by Rahman in Coleman, A.R. Rahman Interview.
31. Wierzbicki, *Film Music*, 145.
32. Ronald Rodman, 'The Popular Song as Leitmotif in 1990s Film', in Phil Powrie and Robynn J. Stilwell (eds), *Changing Tunes: The use of Preexisting Music in Film* (Aldershot: Ashgate, 2006), 120.
33. Royal S. Brown, *Overtones and Undertones: Reading Film Music* (Berkeley: University of California Press, 1994), 5.
34. John Blacking, *Music, Culture and Experience: Selected Papers of John Blacking*, ed. Reginald Byron (Chicago: University of Chicago Press, 1995).
35. Coleman, A.R. Rahman Interview, 20.
36. Royal S. Brown, *Overtones and Undertones*, 5–7.
37. Philip Tagg and Bob Clarida, *Ten Little Tunes: Towards a Musicology of the Mass Media* (The Mass Media Music Scholars' Press, New York, Montreal, 2003), 104.
38. Tagg and Clarida, *Ten Little Tunes*, 313.
39. Tagg and Clarida, *Ten Little Tunes*, 310.
40. Rahman interview with Lindsay Coleman, 2014.
41. Peter Fletcher, *World Musics in Context: A Comprehensive Survey of the World's Major Musical Cultures* (New York: Oxford University Press, 2001), 103.
42. Fletcher, *World Musics in Context*, 103.
43. Fletcher, *World Musics in Context*, 103.
44. Coleman, A.R. Rahman Interview, 17.
45. Tagg and Clarida, *Ten Little Tunes*, 320.
46. Tagg and Clarida, *Ten Little Tunes*, 320.
47. As discussed in Coleman, A.R. Rahman Interview, 18.
48. Qawwali is a vocal tradition of Sufi Islam.
49. Booth, 'That Bollywood Sound', 108.
50. Fletcher, *World Musics in Context*, 249.
51. *Kambhoji*, https://en.wikipedia.org/wiki/Kambhoji, accessed 2 December 2015.
52. Coleman, A.R. Rahman Interview, 17.
53. 'Aaja Zara Mere Dil Ke Sahare', Saregama, 1957, from the film *Ek Jhalak*, performed by Hemant Kumar and Geeta Dutt.

54. 'Om Jai Jagdish Hare', a traditional Hindu devotional song dedicated to Lord Hari.
55. Coleman, A.R. Rahman Interview, 18.
56. This cue is another extract from the *Bombay* theme, recycled in *Fire*.
57. Ronald Rodman, 'The Popular Song as Leitmotif in 1990s Film', 133.
58. Dido's professional website, http://www.didomusic.com, accessed 25 November 2015.
59. John Pugh, 'Never Hear Surf Music Again', performed by Free Blood, published by Rong Music, date TBC.
60. *Geoffrey Himes*, 'SXSW: Danny Boyle Talks Up New Film Trance,' *Baltimore City Paper*, 12 March 2013, retrieved 2 April 2013.
61. *Himes*, 'SXSW: Danny Boyle Talks Up New Film Trance'.
62. *Filmibeat*, http://www.filmibeat.com/celebs/suzanne-d-mello/biography.html, accessed 25 November 2015.
63. *Filmibeat*.
64. Sigur Ros, 'Festival', *Með suð í eyrum við spilum endalaust*, EMI Records, published by Universal Music, 2008.
65. Rahman uses the words "very formulaic" to describe the first bars of 'Jai Ho' when asked if the beginning of the song is a quote of a phrase universal to Bollywood, see Coleman, A.R. Rahman Interview, 20.
66. Fletcher, *World Musics in Context*, 253, summarizing the doctrines of Shārngadeva in the *Saṅgītaratnākara* (13th century).
67. Coleman, A.R. Rahman Interview, 23.

Bibliography

Blacking, John. 1995. *Music, Culture and Experience: Selected Papers of John Blacking*, ed. Reginald Byron. Chicago: University of Chicago Press.

Booth, Greg. 2008. That Bollywood Sound. In *Global Soundtracks: Worlds of Film Music*, ed. Mark Slobin, 85–113. Middletown, CT: Wesleyan University Press.

Brown, Royal S. 1994. *Overtones and Undertones: Reading Film Music*. Berkeley: University of California Press.

Fletcher, Peter. 2001. *World Musics in Context: A Comprehensive Survey of the World's Major Musical Cultures*. New York: Oxford University Press.

Getter, Joseph, and B. Balasubrahmaniyan. 2008. Tamil Film Music: Sound and Significance. In *Global Soundtracks: Worlds of Film*, ed. Mark Slobin, 114–152. Middletown, CT: Wesleyan University Press.

Heldt, Guido. 2013. *Music and Levels of Narration in Film: Steps Across the Border*. Bristol: Intellect.

Kalinak, Kathryn. 1992. *Settling the Score: Music and the Classical Hollywood Film.* Madison and London: University of Wisconsin Press.
Kassabian, Anahid. 2001. *Hearing Film: Tracking Identifications in Contemporary Hollywood Film Music.* New York: Routledge.
Rodman, Ronald. 2006. The Popular Song as Leitmotif in 1990s Film. In *Changing Tunes: The Use of Preexisting Music in Film*, ed. Phil Powrie and Robynn J. Stilwell, 119–136. Aldershot: Ashgate.
Smith, Jeff. 1998. *The Sounds of Commerce: Marketing Popular Film Music.* New York: Columbia University Press.
Tagg, Philip, and Clarida, Bob. 2003. *Ten Little Tunes: Towards a Musicology of the Mass Media.* New York and Montreal: The Mass Media Music Scholars' Press.
Whittall, Arnold. 2001. Leitmotif. In *The New Grove Dictionary of Music and Musicians*, 2nd ed., ed. Stanley Sadie, Vol. 14, 527–530. London: Macmillan.
Wierzbicki, James. 2009. *Film Music: A History.* New York: Routledge.

INTERNET

A.R. Rahman—The Official Site. http://www.arrahman.com/biography.aspx. Accessed 8 July 2016.
Dido. http://www.didomusic.com. Accessed 25 November 2015.
Filmibeat. http://www.filmibeat.com/celebs/suzanne-d-mello/biography.html. Accessed 25 November2015.
Hariharan. http://www.singerhariharan.com. Accessed 26 November 2015.
Himes, Geoffrey. 2013. *SXSW: Danny Boyle Talks up New Film Trance.* Baltimore City Paper, Baltimore, MD, March 12. Accessed 2 April 2013.
Kambhoji. https://en.wikipedia.org/wiki/Kambhoji. Accessed 2 December 2015.

CHAPTER 4

Zbigniew Preisner Interview

Jonathan Godsall

Zbigniew Preisner is a film composer with 66 credits to his name. His most well-known work was with the late Polish director Krzysztof Kieślowski, in particular for the films *Three Colours: Blue* (1993), *Three Colours: White* (1994), and *Three Colours: Red* (1994). In addition to his collaborations with Kieślowski, he has also worked with Hector Babenco on *At Play in the Fields of the Lord* (1991), Louis Malle on *Damage* (1992), and Agnieszka Holland on *Europa Europa* (1990).

The following interview with Zbigniew Preisner was conducted by Jonathan Godsall, via email, in mid-2015.

Q: Do you feel that your musical style, and approach to film scoring more specifically, have changed or evolved over the years? If so, how?
A: Getting older we also get more mature. Our opinions change, taste, etc. Music is composed based on one's emotions. So, as our lives change, the music starts to be different. But is it better? I have no idea.

J. Godsall (✉)
School of Humanities and Performing Arts, Plymouth University, United Kingdom

© The Author(s) 2017
L. Coleman, J. Tillman (eds.), *Contemporary Film Music*,
DOI 10.1057/978-1-137-57375-9_4

Q: Since 1994 you've recorded your music in your own studio. What are the key advantages of owning this facility? Has doing so affected your working method, or even aspects of the music you've written?

A: My studio gives me freedom. I can record how much I want, how long I want and then mix without any time limits. I collected there all the effects I need to mix my music that it would be difficult to find in one other place (I have three Lexicon 224s, two 480s, and one 960). I filled my studio with such analogue devices that let me create my sound. I always fight for the highest quality of recording. In my place I have exactly what I need to do my job.

Q: When someone asks you to compose music for a film nowadays, what are the most important factors affecting your decision to say 'yes' or 'no'?

A: The most important is meeting with the director. When I have good communication, I watch a good film, and I feel we can make something nice together, I say 'yes'. But when I see that the producer is coming between the director and the composer—who *always* know best what music is needed for the film—I mostly resign because it's a fight with windmills.

I'm from a different school, with different aesthetics: most annoying is the fact that everybody is enthusiastic about my music, e.g. for the Kieślowski movies, but would like me to compose music in the style of a dozen or so other composers in the world. That's epigonism, and it leaves no memories.

Q: You have worked with filmmakers from all over Europe, and beyond. Have you noticed broad cultural differences in attitudes towards the style and role of music in film, or does it vary more from filmmaker to filmmaker, production to production?

A: My benchmark is set very high. Please remember that I started with directors like Kieślowski, Agnieszka Holland, Louis Malle, so it's from that perspective that I judge young directors. The same with producers. I have worked with several legendary producers: Saul Zaentz, Francis Ford Coppola and Marin Karmitz. I was lucky to meet Dino De Laurentiis and Carlo Ponti. From that perspective everything seems not perfect. They took risks and weren't afraid of that. That's why we had great movies. Nowadays producers and directors try to check their films at each stage of production, giving out cards to screening audiences, with questions such as what did you like, and what not. My question is whether it's still art, or a compilation of the taste of producers, directors, audience and nobody knows who else.

Q: Collaboration seems to be central to your work as a composer, whether it's with a filmmaker, the musicians who perform your music (particularly regular soloists like soprano Elżbieta Towarnicka), Edoardo Ponti on the staging of *Requiem for My Friend*, Pink Floyd's David Gilmour (for whom you've provided orchestrations), and so on. Is this a fair assessment? How have these collaborators influenced your life and music?

A: A composer who writes mainly film music can't live separated from reality. Music won't be good if it's not performed by the right people. While composing I always know who will perform it. The examples you mentioned are all great people. And, in the case of David Gilmour, we are talking about a musical genius. Once, a musician colleague told me that we should always work with people better than ourselves, so we have a chance to learn. So, all my life I try to learn.

Q: Has a collaborator ever influenced you into taking your music in a new and unexpected direction?

A: If you mean directors, of course everybody wants to have music that is original in his opinion, leaving aside the consideration that not everything 'original' is original. Mostly, these are difficult conversations; directors are afraid to take risks. Once I was asked 'please write innocent music', even when the film in question needed strong music. And it happened the opposite way: I heard minimalistic music in the film but the other side wanted me to thunder with orchestra and choir. That's the job.

Q: You have spoken previously about the importance of matching orchestration—and particularly the choice of solo instruments—to the tone of each film. How do you find that match? What was the thinking behind the cello's prominent role in *Damage*, for instance?

A: Each film has its own music; the composer's role is to write the manuscript of the score and record it. Always, I follow my instinct. It was like that with *Damage*.

Q: There are moments in *Blue* in which Julie seems to experience a synesthetic connection between music and colour. In regard to the *Three Colours* trilogy as a whole, did the colours influence your music, either orchestrationally or otherwise?

A: The music in these films reacts to the script, was a partner, was in our heroes' minds.

My film music always tries to underline what we can't see, but can feel. My music is never illustration, *sensu stricto*.

Q: You have said that prolonged silences, and the amount of reverb you tend to use on your recordings, are important to your music in allowing it to 'breathe'. For me these aspects help to evoke church- and cathedral-like spaces, and the music one might hear in them. Has that been part of your intent, too?

A: My music always speaks to greatest effect in the silence between music. What I compose prepares the audience to listen to silence. When I started to compose film, or other, music, space was always the most important to me. This is my style that can be recognized, and the way I mix music is important for a film for another reason: music with such space never contradicts the dialogue and effects, it's a different background.

Q: There are a number of instances in your collaborations with Kieślowski in which it is unclear where the music is coming from, in the sense of whether it's for the audience's benefit only, or whether the characters can hear it, too (and either in reality or in their minds). As Julie sits oblivious to the old lady's struggle with the bottle bank in *Blue*, for instance, the music sounds initially as if it is being played by a busker, but though we've seen one previously we don't see him in this scene, so other interpretations are possible. Were you consciously striving to create ambiguity in that regard, there and elsewhere?

A: As I said before, I try to describe emotions that we can feel. Sometimes I'm on the audience's side, and think what would be my reaction, sometimes on the side of the actor (or, precisely speaking, the character); then the music gives his emotions to the audience. It's difficult to describe where those positions come from and why. Watching a film I try to analyze and find the best contact with the audience.

Q: In *Blue*, and also *The Double Life of Véronique* (Krzysztof Kieślowski, 1991) particularly, music seems to 'haunt' the characters (and the audience), with fragmented melodies recurring as echoes at various points across the films. We have all experienced a similar thing in our own lives in some way—in having a tune stuck in our heads, for example—but how do you translate that effect for the cinema?

A: In these two films you mentioned, obsession played a very important role. Véronique had the obsession with her alter ego in Poland, Julie in *Blue* had the obsession with her husband's musical themes, after his death. Obsession changed into suffering. Music underlined that suffering or, as in *Blue*, anticipated upcoming emotions. How to make it? I have no idea. I'd like to share it but I don't know.

Q: How do you go about writing music that is supposed to have been composed by a character in a film? Is the process different to when you are writing as yourself, whether for film or for the concert hall?

A: I try to be in the character's skin, and I compose such music. Film music follows different rules, needs to communicate with editing, dialogues, synchronization, so is limited in time. A film is a story and the music must follow it. When I compose music that is not connected with a film I don't have these limits. There is one question left: what to describe, say. It's much more difficult than composing for film.

Q: How do you get 'in the character's skin'? How do you decide what their music will sound like? Did the music of other real-life composers provide any inspiration for that of these characters?

A: In the examples that you mention, where the composer is a character in a film, I try to be that composer. I think about what he wants to say, what musical language and style. It is not very different from other composing for film. Kieślowski once said to me, 'If different should be different, different must be different,' and I follow that rule.

Q: Do you feel that there is a clear distinction between your own style and that of, say, Van den Budenmayer? Or are the voices of the fictional composers you've written as tied up with your own?

A: Van den Budenmayer is my alter ego. Or maybe I'm his. Our styles are similar, but fortunately I'm still composing. Van den Budenmayer died with Kieślowski.

Q: Are you willing to expand on how your styles are similar (and different)? Does Van den Budenmayer's music have particular traits that distinguish it from yours?

A: I think that anybody who knows my music can, without problems, say that the styles are similar. Van den Budenmayer identifies himself clearly to the audience, in both the music and the lyrics he chose. In *Decalogue IX* (Krzysztof Kieślowski, 1990), when he appears for the first time, he uses lyrics from a Dutch poet, Frederik van Eeden, a brief passage about water lilies. In *The Double Life of Véronique* he quotes from 'Purgatory' and 'Heaven' in the *Divine Comedy* by Dante.

Q: Your film music, including that written 'by' fictional composers, can be heard outside of its filmic contexts, and indeed alongside your concert music, both live and in recorded form. Do you see distinctions between categories of your output, in respect of how the music works for listeners on its own terms?

A: I'm not a fan of releasing every film score on a soundtrack album. Some music can be heard without film, some not. More and more I'm convinced that, when releasing a soundtrack, the music needs to be edited so that it reflects its function in the film. In other words, between the music in the film, we have dialogue, scenes, etc., that we don't have on an album. I have a lot of music composed for films, that I never released because I think it has no sense outside of those films.

Q: Parts of your *Requiem for My Friend* have been used in Terrence Malick's *The Tree of Life* (2011) and Paolo Sorrentino's *The Great Beauty* (2013). Have you seen these films? How do you feel about the redeployment of your music in this way?

A: I saw these films and I'm satisfied with the way the directors used my music. The most spectacular was what Terrence Malick made in *The Tree of Life*—the Lacrimosa there sounds as if it was composed for that film.

CHAPTER 5

Music by Zbigniew Preisner? Fictional Composers and Compositions in the Kieślowski Collaborations

Jonathan Godsall

Zbigniew Preisner is a composer of many voices. The different facets of his output are evidenced by concerts of his music that took place in London in 1999 and 2007.[1] The first half of each was devoted to a concert work: in 1999, *Requiem for My Friend*, Preisner's first such piece, written in honour of the recently deceased director Krzysztof Kieślowski; in 2007, *Silence, Night & Dreams*, a large-scale song cycle. The expansion of Preisner's non-film output since *Requiem*—with 2015's *Ten Pieces for Orchestra* the most recent addition—has coincided with a relatively quiet spell in his film-scoring career, with only a handful of assignments having been completed in the last decade, but it is as a film composer that Preisner remains most famous.[2] In both 1999 and 2007, it was his music for film—and particularly for the films of Kieślowski, with whom he collaborated regularly from 1985's *No End* to 1994's *Three Colours: Red*, the director's final film—on which the second halves of the concerts focused.

J. Godsall (✉)
School of Humanities and Performing Arts, Plymouth University, Plymouth, United Kingdom

Perhaps surprising for anyone not familiar with Preisner's oeuvre, however, would be the opinion of Jonathan Broxton and James Southall, writing of the 1999 concert that '[t]he highlight of the second half [...] was undoubtedly the performance of Van den Budenmayer's *Concerto in E Minor* from *The Double Life of Véronique* [Krzysztof Kieślowski, 1991]'.[3] The same piece also featured in the later event. How could another composer's work be the highlight of a concert of Preisner's music? The answer, of course, is that Van den Budenmayer *is* Preisner, or rather, a pseudonym of Preisner's. In *Véronique* the *Concerto* is performed in a key scene, and elsewhere in the same film (set in the then-present day) we are informed that Van den Budenmayer was a Dutch composer who lived from 1755 to 1803, but who was 'discovered only very recently'. In reality, though, and along with other pieces 'by' Van den Budenmayer and similarly fictional composers featured in other Kieślowski films, the *Concerto* was written by Preisner.

Preisner's fictional voices are the concern of this chapter. That the *Concerto*, a piece effectively written by Preisner not as himself but while pretending to be someone else, was the 'highlight' of that 1999 concert for at least some in the audience is still striking, and illustrates the centrality of such music to his identity as a composer. It is thus an important avenue for exploration in this sense, but also, I will argue, forms an intriguing case study situated within a wider field as yet largely unexplored by musicology.

Fictional Music in Theory and Practice

The *Concerto in E Minor* is an example of *fictional music*, which I define generally as original music, existing within a work of fiction's storyworld, which the work implies has been composed by one or more of its fictional characters. In *Véronique* the *Concerto* supposedly written by Van den Budenmayer features in a diegetic concert performance, during which Weronika (Irène Jacob)—the protagonist of the first part of the film, and the soprano soloist for the piece—collapses and dies. Excerpts from it are also performed by other characters in the film, as for instance when Véronique (also Jacob)—Weronika's double, and the focus of the longer second part of the film—leads her school pupils in a rendition of its principal theme.

Given this manner of its representation, the *Concerto* is more particularly an example of *observable-in* fictional music. This term I borrow from Paisley Livingston's discussion of 'nested art', the broader phenomenon of one artwork being nested within another. Livingston distinguishes between 'artistic structures presented or made observable-in some artistic representation' (what he terms nested artworks) and 'those merely described or evoked, the underlying point being that what nesting makes possible is a direct gauging or appreciation of an artistic structure on display'.[4] The *Concerto* is observable-in *Véronique* because it was actually composed by Preisner and recorded by real musicians, meaning that the film's audience can hear it as music. Other such filmic examples range from the *Warsaw Concerto*, composed by Richard Addinsell for performance (and supposed composition) by the piano-virtuoso main character of *Dangerous Moonlight* (Brian Desmond Hurst, 1941), to the songs of the titular band in *This Is Spinal Tap* (Rob Reiner, 1984).[5] Examples realized by Preisner and featured prominently within Kieślowski films include other pieces by Van den Budenmayer heard in *Decalogue IX* (1990), *Three Colours: Blue* (1993) and *Three Colours: Red* (1994), music by unnamed composers in *Decalogue II* (1990) and *Véronique*, and music by the central composer characters in *Three Colours: Blue*.

In *Blue*, Preisner's *Song for the Unification of Europe* is a piece fictionally begun by the character Patrice de Courcy (Hugues Quester), a celebrated composer, but left to be completed by his wife, Julie (Juliette Binoche), and friend Olivier (Benoît Régent) following the deaths of Patrice and his and Julie's daughter. The *Song* is notable for appearing not only sonically, but also in part via notation that is legible to the film's audience. This exemplifies another manner in which fictional music can be observable-in any kind of visual or indeed literary artwork, and also illustrates Livingston's further notions of 'partial nesting' (given that we only see certain pages or staves of the scores) and of the representation of works that are themselves somehow partial or incomplete (given that we see manuscript scores to which changes can be and are made by Julie and Olivier).[6] In general, though, observable-in fictional music that is more specifically *audible-in* is the most significant possibility attached to art forms with a sonic component, with non-film examples ranging from the 'Prize Song' of Richard Wagner's *Die Meistersinger von Nürnberg* (1868) to the country hits of television show *Nashville* (2012–). By contrast, novels in particular have encouraged authors to conjure wonderful *ekphrastic* compositions, as for instance in Thomas Mann's *Doctor Faustus* (1947) or Anthony Burgess's *A Clockwork Orange* (1962).

One gets a sense here of how Preisner's fictional music fits into a bigger tradition. It is a uniquely extensive case within that tradition, though, given the network of fictional composers and compositions developed across multiple collaborations with Kieślowski, to be considered further below. Nonetheless, it will still illustrate general aspects of the concept and category of fictional music, particularly of the audible-in type. This phenomenon has so far been underexplored in musicological scholarship, previous studies of particular cases having not addressed the functions and attributes shared by examples of such music beyond a particular text, genre or medium.[7]

Peter J. Rabinowitz has outlined his own definition of fictional music as simply 'music that pretends to be a different performance of some other music'.[8] His concern with the phenomenon's presence in concert music and opera can be expanded to include other art forms (music by Preisner, performed by real musicians, pretends to be music by Van den Budenmayer performed by characters in *Véronique*, for instance), and in any case usefully highlights that fictional music can be nested within other music. Furthermore, an interesting implication of his definition is that fictional music need not be nested at all, though we might say that the music in such cases still appears to generate its own nest (its own fiction, at least), as with Peter Schickele's compositions as P. D. Q. Bach. While I adopt these ideas, though, Rabinowitz also includes in his category quotations of existing, real pieces that are presented within larger musical contexts, as for example in the works of Charles Ives. Rabinowitz's theories of how we listen to this 'music pretending to be other music' justify his broader remit, and indeed will be drawn upon later in this chapter, but overlook differences between music with its own history and music that is explicitly new, which have implications for both the creators and audiences of texts that include such music. I have appropriated Rabinowitz's term because his definition corresponds to meanings of the adjective 'fictional' less straightforwardly than my own, and is not widely used.[9]

Here, it is nonetheless worth overlooking some differences to consider the telling similarities between examples of fictional pieces such as in *Véronique* and *Blue* and cases of the filmic representation of real, pre-existing compositions, all of which fall under Livingston's even broader umbrella of 'nested art'. Take *Amadeus* (Milos Forman, 1984). Like those Kieślowski films, this has a musical protagonist, albeit a real one: Mozart. And, as in those other films, we witness diegetic musical performances, though the music performed is again now real music that we might say 'plays itself' in the manner of a real person appearing as themselves within a fiction film.[10] A particularly strong comparison is with *Blue*, given the composer characters and that the films both depict the compositional process. In *Amadeus*, this occurs most famously in the deathbed sequence of Mozart (Tom Hulce) dictating the 'Confutatis' of his *Requiem* to rival Salieri (F. Murray Abraham). The music here is sung by both characters, but also exists in orchestrated form in a seemingly shared internal diegetic space to which the film's audience is given access via a process of internal focalization, meaning that we can hear the piece taking shape as Salieri takes down each part in turn.[11] In *Blue*, an equivalent scene features Julie and Olivier working on the completion of Patrice's *Song for the Unification of Europe*. We hear the piano at which they work but also other instruments not present in the room, this orchestration evolving in real time as Julie suggests changes to the score. Again, we might think of this latter soundtrack component being heard internally by Julie and/or Olivier, though it is present primarily for the audience's benefit.

One difference is that the *Requiem* escapes the bedroom during the *Amadeus* sequence: images from that locale are intercut with others of Mozart's wife and son travelling back to Vienna to be with him, but the music (including Mozart's sickly sung dictation of it) continues uninterrupted. This does not occur in the composition scene in *Blue*. The broader strategy of which the deathbed 'escape' is just one example in *Amadeus* can be observed elsewhere in Kieślowski's film, though, and indeed in *Véronique* and other of the director's films featuring Preisner's fictional pieces, including some that do not focus on musical characters. Music that appears diegetically can seep out of the narrative into the film's narration, and so function not merely as an element furnishing a believable storyworld but also as 'film score'. In *Amadeus* and other Mozart biopics that Guido Heldt has studied, this 'links the life and work in a myth-making (or more often myth-reinforcing) feedback loop': 'in some films Mozart *becomes* Don Giovanni, not just through actions, but through the music; in some films, the Requiem indeed presages his own death, fulfilling the biographical myth, but fulfilling it because of the way the medium works'.[12] While Kieślowski's films do not interact with historical biography in the same way, their fictional compositions often have similarly symbolic roles to play, and fulfil these by moving fluidly between levels of narration (with their positioning in relation to the diegesis commonly ambiguous) as well as through their own musical attributes.

In *Blue*, for instance, Nicholas Reyland identifies two themes by Van den Budenmayer, and argues that Julie, the film's protagonist, 'must supplant one [...] with another in order to progress' with her life after the deaths of her husband and daughter.[13] The first theme is played by an ensemble at their joint funeral, and so is associated with the tragic event that threatens to metaphorically (and perhaps literally) end Julie's life, too. The second, though, is a theme that Julie, following the apparent intentions of her husband, weaves into her completion of his *Song for the Unification of Europe*. This Budenmayer theme, then, represents the closure and control that will allow her to move forward. Though musically similar to the first in many respects (some of which will be considered below), it hints at a major key and so has what Reyland describes as a 'yearning quality', where the first sits unwaveringly in the minor.[14] It is the second theme that comes to predominate on the soundtrack; Reyland states that '[n]ot to hear this musical exchange is to miss something crucial in *Blue*'s plot'.[15] And, importantly, neither theme is heard only in diegetic performance. Quite whether they are then always (or ever) truly non-diegetic is a matter for individual interpretation; the film also allows its audience to conceive of cues being internally diegetic (though never as clearly as in the aforementioned composition scene), or else as somehow supernaturally diegetic (on the idea of which more below). The music can signify different stages in Julie's life in any of these positions, the more significant factor being its detachment from obvious diegetic motivation. At the least, the boundary between narrative and narration is blurred, creating ambiguity emblematic of the film's broader interpretive openness.

In *Véronique*, too, the *Concerto* echoes between the lives of Weronika and Véronique, not only through its simple diegetic occurrence in both. At the very beginning of the film, for example, we see Weronika in childhood, and hear a foreshadowing of her fate. A presumably non-diegetic recorder plays what is later revealed to be the main theme of the *Concerto*, but the melody is cut off abruptly before resolution, much as Weronika will later collapse and die during a performance of the same piece. Elsewhere, recurring fragments of the *Concerto*, both diegetic and not, function much like the repeated visual motifs of reflection and refraction also present throughout the film, contributing to the uncanny atmosphere through which we perceive the doubled lives of the doppelgängers (an atmosphere to which the music's literally unreal status perhaps generally contributes, here and in other Kieślowski films). There is, in fact, very little music in *Véronique* that does not originate in some respect from the fictional Van den Budenmayer composition.[16]

It is not only within individual films but also across the collaborations of Kieślowski and Preisner that fictional pieces of music can work in these ways. Intertextual connections are a feature of Kieślowski's films more generally: the character of Weronika in *Véronique*—a singer with a heart condition—is prototyped by a minor character in *Decalogue IX*, for instance, while actor Aleksander Bardini appears in multiple films (bookended by roles as a lawyer in both *No End* and *Three Colours: White* [1994]). Musically, the centrepiece of a network that spans from Preisner and Kieślowski's earliest collaboration to their last is Van den Budenmayer, both generally and through the recurrence of specific pieces.

One such recurrence, apparently requested by Kieślowski himself, is of the Van den Budenmayer 'funeral music' in *Blue*,[17] which first appeared in *No End* without being attributed to any particular fictional composer. In the earlier film, the theme is initially heard at moments when Antek (Jerzy Radziwiłłowicz), the recently deceased husband of protagonist Ula (Grażyna Szapołowska), either actually appears as a ghost or is implied to be in Ula's thoughts. These occurrences, in which the melody is orchestrated in different ways, are all most safely interpreted as non-diegetic: no source is actively implied, and significantly neither Ula nor her son Jacek (Krzysztof Krzemiński) is shown to hear the music. Yet near the end of the film, Jacek plays the same melody on their piano (and is shown to write on manuscript paper just prior to doing so, suggesting that he is transcribing or even composing the music) and a shocked Ula bursts into the room, before leaving in tears as Jacek turns back to the piano somewhat indifferently. This event calls the melody's prior status into explicit question, where in *Blue* and *Véronique* the ambiguity of music's positioning in relation to the diegesis is not so highlighted.

The *No End* theme seems to represent Antek not only for the film's audience, but also for its characters; this is the clearest explanation for Ula's anguish. In playing the melody and then appearing to take more interest in it than in his mother's distress, Jacek might be seen to be expressing a connection to his father that he does not share with her. Joseph Kickasola reads a political dimension into this, noting Antek's role as a lawyer defending members of the Solidarity movement and Jacek's apparent nascent interest in that movement, and moreover naming the tune as Jacek Kaczmarski's protest song 'Mury',[18] an 'unofficial hymn' of Solidarity.[19] Importantly, however, its melody is shaped differently to that of 'Mury' (which was written to the tune of Lluis Llach's Catalan protest song 'L'Estaca'), though it is similar in its phrasing and range and so was perhaps designed to evoke Kaczmarski's song. Indeed, Reyland spots a resemblance to the Polish hymn 'Holy God' that he confirmed as deliberate in his own interviews with Preisner.[20] Again, though, the melody is similar but clearly not the same; the theme in *No End* is original and thus fictional music (Figs. 5.1, 5.2, and 5.3).

Given the appearance of Antek's ghost at various points in the film, a supernatural interpretation of the music's recurrence and eventual diegetic utterance would not be inappropriate (though this is not to say that it *would* be an inappropriate way of understanding the ambiguous status of music in *Blue* and *Véronique*; the supernatural is emphasized in *No End*, but might also explain *Véronique*'s doublings, for instance). Has the tune also been a ghost, literally haunting Ula and Jacek? (Does Jacek even play it? After all, the camera cuts away to shots of Ula in another room at the moment we hear the piano.) Reyland suggests that 'the music's crossing between afterlife and life, nondiegetic score and diegesis, anticipates the border crossing Ula will undertake' upon her eventual suicide, implying a ghostly reading on his part.[21] The connection to either or both 'Mury' and 'Holy God' hints, though, at a straightforward reason for the association with Antek the melody seemingly holds for Ula and Jacek, namely that they associated it with him at a time prior to the film's narrative. Ula might even have been hearing it internally at some or all of its earlier moments of occurrence during that narrative (in which case 'haunting' could still be an appropriate description of its relationship to her, if in a more mundane sense). While its evocation of a protest song suggests an association with Antek's *life*, the theme's resemblance to a hymn (and its rather funereal musical character) points instead to Antek's death, and specifically his funeral. This second connection is then, of course, supported by the same music's later appearance as *Blue*'s first Van den Budenmayer theme, played at the funeral of Julie's husband and daughter.

That this apparent confirmation occurs only in another film eight years later is precisely the point: *No End* might imply this reading, but leaves its audience to fill in the gaps. Whether Kieślowski and Preisner intended the theme's use as funeral music in *Blue* to reflect back on *No End* in this way is unclear; in any case, it does. Its repetition also more generally connects

Fig. 5.1 *No End* melody, Jacek's piano version. Music by Zbigniew Preisner. © Copyright 1985 Amplitude Publishing. Used by permission

Fig. 5.2 'L'Estaca' (first two phrases, transposed from A minor into G minor for ease of comparison). © Copyright 1968 by Lluis Llach Grande; SEEMSA, Alcalá 70, 28009 Madrid (Spain). Used by permission

Fig. 5.3 Refrain from 'Holy God' ('Święty Boże', traditional Polish church song)

the mourning processes of the two widows, emphasizing the importance of Julie supplanting this theme with the other, given that Ula's inability (or unwillingness) to escape it leads to her suicide. Such is the multidimensional manner in which Preisner's fictional pieces can function both within and between Kieślowski's films.

Composing Fiction

The nature of the regular and trusting collaboration between Kieślowski and Preisner was key to the construction of the unique universe of fictional music that envelops their films, both in the sense of allowing that universe to develop over the course of multiple projects, and in that of pushing the music to the foreground in many of them. Preisner has said that 'the music in [Kieślowski's] films was considered as part of the initial concept',[22] and that

> [f]or *Véronique* I recorded about 80 per cent of the music before the film was shot and for *Blue* I recorded almost all the music before the shooting. The music was already prepared for in the scripts; Krzysztof and his co-screenwriter generally made very precise indications in their scripts with instructions, such as 'Here the music will play for 45 seconds or one minute ten seconds'.[23]

Kieślowski himself remarked that '[i]n a way, [*Blue*] was shot as an illustration of the music'.[24]

What are the processes by which a real person goes about writing music 'in character' as a fictional one, though? This is an intriguing question to be asked in relation to any fictional music (even if it is only described and not actually composed); the peculiarity of this creative process provides much of the justification for defining and exploring this category in the way I suggest. That there is a whole genre of such music within the Preisner-Kieślowski collaborations—including multiple pieces 'by' the same fictional composer, and similar pieces 'by' multiple different fictional composers, all of which can be compared—makes that genre in many respects the ideal fictional music case study.

The creative process here must be mostly inferred through examination of Preisner's pieces as they exist in their final forms, though. Preisner has said little about how he composes 'in character' in previous interviews, and remarks in our interview only that 'I try to be that composer. I think about what he wants to say, what music language and style.'[25] A tendency not to intellectualize his own process is present in regard to other aspects of his work and indeed in other interviews, too, and so does not relate specifically to the subject of his fictional alter egos. Nonetheless, that Preisner acknowledges the notion of his playing a role in these cases, allowing fictional musical voices to speak through his own, validates a useful way of conceptualizing this process from a scholarly perspective.

Imitation is probably the most obvious method of writing in another voice, as evidenced by the abundance of examples of pastiche and emulation in cases of fictional music. The Beatles-alike songs of make-believe band The Rutles, as already usefully discussed by John Covach,[26] present only the most obvious examples of pieces that might be fruitfully studied as instances of applied musical analysis and criticism (obvious because their targets and lovingly satirical intent are so apparent). In the case of alleged late-eighteenth-century Dutch composer Van den Budenmayer, Preisner at least eschewed possibilities for imitation of music by historically or culturally appropriate figures, describing his alter ego's style as 'close to Neo-Romanticism, with its mixture of Classical Romanticism and the compositional techniques of contemporary music'.[27] While the evident (and at least partly intentional) relation of the *Blue/No End* funeral music to pre-existing melodies discussed above does not point to the Netherlands either, though, it does point to Preisner's imitative abilities.[28] Citing his own interviews with Preisner, Reyland also suggests then-recent compositions of Krzysztof Penderecki's late neo-Romantic style as a model for the *Song* of *Blue*'s present-day composers, and intriguingly points out that Preisner 'vehemently dislikes' this style, an issue to which I will return shortly below.[29]

External models aside, Reyland hears a common 'Budenmayeran quality' in the two themes in *Blue*, noting among other attributes that they are both in minor keys (notwithstanding the second theme's suggestion of its relative major, mentioned above), have similar slow tempi, and share 'aspects of phrasing and rhythm'; dotted figures are the most obvious of the latter (Figs. 5.4 and 5.5).[30] The main theme of the *Concerto* in *Véronique*, too, shares all of these attributes, as well as the combination of stepwise and chordal melodic movement present in both *Blue* melodies (Fig. 5.6).[31] And the cadential melody of the song that first appears in *Decalogue IX*, and later recurs in *Red*, also exhibits those melodic characteristics, further pivoting around the second degree of the scale in a manner common to Van den Budenmayer's other conclusions (Fig. 5.7). This all suggests that Preisner follows certain compositional 'rules' when writing in character.

The living composers in *Blue*—Julie and Olivier—share the 'conservative diatonic palette' that Reyland identifies as underpinning Van den Budenmayer's work,[32] and also have their own recognizable traits—their own generative 'rules', perhaps—in being differentiated through stereotypically feminine and masculine musical voices. In the composition scene mentioned earlier, for example, Julie feminizes an orchestration previously completed by Olivier, removing percussion and trumpet from the first melody, and settling on a solo recorder instead of a piano for the second.[33] Both of these melodies in fact appear to be inventions of Olivier and not Patrice, or at least are notable for not appearing in Julie's own eventual completion of the *Song* as heard in the film's celebrated final montage.[34] The rapid rising gesture that opens the first, with the strong pitches of a

Fig. 5.4 Van den Budenmayer funeral music in *Blue*. Music by Zbigniew Preisner. © Copyright 1994 MK2 SA, Chester Music Limited. All Rights Reserved. International Copyright Secured. Used by permission of Chester Music Limited

Fig. 5.5 Second Van den Budenmayer theme in *Blue* (as initially heard in Julie's version of the *Song*). Music by Zbigniew Preisner. © Copyright 1994 MK2 SA, Chester Music Limited. All Rights Reserved. International Copyright Secured. Used by permission of Chester Music Limited

Fig. 5.6 Main theme, Van den Budenmayer *Concerto in E Minor* from *Véronique*. Music by Zbigniew Preisner. © Copyright 1991 Delabel Editions SARL/ New Music BV. Used by permission of Sony/ATV Music Publishing (Germany) GmbH

Fig. 5.7 Cadential melody, Van den Budenmayer song from *Decalogue IX*. Music by Zbigniew Preisner. © Copyright 1989 Amplitude Publishing. Used by permission

minor triad outlined over a stable bass, might be interpreted as particularly masculine (Fig. 5.8).

This theme is first heard around ten minutes prior to the composition scene: Olivier plays it on his piano for Julie, albeit lightly and with an arpeggiated accompaniment in the left hand. Olivier is in love with Julie, and the manner in which he intently focuses on her as he plays suggests a desire for her approval not only musically: the masculine nature of the theme promotes a reading of the scene as an awkward attempt at seduction, in response to which Julie appears unmoved. A few minutes later, however, and indeed after the final utterance of the funeral music connected with Julie's previous life (among other significant events), the theme returns

Fig. 5.8 Olivier's theme from *Blue*. Music by Zbigniew Preisner. © Copyright 1994 MK2 SA, Chester Music Limited. All Rights Reserved. International Copyright Secured. Used by permission of Chester Music Limited

without diegetic motivation, still for solo piano but now in the more forceful guise shown in Fig. 5.8. Here it seems to cue Julie's return to Olivier's apartment to work on the music with him, and so also their eventual sexual relationship, in which Olivier is portrayed as dominant by the final montage's image of Julie pressed between him and a fish tank.[35]

That the fictional music in Kieślowski's films is often required to play such symbolic parts, as also seen with other examples discussed above, would have made Preisner's task in composing it all the more difficult. This music must do multiple things at once, and its general success in doing so forms the basis for Reyland's defence of the *Song* in particular against those who criticize that piece for not sounding like the great twentieth-century concert music *Blue*'s plot arguably requires it to be.[36] Indeed (and recalling Preisner's own opinion of the neo-Romantic Penderecki repertoire on which he might have modelled the piece), Reyland wonders whether the *Song*'s 'very artifice might not also be a carrier of meaning', asking, '[t]o what degree do Preisner's neo-romantic avatars satirize a tradition he disdains?'[37]

The Fictional and the Real

Preisner himself calls *Blue*'s *Song* 'pompous'.[38] Its fictional status as an anthem for European unification places it in what Kieślowski described as a context of 'elevated tones and exceptionally weighty words—to put it positively—or bombast—to put it negatively',[39] and suggests that the composer commissioned to write it—Patrice—is more conservative populist than high-art progressive (as does the media coverage of his death shown in the film).[40] To hear it as at once unadventurous and pretentious is therefore not only possible, but seemingly authorially sanctioned.

Why, then, did the piece appear as the finale to both concerts of Preisner's music mentioned at the start of this chapter, and indeed on the 1995 'best of' compilation album *Preisner's Music* (itself a recording of a live event), in that latter case with no reference in the track listing or liner notes to any fictional composer?[41] The apparent care that Preisner takes over releasing his film music for extra-filmic consumption—summarized by his statement in the interview here that 'some music can be heard without film, some not'[42]—might be read as incompatible with the 'pompous' *Song*'s straightforward presentation for such consumption, given that some listeners inevitably will not have seen *Blue*. Then again, music composed *as* (fictional) concert music is in one sense a logical choice for presentation in that manner. And the success of the *Song* outside of its filmic context could be taken as an example of the gap that inevitably exists between intention and reception, and moreover as calling into question the validity of suggestions that the piece is not 'good' real-world concert music, in a way at least.

As for the Penderecki connection, the accessible style and harmonic soundworld that the older composer's late neo-Romantic works share with Preisner's fictional compositions are complemented by more specific similarities. The orchestra, choir and soprano soloist scoring of *Blue*'s *Song*, for example, in fact most obviously prefigures that of Penderecki's *Symphony No. 7* ('Seven Gates of Jerusalem'), a 1996 work for orchestra, choir, vocal soloists and narrator, and *Credo*, from 1998 and for orchestra, choir, children's choir and vocal soloists. The more intriguing pre-echo, though, particularly in light of his apparent distaste for this style, is of some of Preisner's own concert music, which we might reasonably understand to represent his own voice most directly.

Given the tendency of fictional pieces in Kieślowski's films to escape the diegesis, it is often hard (and, arguably, pointless) to distinguish between those pieces and Preisner's 'own' scoring for the purposes of analysis. This blurred line between 'real' and 'fictional' aspects of the composer's output also exists on a larger scale. Preisner acknowledges in our interview that his and Van den Budenmayer's styles are 'similar',[43] for instance, which is to be expected given that Preisner's fictional voices emanate from the same background of (a lack of formal) training and influence as his own.[44] Perhaps more interesting is the possibility that composing 'in character' has provided opportunities for the *development* of his own voice.

Requiem for My Friend, Preisner's first concert work, was, after all, composed only after the collaborations with Kieślowski that gave rise to those opportunities. It features stylistic traits that illustrate the blurred general divide between real and fictional, including writing for solo recorder (and specifically the recorder of regular collaborator Jacek Ostaszewski) that echoes the prominent use of that instrument not only in fictional contexts (as in the *Blue* composition scene mentioned above) but also, for example, on the score to the fictional-music-less *Decalogue I* (1989). More particularly, though, the *Requiem*'s solo soprano part was written specifically for (and has since been performed and recorded by) the voice of Elżbieta Towarnicka, most familiar from the solo roles similarly taken for *Blue*'s *Song*, *Véronique*'s *Concerto*, and the Van den Budenmayer song heard in *Decalogue IX* and *Red*. And its second half—titled 'Life', and scored for orchestra, choir, and other vocal and instrumental soloists alongside Towarnicka and Ostaszewski—notably has more in common with the 'monumental' sound of pieces by Van den Budenmayer and the composers in *Blue* than it does with the restrained, sparse cues that otherwise characterize Preisner's scores for Kieślowski and others.

Of course, the nature of a film composer's regular scoring work might force them to write music in a 'voice' that does not come naturally, which could itself act in the development of their own 'sound'. Fictional music undoubtedly presents particular opportunities and challenges in this regard, though. A piece of fictional concert music will inherently have more in common with a real concert piece than a film score cue in many respects. But while a developmental reading is therefore tempting in Preisner's case, it might equally be true that consistency between his real and fictional work is owing to nothing more than a relatively unchanged, pre-existing response to the demands of concert composition, for which the Kieślowski collaborations simply provided the first opportunities.

Either way, the resemblance to fictional pieces of the *Requiem* in particular remains, and if anything is highlighted by Preisner's freer exploration of other aspects of his voice in later concert works. Pop and jazz influences are audible in the *Requiem*'s solo saxophone writing, for instance, but more fully characterize many of the rhythms, harmonies and simple lyrical melodies of *Ten Easy Pieces for Piano* (1999). And a 'New Age' aesthetic is apparent in subsequent large-scale works such as *Silence, Night & Dreams* (for orchestra, choir, and instrumental and vocal soloists). While this broader fluidity of Preisner's voice could suggest that his fictional compositions have played a less important part in the evolution of his style than proposed above, in order to account for that fluidity we might

78 J. GODSALL

nonetheless forward the idea of 'playing different characters' as one way of understanding his approach (and perhaps that of other composers with similarly varied outputs) to writing individual works of any kind.

What about the questions raised by the potentially critical pomposity of *Blue*'s *Song*, though? Similarities of the *Requiem* to that piece are not only broad: the later work's 'Kai Kairos' movement features what appears to be a quotation of Olivier's masculine-flirtation theme (Fig. 5.8 above), arguably the most pompous music in *Blue* (Fig. 5.9).

It is unclear whether this was a deliberate quotation, and if so what the reasoning was behind it. In any case, the musical similarity encourages us to interpret the movement via *Blue*, and to search for potential authorial intent in so doing. The movement's lyrics are adapted from Ecclesiastes 3:1–8 ('To every thing there is a season, and a time to every purpose under the heaven; [...]'), with the theme heard directly after an opposition of time 'to mourn' and time 'to dance'. Are we to recall the role of Olivier (and this melody) in moving Julie from a state of mourning to one of dancing (figuratively), one enactment of the text's meaning? Maybe so, but then what is to stop us from understanding this music as satire in the same way that the *Song* might be understood? Are we meant to not take the *Requiem* (or its second half, at least) seriously? Given its dedication to

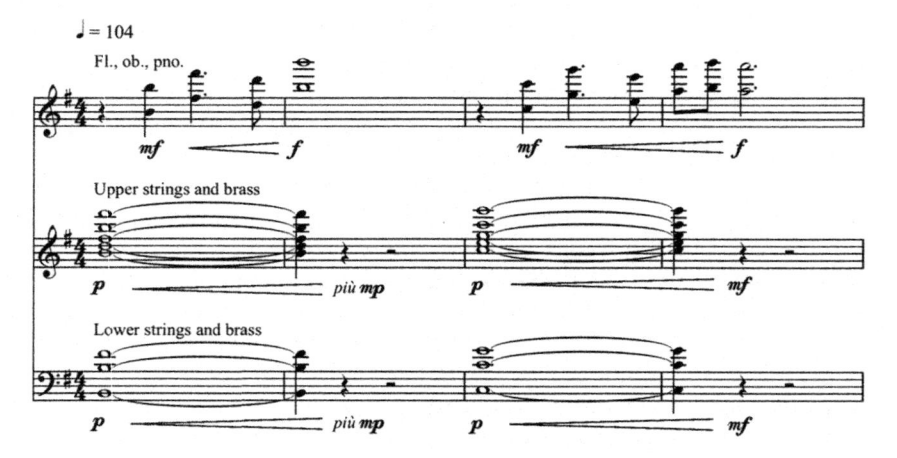

Fig. 5.9 *Requiem for My Friend*, 'Kai Kairos', bars 84–87. Arranged by Zbigniew Preisner. © Copyright 1996, Chester Music Limited. All Rights Reserved. International Copyright Secured. Used by permission of Chester Music Limited

Kieślowski, this is surely not the case. Preisner refers to the work's final 'Prayer' movement being 'very personal':

> I am asking for the strength to go on living in this sad situation. In my life, there were only very few people I wanted to spend time with. One of them was Krzysztof. This prayer is also a request, that such friendship could be found once more.[45]

The lack of clarity here owes broadly to a blurring of the real and the fictional. The line between these states is being crossed in much of what has been discussed above. Most notable is that fictional music audible-in a work of fiction inherently straddles that line: such music is fictional and yet also inarguably real, because we can hear it. The relationship of a fictional piece—a fictional *utterance*—to reality is thus very different to that of fictional *entities* such as characters or physical objects. In this specific case, there are intriguing convolutions. The music of *Blue*'s composition scene is, as Reyland notes, 'music that *might* be, rather than music that was or yet is', for example.[46] And yet, through realizing music that does not and might never formally exist (as a published, performed, publicly available composition) in the fictional storyworld, Preisner creates music that does and always will exist in that way for us. Conversely, the films also imply the existence of music that the fictional audience has heard and will hear—earlier works by *Blue*'s Patrice, for instance—but that we cannot.

The presence and presentation of Preisner's fictional music in concert, on record, as published sheet music and elsewhere in real life takes this further, with fictional pieces appearing alongside and even within real ones. While the appearance of Olivier's theme in Preisner's *Requiem* provides an apparent example of self-quotation, note also the sampling of *Véronique*'s *Concerto* in German rapper Spax's 'Psycho' (2003) and Philadelphian hip-hop duo OuterSpace's 'Written in Blood' (2011) (the latter containing the rather appropriate-to-*Véronique* refrain lyric 'Live life after death'), and of the *Blue/No End* funeral music in 'La Quête' (1998) by Québécois hip-hop group La Constellation. Van den Budenmayer's music here escapes even further into reality (in cases of life-art imitating art-art, given Julie's quotation of another Van den Budenmayer melody in her completion of the *Song*).[47]

The real-world existence of this music can, moreover, have implications for interpretation of the film(s) from which it originates. As a simple but significant example, while I have suggested above that the reappearance of music from *No End* in *Blue* clarifies our understanding of its meaning for the earlier film's characters, a not dissimilar process in fact clarifies its *identity* in both films, for in neither is there any mention of its having been composed by Van den Budenmayer. Reyland points to *Blue*'s screenplay and cue sheet as confirming its alleged origin,[48] but more relevant for the majority of audience members would be *Blue*'s soundtrack release, which labels it similarly.[49]

More generally, and particularly given that the para- and extra-textual forms of these pieces are often somehow different than those heard in the films (*Blue*'s soundtrack release features organ versions of both Van den Budenmayer themes, for instance, which are not heard in the film and so seem to offer a glimpse of a bigger oeuvre), these other existences of Preisner's fictional compositions do not just extend the 'experiences' of Kieślowski's films beyond the end credits (in the manner of other cases of film music's real-world reception in, say, concert-hall performances). More specifically, they extend their *fictions* into the real world. In the terms of Kendall Walton's conception of fiction, they are 'props' that allow and, if encountered, prompt the continuation of the games of make-believe that audiences are initially encouraged to play by Kieślowski's films. Those films set the 'principles of generation' that mandate our imagining that the pieces were composed and interacted with by fictional characters. When the pieces are later heard elsewhere they can thus, like the tree stumps imagined to be bears as per the rules of a child's game of make-believe, renew our investment in the fictional worlds that originally surrounded them.[50]

Rabinowitz puts forward a similar idea of the audience playing a role, applicable here despite his wider definition of fictional music. He states that, in order to fully comprehend and appreciate such music, 'we must listen to [it] simultaneously as what it is and what it appears to be', and suggests that doing so might involve our pretending to hear that music in a different time and/or place—those of its fictional reception, rather than those in which we actually hear it—and moreover in a different evaluative light.[51] The latter point sets up another riposte to those critics who argue that *Blue*'s *Song* is of inadequate quality, namely that those critics are not 'playing the game', though they are of course entitled not to do so.[52] Given the potential for Preisner's fictional pieces to be encountered in real-world contexts that might not highlight their fictional status at all, and/or by audiences not familiar with Kieślowski's films, differences of opinion might also occur for more innocent reasons; this is music that leads a double life, like *Véronique*'s doppelgängers.[53] Rabinowitz asserts that it is often the context in which such music is presented that cues us to listen in the manner he suggests, and this is probably particularly true with fictional pieces like Preisner's, which are not obviously silly or satirical in the manner of, say, the songs of Spinal Tap.[54] When Preisner's compositions fly their fictional nests, they can easily defy Rabinowitz's ideal mode of interpretation. Much as the filmic roles of these pieces are characterized by ambiguity and by the music's moving freely in and around narrative spaces, then, so in the real world this fictional music, precisely because of such music's peculiar relationship with reality, displays a fluidity of identity and of the potential interactions that it directly invites. In this sense, it is arguably the music most representative of its multivoiced composer.

Notes

1. The programme of the 1999 concert can be inferred from reviews. See Jonathan Broxton and James Southall, 'Zbigniew Preisner—In Concert: *Requiem for My Friend*', Movie Music UK, http://web.archive.org/web/20081020230549/http://www.moviemusicuk.us/preisint.htm, accessed 13 August 2015, and Tess James, 'Review of Zbigniew Preisner, *Requiem for My Friend*', Music Theory Online, vol. 5, no. 4 (September 1999), http://www.mtosmt.org/issues/mto.99.5.4/mto.99.5.4.james.html, accessed 13 August 2015. For the programme of the 2007 concert, see Zbigniew Preisner, *Silence, Night & Dreams*, Barbican, 2 December 2007, programme, http://www.barbican.org.uk/media/events/6112preisnerproglowresforweb.pdf, accessed 13 August 2015.
2. At the time of writing, some of his non-film compositions—including *Ten Pieces*—have not been performed outside of the recording studio, but I will nonetheless describe them as 'concert music' below for the sake of consistency and clarity.
3. Broxton and Southall, 'Zbigniew Preisner'.
4. Paisley Livingston, 'Nested Art', *Journal of Aesthetics and Art Criticism*, vol. 61, no. 3 (Summer 2003), 238.
5. For a discussion of several examples including the *Warsaw Concerto*, see Ben Winters, *Music, Performance, and the Realities of Film: Shared Concert Experiences in Screen Fiction* (Abingdon: Routledge, 2014), 47–66. On the songs of Spinal Tap, see John Covach, 'Stylistic Competencies, Musical Humor, and *This Is Spinal Tap*', in

Elizabeth West Marvin and Richard Hermann (eds), *Concert Music, Rock and Jazz Since 1945: Essays and Analytical Studies* (Rochester: University of Rochester Press, 1995), 399–421.
6. See Livingston, 'Nested Art', 238–40.
7. These studies, two of which are named in endnote 5 above, of course use different perspectives to aim at different goals. John Covach's essay on *This Is Spinal Tap* explores how listeners' knowledge of certain musical styles affects perception of that film's musical humour, for instance. Covach, 'Stylistic Competencies'.
8. Peter J. Rabinowitz, 'Fictional Music: Toward a Theory of Listening', in Harry R. Garvin (ed.), *Theories of Reading, Looking, and Listening* (London: Associated University Presses, 1981), 198.
9. My definition in fact more closely matches the concept of 'imaginary music' that Rabinowitz coins (but does not fully define or explore) in a discussion of music in Burgess's *A Clockwork Orange*: Peter J. Rabinowitz, '"A Bird of Like Rarest Spun Heavenmetal": Music in *A Clockwork Orange*', in Stuart Y. McDougal (ed.), *Stanley Kubrick's* A Clockwork Orange (Cambridge: Cambridge University Press, 2003), 109–30. My objection to this term is largely nomenclatural, for while the sound of *ekphrastic* music in a novel will have to be imagined by a reader, viewers need not imagine that of a film's audible-in music. 'Fictional music' better reflects the cross-media concept I have outlined.
10. A difference between Mozart's character and his music in *Amadeus* is that the character is a fictionalized version of a real, historical figure, whereas the music *is* the real music, at least compositionally. It is presented in fictional (or fictionalized) performances, however. To paraphrase Rabinowitz, these are performances that pretend to be different performances of the same music.
11. On the application of the narratological concept of focalization to music in film, see Guido Heldt, *Music and Levels of Narration in Film: Steps Across the Border* (Bristol: Intellect, 2013), 119–33.
12. Guido Heldt, 'Playing Mozart: Biopics and the Musical (Re)invention of a Composer', *Music, Sound, and the Moving Image*, vol. 3, no. 1 (Spring 2009), 25. Emphasis original.
13. Nicholas W. Reyland, *Zbigniew Preisner's* Three Colors *Trilogy:* Blue, White, Red—*A Film Score Guide* (Plymouth: Scarecrow Press, 2012), 185. My thanks to Nick for his authoritative book (on which I draw heavily below) and informal discussions with me about this topic.

14. Ibid., 202.
15. Ibid., 185.
16. The notable cues that do not relate to the *Concerto* are also examples of fictional music: the piece that Weronika sings with her choir at the beginning of the film, and the piano accompaniment that Alexandre uses for his puppet show at Véronique's school. A composer is not named in either case.
17. See Reyland, *Zbigniew Preisner's* Three Colors *Trilogy*, 171.
18. Joseph Kickasola, *The Films of Krzysztof Kieślowski: The Liminal Image* (New York: Continuum, 2004), 156–7.
19. José M. Faraldo, 'Spain: The Common Experience of Transition and a Military Coup', in Idesbald Goddeeris (ed.), *Solidarity with Solidarity: Western European Trade Unions and the Polish Crisis, 1980–1982* (Plymouth: Lexington Books, 2010), 59.
20. Reyland, *Zbigniew Preisner's* Three Colors *Trilogy*, 15.
21. Ibid., 98.
22. In Mark Russell and James Young, *Film Music: Screencraft* (Woburn: Focal Press, 2000), 167.
23. In Geoffrey Macnab and Chris Darke, 'Working with Kieślowski', *Sight and Sound*, vol. 6, no. 5 (May 1996), 20.
24. Quoted in ibid., 22.
25. Jonathan Godsall, Zbigniew Preisner Interview, this book, Chapter 4, 61.
26. John Covach, 'The Rutles and the Use of Specific Models in Musical Satire', *Indiana Theory Review*, vol. 11 (1991), 119–44.
27. In Macnab and Darke, 'Working with Kieślowski', 20.
28. The most famous example of imitation in his scoring is a non-fictional cue in *White*. Preisner explains: 'When, finally, the hero arrives back in Warsaw and is thrown on to a garbage dump he surveys his surroundings and exclaims, "Home at last". The music becomes very like Chopin, a Polish cultural icon—it was ironic. At that time Poland was one huge garbage dump.' In Russell and Young, *Screencraft*, 168.
29. Reyland, *Zbigniew Preisner's* Three Colors *Trilogy*, 40.
30. Ibid., 202.
31. The similarities are such that, argues Reyland, '[i]t is even just about possible to imagine that the [second Van den Budenmayer theme in *Blue*] is a reminiscence (misremembered by Patrice?) of the [...] Concerto heard in *Véronique*.' Ibid., 415n129.

32. Ibid., 75.
33. Olivier later declines Julie's assistance, asserting that 'this music can be mine. A little heavy and awkward, but mine'.
34. Reyland notes practical and other reasons for this, pointing out that the theme was present in Preisner's manuscript score for Julie's version. Reyland, *Zbigniew Preisner's* Three Colors *Trilogy*, 422–3n128. The final form of Julie's version in the film nonetheless suggests this authorial attribution, though the question of who authors much of *Blue*'s fictional music is a murky one more generally, as Reyland also explores. See ibid., 130–2.
35. As Reyland puts it, 'a man is back on top in Julie's life and she is shown here to be not just subjugated but suffocating in her new position'. Ibid., 235.
36. He argues that '[t]he most tedious subtext to criticism of the [*Song*] is a damning of the music as if it were being offered as a piece of actual Western art music, as opposed to a fictionalized representation thereof performing unique symbolic functions in the context of a narrative film.' Ibid., 125.
37. Ibid., 75, 40.
38. In ibid., 126.
39. In Paul Coates, '"The Inner Life Is the Only Thing that Interests Me": a conversation with Krzysztof Kieślowski', in Coates (ed.), *Lucid Dreams: The Films of Krzysztof Kieślowski* (Trowbridge: Flicks Books, 1999), 174. Quoted in Reyland, *Zbigniew Preisner's* Three Colors *Trilogy*, 125.
40. Geoff Andrew, *The* Three Colours *Trilogy* (London: British Film Institute, 1998), 88n10. Quoted in Reyland, *Zbigniew Preisner's* Three Colors *Trilogy*, 125.
41. Zbigniew Preisner, *Preisner's Music* (Virgin 7243 8 40799 2 5, 1995). CD.
42. Godsall, Zbigniew Preisner Interview, 62.
43. Godsall, Zbigniew Preisner Interview, 61.
44. See Reyland, *Zbigniew Preisner's* Three Colors *Trilogy*, 20–1.
45. In James, 'Review of Zbigniew Preisner'.
46. Reyland, *Zbigniew Preisner's* Three Colors *Trilogy*, 226. Emphasis original.
47. Consideration of the sampled music's functions and effects in those songs is beyond the remit of this chapter. The sampling of Addinsell's *Warsaw Concerto* in DMX's 'What's My Name' bears comparison in

terms of the sample's fictional status, and is discussed in Michael Long, *Beautiful Monsters: Imagining the Classic in Musical Media* (London: University of California Press, 2008), 33–41.
48. Reyland, *Zbigniew Preisner's* Three Colors *Trilogy*, 184.
49. Zbigniew Preisner, *Trois Couleurs: Bleu—Bande Originale du Film* (Virgin 72438 39027 2 9, 1993). CD.
50. See Kendall Walton, *Mimesis as Make-Believe: On the Foundations of the Representational Arts* (Cambridge: Harvard University Press, 1990). The potential for solely non-diegetic cues (and 'real' diegetic music) to prompt such make-believe when heard outside of the cinema would be an interesting topic for future thought. If one agrees with Ben Winters' suggestion that a film's characters can experience the music conventionally thought of as non-diegetic that surrounds them, the specificity of fictional music's ability to act in this way disappears entirely, though the distinctions between it and other kinds of music in this regard might not be concrete in any case. See Winters, *Music, Performance, and the Realities of Film*, 172–98.
51. Rabinowitz, 'Fictional Music', 199–203.
52. Walton notes that, while art appreciation will generally involve playing games of make-believe, art criticism will often not, for it might instead attend solely to questions of *how* the art functions. Walton, *Mimesis as Make-Believe*, 53.
53. Preisner has in the past also claimed Van den Budenmayer to be a real composer, as for instance in Mikael Carlsson and Peter Holm, 'The Double Life of Zbigniew Preisner', *Music from the Movies*, May 1997, 40–1.
54. Rabinowitz, 'Fictional Music', 207–8n12.

Bibliography

Broxton, Jonathan, and James Southall. 2015. Zbigniew Preisner—in Concert: *Requiem for My Friend. Movie Music UK.* http://web.archive.org/web/20081020230549/http://www.moviemusicuk.us/preisint.htm. Accessed 13 August 2015.

Carlsson, Mikael, and Peter Holm. 1997. The Double Life of Zbigniew Preisner. *Music from the Movies*, 38–42. May.

Covach, John. 1991. The Rutles and the Use of Specific Models in Musical Satire. *Indiana Theory Review* 11: 119–144.

———. 1995. Stylistic Competencies, Musical Humor, and *This Is Spinal Tap*. In *Concert Music, Rock and Jazz Since 1945: Essays and Analytical Studies*, ed.

Elizabeth West Marvin and Richard Hermann, 399–421. Rochester: University of Rochester Press.

Faraldo, José M. 2010. Spain: The Common Experience of Transition and a Military Coup. In *Solidarity with Solidarity: Western European Trade Unions and the Polish Crisis, 1980–1982*, ed. Idesbald Goddeeris, 51–73. Plymouth: Lexington Books.

Heldt, Guido. 2009. Playing Mozart: Biopics and the Musical (Re)Invention of a Composer. *Music, Sound, and the Moving Image* 3(1): 21–46.

———. 2013. *Music and Levels of Narration in Film: Steps Across the Border*. Bristol: Intellect.

James, Tess. 1999. Review of Zbigniew Preisner, *Requiem for My Friend*. *Music Theory Online* 5(4). http://www.mtosmt.org/issues/mto.99.5.4/mto.99.5.4.james.html. Accessed 13 August 2015.

Kickasola, Joseph. 2004. *The Films of Krzysztof Kieślowski: The Liminal Image*. New York: Continuum.

Livingston, Paisley. 2003. Nested Art. *The Journal of Aesthetics and Art Criticism* 61(3): 233–245.

Long, Michael. 2008. *Beautiful Monsters: Imagining the Classic in Musical Media*. London: University of California Press.

Macnab, Geoffrey, and Chris Darke. 1996. Working with Kieślowski. *Sight and Sound* 6(5): 16–22.

Preisner, Zbigniew. 1993. *Trois Couleurs: Bleu—Bande Originale du Film* (Virgin 72438 39027 2 9). CD.

———. 1995. *Preisner's Music* (Virgin 7243 8 40799 2 5). CD.

———. 2007. *Silence, Night & Dreams*. Barbican, 2 December. Programme, http://www.barbican.org.uk/media/events/6112preisnerproglowresforweb.pdf. Accessed 13 August 2015.

Rabinowitz, Peter J. 1981. Fictional Music: Toward a Theory of Listening. In *Theories of Reading, Looking, and Listening*, ed. Harry R. Garvin, 193–208. London: Associated University Presses.

———. 2003. 'A Bird of Like Rarest Spun Heavenmetal': Music in *A Clockwork Orange*. In *Stanley Kubrick's A Clockwork Orange*, ed. Stuart Y. McDougal, 109–130. Cambridge: Cambridge University Press.

Reyland, Nicholas W. 2012. *Zbigniew Preisner's Three Colors Trilogy: Blue, White, Red—A Film Score Guide*. Plymouth: Scarecrow Press.

Russell, Mark, and James Young. 2000. *Film Music: Screencraft*. Woburn: Focal Press.

Walton, Kendall. 1990. *Mimesis as Make-Believe: On the Foundations of the Representational Arts*. Cambridge: Harvard University Press.

Winters, Ben. 2014. *Music, Performance, and the Realities of Film: Shared Concert Experiences in Screen Fiction*. Abingdon: Routledge.

CHAPTER 6

Carter Burwell Interview

Lindsay Coleman

A memorable composer whose work is often a welcome hallmark in celebrated films such as *Miller's Crossing* (Coen brothers, 1990), *The Man Who Wasn't There* (Coen brothers, 2001), *Rob Roy* (Michael Caton-Jones, 1995) and *True Grit* (Coen brothers, 2010), Carter Burwell is probably best known for his now 30-year collaborative relationship with the Coen brothers. In addition to them he has also worked closely with Todd Haynes in television productions such as *Mildred Pierce* (2011), and the recent *Carol* (2015). Likewise he has collaborated for many years with Bill Condon on *Gods and Monsters* (1998) and the final two *Twilight* (2011 and 2012) films.

The following is the transcript of a Skype interview conducted with Burwell in late 2013. The interview was conducted by Lindsay Coleman.

Q: John Corigliano mentioned that the love theme of *Altered States* (Ken Russell, 1980) was based on a single moment in Blair Brown's performance in that film. How specific is your inspiration for character themes?

A: With Gabriel Byrne's performance in *Miller's Crossing*, that was the first instance where I was conscious that what the actor was giving was in turn providing me inspiration for the score. Another aspect of that is that, when I am approaching a film, I will usually pick two or three key scenes where, if the music works there, odds are it's

L. Coleman (✉)
Nunawading, Australia

going to work in other places also. That's part of the same issue. I'll take one scene. It might explicate the character. It might capture the paradox of the film. Or it might be especially difficult. I'll start there, and there may be something, some particular moment in the scene which becomes a clue to the music. I have to tell you, though, it's very unpredictable [laughs].

Q: Your comment on *Miller's Crossing* suggests a certain irony or perversity on your part. His performance is a provocation to you as composer.

A: That's right. And it's not unusual in the Coen brothers' films. They will often paint deliberately opaque characters. When we talk about the music, they are still quite opaque in our conversations. Another example of an opaque character is Billy Bob Thornton in *The Man Who Wasn't There*. He was intentionally the hole in the middle of the film. That is why the film has that title. When we talked about him Ethan came up with this one adjective—and it can be a lot even to get them to come up with one adjective for their characters—he said, 'he has yearning'. The point, really, is that he is yearning for something completely unspecified. He doesn't know what it is. We don't know what it is. But you have to believe that that character is after something, wants something. We thought that was what would pull the audience in. So I looked at his vacant gaze, and tried to write the something which was trapped, yet also suggest some kind of vague aspiration.

Q: Why did you feel the piano was so well suited to your score for that character? Was it because of his relationship with the Scarlett Johansson character, who of course plays the piano?

A: It was. We all agreed right from the start that that was going to be a logical sound for him. It, of course, also helped tie the score in with the Beethoven Sonatas. If the score hadn't featured piano then the Beethoven music and the score would have really been two separate musical worlds. That might have worked. But that was not what we wanted. We wanted it to be a little bit more integrated.

Q: Dario Marianelli talked about how judicious he had to be in his use of extracts of Beethoven on *The Soloist* (Joe Wright, 2009). Was that the same for the Piano Sonatas in *The Man Who Wasn't There*?

A: They were chosen while we were working on the film in post-production. We tried to pick what would not be classified as the more intellectual pieces. They had to be something which would somehow fit Billy Bob Thornton's character. They're not very complex musically, they're not the late pieces. They're the things his character would like. He would hear them and they would make him strive for some ill-defined something. They're sort of simple. Some of them don't sound like Beethoven, they're so simple. Some of them are more of what we would imagine as the clichéd pieces of Beethoven. Again that fits the character. They speak to a desire for the sublime he obviously will never achieve.

Q: *A Serious Man* (Coen brothers, 2009) is a mysterious film. How does one go about scoring such an opaque narrative, in turn full of mysterious characters?

A: It's a good question. As a composer there are things which I do, which you can see in that score, which are mechanisms which help me achieve a feeling of mystery. One such mechanism is the meter. The harp part which repeats is three-against-four. Are we in three or are we in four, you cannot tell. The melodies, which play through it, are in turn going against it, obscuring the meter. I can't tell where the bar lines are. That's something which I will do. There are things you can do harmonically also, when each instrument comes in—it's a simple score built largely of solo instruments—sometimes they'll come in in a different tonality than what you are expecting. I'm a very simple composer, so I rely on simple means such as this to convey mystery.

Q: You seem to have a strong relationship with Howard Shore.

A: We see each other every three years, but I like Howard a lot. We are both New York-based cats. His background with David Cronenberg has a lot of similarities with my work with the Coens. They are all filmmakers who occasionally are called on to do mainstream things. Howard does more mainstream things than I do. I sometimes go to ask him for advice.

Q: He makes bold decisions in terms of time signature. You mentioned being a 'simple composer'. Do you find that intimidating, inspiring?

A: I think it's great! Whenever any composer puts anything into a film score which is outside the middle-brow—I'm sorry but so much of film composition is mediocre, middle-brow—tradition of film music I always take my hat off to them. Any time people do complex meters, microtonality, Jerry Goldsmith, *Planet-of-the-Apes* type instrumentation … those kinds of challenges are not set by the filmmaker, they are set by the composer themself. Filmmakers don't ask composers to step out and experiment in that manner, at least I have never experienced that. I admire that. Also, a film like *Lord of the Rings* (Peter Jackson, 2001–2003), it's wall-to-wall music, certainly more than 100 minutes, for each of the respective scores he wrote for those films; it's a real challenge to keep it fresh, to keep it moving, to stop it from settling into a *mass*. I think part of what Howard was doing with such choices was to achieve exactly that.

Q: You use the program Sibelius to compose. Do you feel it would be appropriate to compose anything, or more film music specifically?

A: I don't think it is in any way particularly appropriate to film music over anything else. I've never interpreted it that way. I compose in a hybrid environment. I start at the piano, then I go into a piece of software called Digital Performer. I find it is faster. Then I'll go into Sibelius as a last step to make it legible. It has all the same limitations that music notation has. That's what it is designed for. It's a music notation program. I don't come from a music conservatory background. I was just working on something with a guitarist called David Torn, and sometimes I'll just put down whole notes and it becomes about the adjectives I'll use to explain to David. I'll say 'here a whole note, but I want it to say this, I want it to do that'. I can't do that with a symphony orchestra. Or maybe I could if I were Ligeti! [laughs]. Ideally it's somewhere in between. You have a certain amount of notation. I like it if it's free. Howard, I know, also likes this. Tom Newman, I know, is the same. I think it is lovely to get away from the page.

Q: A side point, but I was fascinated by how you knew the frequency of a refrigerator in a scene in *No Country for Old Men* (Coen brothers, 2007) was running at 60 hertz. How did you know that?

A: I knew that because our electricity runs at 60 hertz here in the States. Like most musicians I know, I am tortured when I walk into a room because there is always a background hum. It might be a refrigerator, an air-conditioner, etc. 60 hertz suffuses our environment here, and all the harmonics of 60 hertz. It's something we have to live with. Interestingly, it was something we could use in the scene. It's a musical note, but so low you don't think of it as a music note. It is close to a B natural.

Q: The bowing on the fiddle solos in *Fargo* (Coen brothers, 1996) is very distinctive. Was that something you had a role in, or was it down to the performer?

A: It was very much down to the performer. I happen to know that this guy, Paul Peabody, is classically trained; he is the concert master for the the Metropolitan Opera, but he also has an abiding interest in folk fiddling from around the world. He would know the difference between ornamentation from Ireland or Scandinavia, for instance. Or Scottish ornamentation. It's a subtle thing, but he would know the difference. I would talk with him beforehand and say I wanted it to sound like a hardanger fiddle. He suggested we not actually use a hardanger fiddle, because they are pretty hard to play, but instead take a concert violin and tune it up a whole step, give it a more strident tone, and that we use two of them. A player would stand next to Paul and concentrate on all of the drone notes; that way Paul could concentrate on all of the melodies, all of the figures. It was very much about the performer.

Q: Was that his consistent style, or did you just go with the take which you and he liked the most?

A: We knew that we were after a Norwegian hardanger style. We discussed how much ornamentation, when to pull it back a bit. The nice thing about Paul, because he comes from a classical background, he has that whole repertoire. He's not married to anything in his folk fiddling. We can say, oh that's good, but can we give it a richer tone? Can we capture some pathos here? He can translate those kinds of adjectives into a folk fiddle style.

Q: What is interesting to me about *Fargo* is the number of jokes which people get, or don't get, when watching the film. How is the score affected by that, because arguably you don't want the score to get in the way of what might be called invisible, or non-obvious, laughs?

A: It's a good question. This is where the fact that the Coens and I have a similar sensibility really comes into play. There is something about their pacing, their editing, which can bring humour to things that are not obviously funny at all. In *No Country for Old Men* there is nothing obviously funny about that story at all. At *all*.

Q: I was laughing my head off in the coin scene.

A: That's right, there are laughs all through it! There are certain bizarre, funny elements like Javier Bardem's hair. But there are also things to do with pacing, how long they spend on a shot. It will just linger an extra second. It's awkward, and creates a discomfort that you want to release with a laugh. I can't analyse it. But it is *there*. My sensibility is similar; it's a dry, dark sensibility. The way I write music seems to fit. It's good fortune!

Q: I always find the coin scene funny because the Javier Bardem character seems very disappointed when he is not able to kill the guy. You really get a sense he was hanging out for it. He wanted to, but the guy picks the right side of the coin, and now he can't.

A: He's an ethical guy [laughs].
Q: What I find interesting about *Mildred Pierce* is that all of the title character's strengths and weaknesses are revealed and clear, almost from the first scene. What is that like to work with, in terms of themes, where the character has an arc of semi-realization of her own flaws as a person, but they are there on display for the audience for the entire five hours of the series?
A: It's an interesting question. The best answer is that the music isn't really about those things. The fact that they don't change doesn't really affect the music. You're right, there's a lot that doesn't change. The role of sexuality, there is development there. She does experience a change there. Her relationship with her daughter, it is intense and tragic. It was the first time I'd done episodes, worked on a television series. So I was aware that there was some need for common themes. We knew we needed something to play at the beginning of episodes. It needed to be appropriate to a female lead of that period. This is what brought me to woodwinds. I felt they would be appropriate. With woodwinds you can do something which fits the period, might have been used to score *Mildred Pierce* in the thirties, but also with woodwinds it's possible to become tough and loud with them. That's why I chose that instrumentation. I wanted her theme to be tough, like she is tough. I wanted to focus on the parts of her life which do change. Her character, as you say, may not change at all, but her circumstances change tremendously.
Q: In the series, ten, fifteen years pass, and you feel that the characters end back where they started. It's interesting from a dramatic point of view.
A: Oh it is, I agree. I think James M. Cain was writing a radical feminist book at the time. Why he chose to end it back at the beginning, I will admit, is a mystery to me.
Q: There is an incredible moment where Mildred and her husband sit down after finalizing their divorce, and they start to weep. How do you score a moment of such emotional complexity?
A: You have to be extremely respectful and gentle. It's all there on the screen. It doesn't need anything. Music is really just lending a little support. I'm personally the kind of composer who prefers to leave things unsaid. I'm happy to leave things *without* music.
Q: There was some score for it.

A: There is some score there; I certainly remember it in the part where they get up. Todd Haynes is an ardent lover of melodrama. He's not ashamed to put music in, and sometimes he has to pull me along with him. In a scene like that you really have to be very respectful of what is happening in the scene. It is as though you were a person in the room with them.

Q: The question is asked in *Mildred Pierce* whether the character of Veda has the soul of an artist, or not. How was your score influenced by that question?

A: That's an interesting question.

Q: I don't think the question is answered. It seems to be up to us, the audience, to determine.

A: Yes, I agree. She certainly has an artistic temperament. I don't recall it was ever necessary for me to make a decision on that in terms of score. I'm really writing from Mildred's perspective; I don't ever take Veda's. Mildred never pretends to know anything about music. She just wants the best for her daughter.

Q: So your approach is different to the barber character in *The Man Who Wasn't There*?

A: Exactly. Mildred could care less about music. I think the way that Todd understood it, having your daughter take piano lessons, it was the ultimate bourgeois aspiration, and that is why Mildred takes it so seriously. It is the ultimate statement of bourgeois lifestyle of that period. When Veda comes back as a singer, it's so *bizarre* to me. I love the scene where the teacher describes her as a snake to Mildred [laughs]. This whole artistry thing, it's a whole mystery to Mildred. She has no way to judge it, doesn't know what it means. I have to view it all from Mildred's point of view. I don't care if Veda's good, or bad, or capable. Veda becomes what Mildred wants. She becomes this object of desire for Mildred, and that also comes to destroy her. I found I just had to view it that way.

Q: *The Hi-Lo Country* (Stephen Frears, 1998) and *Fargo* have epic scores. The score of *Fargo* in particular does lend an epic quality to the events you are seeing.

A: Right, I think that is right! That's where the humour in the score come from because what you are seeing, though it might sometimes be criminal, is always banal. The epic quality of the music is what makes things comedic, that the music takes so seriously all these silly things which are happening. That was how I hoped to inject comedy into the score.

Q: The track 'Moose Lake' is very light, really floats, as compared with the main *Fargo* theme. There is that alternating between light and dark on a track-by-track basis. Why go in that direction as opposed to a stirring, epic approach throughout?

A: It's a good question. Such a good question I'll have to give it a moment's thought. I'll wander towards an answer maybe. On principle I like the mix of light and dark. I don't like it if a score is entirely one way or the other. This is why I'm a terrible romantic comedy composer. I can't do just light. I also can't do just dark. It's just my attitude towards life. That fits the Coens very well. There are always horrible things going on in their films, yet these moments are presented with an element of humour. And in *Fargo* there is this element of pathos. They never really put it into their films. But because of Frances McDormand, her performance, there is an element of warmth in the film. That allows for real contrast. That said, it's not as though the light parts and dark parts go with any particular characters. It's all shuffled up. I think it's important that when the murderers are burying the money, it's light. Then, for Fran, something dark. I personally like it when the music from the film steps back from the story. When Steve Buscemi is injured, and burying the money, there is music all through it, but the music is not telling you anything about that scene at all. The music is saying 'you don't have to be involved in that character, you don't have to be in the action you are seeing'. You can enjoy the rhythm of it, the sound of it, the way it looks. The music doesn't have to comment on the character, or the plot, or the emotions of the scene. I love it when music does that. Some of my favourite scores, the films of Terrence Malick for instance, the music is always standing back from the action.

Q: Hans Zimmer for *The Thin Red Line* (1998)?

A: Yes. I'm thinking more of *Badlands* (1973), or *Days of Heaven* (1978). Terrible things are happening on-screen, but the music sits back with the world itself. I like having moments like that. *Fargo*, there are scenes like that. But it is also interspersed with scenes where the music is playing up the film noir elements of a scene.

Q: As they drive past the statue of Paul Bunyan and the Blue Bull there is a beautiful cue. It has no major narrative significance, seeing the bull. Were you self-conscious about giving the shot such a beautiful cue?

A: Yes, I was [laughs]. I was thinking about that before you mentioned it. It is a great example. Whatever you put over that scene in music will be absurd, because the scene's very existence is absurd. So I put in a grand cue [laughs]. It's like the opening of *Fargo*. All that is happening is a guy is riding through the snow. And the score gets bigger, and bigger, and more bombastic. Then again, I think that is my idea of what is funny. That idea of grand music against banal goings-on.

Q: *True Grit* is a Coen brothers film, but it is also Joseph Campbell's hero narrative as well. How did that influence your approach?

A: I don't think that really informed the score until the very end of the film. We had an overall concept for the score, Ethan and I, which we both arrived at independently. It was the idea to use hymns as the basis of the score. For me it came from reading the book. It is so full of church language. That isn't really shown in the film. But I realized, if the audience knew of this church background, it would inform a lot of the character Mattie's behaviour. I thought using hymns would explain why a girl would do these things. She has such a strong sense of right and wrong, of her own righteousness. She feels she's one of the elect. When I got to the end of the score, which I came up with chronologically, and he is carrying her after she is snake-bit, we realized that we weren't clear on what the scene was really about. We realized it was really calling for some sort of emotional closure.

Q: Rooster Cogburn also says 'I am spent'. He doesn't die in the scene, but that is the end of him as a character in the story.

A: Yes, that's right. Anyway, going over the score, Ethan said, 'We need more warmth here, more emotion. I'm pretty sure there is a card on this film which says "produced by Steven Spielberg". We need more closure.' It's exactly as you said; it's not entirely a Coen brothers film! The Coen brothers will leave you bereft of closure. So we knew we needed more. We needed to tie the characters of Rooster and Mattie together. The two are always arguing, bickering, but there was no real emotional glue. I created a theme which was for them, and only for them, coming to fruition in that final sequence where he is carrying her. Joel and Ethan then went back and shot more footage, of the scene where he comes down to her in the cave. There were shots of him looking at her, her looking at him. There just wasn't enough of that in the movie, of them interacting in an emotional way, other than bickering. Just a few of those in that heightened scene. Taking that theme, playing it out at the end, we attempted to create more of a complete arc for the two of them. To us it had to do with this being the key relationship of the movie. Everyone *knows*

Q: that. But it hadn't really quite gelled. We used music, and a couple of extra shots.

Q: So, seconds of film, and seconds of score, can really make that much of a difference?

A: Oh, it *really* can. The Coens are very careful filmmakers. A couple of shots in the cave really helped.

Q: It's also worth noting that she kills Cheney to avenge her father. She's only 14! The audience wants it, but at the same time it is chilling if you stop to think about it.

A: I agree. She does this, and it's almost in cold blood; she could choose not to do it. I kind of wanted to play that discomfort, my discomfort at her choice. Joel and Ethan wanted more of a feeling of 'tah-dah, we've finally killed the bad guy!' Whatever score is in there probably plays both.

Q: There are some atonal qualities in that moment.

A: Good. I thought the audience should be given a moment to think about what just happened. It's an interesting moment. I like the chance to stop and think about it a moment.

CHAPTER 7

Burwell and Space: Inner, Outer, Environmental and Acoustical

Andrew Waggoner

INTRODUCTION

The film music of Carter Burwell is unusually effective in its forceful communication of dramatic tone through the simplest, most stripped-down means possible. This elemental quality is certainly, in part, the product of Burwell's early life in the 'downtown' pop-music scene of the mid-seventies, lived in the context of clubs like the iconic CBGB, playing in bands such as Thick Pigeon and The Same, and bringing a post-punk sensibility into a synth-based music that was texturally simple, and melodically clear. What is ultimately important here, however, is the degree to which Burwell has simultaneously transcended the limitations of his earliest work in punk and art-rock, and retained their unvarnished simplicity, putting it at the service of a specific dramatic point of view. Whether the source material of one of Burwell's scores lies in folk music (as it often does), or hymnody (on occasion), or a kind of generalized, rock-based harmony refracted through an orchestral setting (most of the time), they all impart an immediate sense of place and of the varied, complex human relationships

---

A. Waggoner (✉)
Professor of Composition, Setnor School of Music, Syracuse University, Syracuse, New York, USA

© The Author(s) 2017
L. Coleman, J. Tillman (eds.), *Contemporary Film Music*,
DOI 10.1057/978-1-137-57375-9_7

that unfold within it. This is accomplished principally through a specific, tripartite approach to the medium that works as follows:

- the constellation of the score around a small group of related and memorable gestures,[1] sharply etched in terms of both rhythm and timbre, and carrying profound metonymic potential
- the interaction of these gestures with the acoustical space of the film, its 'natural' environment, and, as a result, the film's overall sound design
- an apparent disconnect between each film's putative genre, or theme, and the music's affective character, yielding a subtle and often complex understanding of the characters' varied relationships to the space, that is, the physical world of the film, and to their own interior, psychological spaces

Our experience of a Burwell score, then, is one in which varied repetitions of a simple, yet strongly *physical*, set of musical gestures combine and recombine with image over time to produce a seemingly limitless range of emotional and dramatic significations. We'll follow this process through four Burwell films that are especially illustrative of his work: *Miller's Crossing* (Coen brothers, 1990), *Fargo* (Coen brothers, 1996), *Gods and Monsters* (Bill Condon, 1998) and *True Grit* (Coen brothers, 2010), with an ear towards a deeper hearing of the narrative opening-out each score effects, revealing aspects of place, time and character that would otherwise remain inaccessible to us.

The Materials

As stated previously, the materials of any Burwell score are simple, direct and physical in their sense of gesture. Burwell has said, 'I'm a very simple composer, so I rely on simple means.'[2] Simple, but not simplistic, for the dramatic and affective range of Burwell's music is made possible by the syntactic openness of the stuff of which it is made. This is a quality often difficult to quantify; one 'knows it when one hears it'. But in Burwell's case it reveals itself immediately, and withstands scrutiny, for it is a function not just of a sense of openness, of symbolic and syntactic possibility, within the ideas themselves (this may be sensed but resists explication), but more importantly within and between the varied micro-fragments that make up each motive. This sense of relationship, of motivic interdependence, is what opens the material up to constant recombination and resignification.

In *Fargo*, for example, the incisive, rhythmically accented Scotch snap figure in the hardanger fiddle-inspired violin writing is joined with a bassline and resultant harmonic progression redolent of the obsessive, repeating bass figures from the ancient Spanish song 'La Folia' ('Madness!'). The combination is musically seamless, but culturally and psychologically confounding: the Norwegian fiddle style is most certainly rooted in the Minnesota of the film, while 'La Folia' is not; it seems to get at something deeper, older, darker, more persistent in its tracing of the long arc of human obsession and violence. Both the rhythm and the repeating bassline of 'La Folia' were associated with the sarabande, the dance brought to Spain by the conquistadors, and subsequently banned at court for what was read as its obsessive lasciviousness. Repeating bass/harmonic patterns have always been both beloved and feared; whether set in an affect of joy or despair, what always emerges is their *physicality*, and a concomitant sort of delirium that they seem to induce (think of the now-gleefully ridiculed clip of the evangelical pastor fulminating against early rock and roll: '*It's the beat! It's the beat! It's the beat! It's the beat!* …'). The principal music from *Fargo* embraces all of this, and more.

In *Miller's Crossing* the elements are more clearly fused at the musical surface, and feel firmly planted in the cultural soil of the film; they seem to reflect our gaze, which is clearly through the eyes of the Irish gangster Tom. Burwell counterpoints the Coens' grimly comic take on the murderous venality of early-twentieth-century Irish- and Italian-American mobs with another Scotch snap figure, this one building in additive fashion through ascending major and minor thirds, to describe an Irish tune (adapted from the folksong 'Lament for Limerick') that is both jocular and profoundly human; it has both surface lightness *and* a capacity for pathos. What is modular here is the relationship between the melody and a similarly ascending bassline. Each time we hear the melody we follow the progress of this twofold rise, and each time we find that it settles at a different point along the registral spectrum, with melody and bass often coming unstuck from each other such that one goes up while the other returns down the way it came. This changeable, at times abortive, voice-leading process finds its fullest, most unified expression (on the subdominant, always voiced *below* the tonic) only at signal moments in the film, such as the tentative reunion in the last scene between Tom, played by Gabriel Byrne, and the childlike and gleefully corrupt Leo, played by Albert Finney, boss of the Irish criminal and political machine. And, while the reunion may be tentative, the musical arrival is not. It tells us more about what the rapprochement means to these two hard-boiled human archetypes than the screenplay could ever reveal.[3]

True Grit's score is unique among Burwell's films with the Coens in that it is based almost entirely on found material, in this case nineteenth-century American Protestant and camp meeting hymns. Hovering over fully a quarter of the the score is Anthony Schowalter and Elisha Hoffman's 'Leaning on the Everlasting Arms'; Burwell deftly mines this simple but distinctive melody for most of the film's motivic material. He makes especially good use of the original's heavily agogic treatment of the word 'leaning', as the line drops in successive, rhythmically accented thirds, a kind of American frontier incarnation of the renaissance 'sigh' figure, itself cast in repeating *appoggiaturas,* or 'leaning tones'. The film is difficult to peg, in both psychological and genre terms, and Burwell has commented on his own uneasiness with its starkness, and apparent lack of humanity (Lindsay Coleman, Carter Burwell Interview, this book, Chapter 6, 95–96; c.f. also Baldwin et al., *Art of the Score*). This conflict seems to have drawn him to an unusually rich and fluid approach to spinning out the musical material. An especially lovely example of this is in his setting of 'Talk About Suffering', late in the film, wherein the song's pentatonic material is refracted into the instrumental texture to provide an ominous background hum of pentatonic harmony. We'll return to this moment later on, as it acts as one of the film's most significant aural markers of place and cultural position.

Gods and Monsters is, of course, not a Coen brothers film. Directed by Bill Condon, its uniqueness lies not in any ironic, mythic strangeness, but rather in its depiction of the aging film director James Whale (a real person, with a real and well-known history), best known for having made *Frankenstein* (1931), *Bride of Frankenstein* (1935), and *The Invisible Man* (1933), and played with a kind of reckless mastery by Ian McKellen. The film's fascination, then, is not structural but personal. Burwell efficiently zeros in on the deep fissures in this compelling and deeply wounded character with a principal melodic/harmonic motive built out of two half-steps, one which forms a tritone with the bass, opening out to a perfect fifth; the other forming alternating major and minor thirds with the bass, thus shifting modality from major to minor in a way that generates and maintains a high degree of harmonic uncertainty and resultant emotional tension. The treatment is more conventional than in Burwell's work with the Coens, but it is, nonetheless, highly effective.

Motive, Acoustical Space, and Place

Much film music, both good and bad, still hews to an essentially operatic, *leitmotivic* approach to amplifying a film's key narrative elements, and generating filmic meaning. In this way of working, specific visual signifiers (characters, settings, symbolically important objects, etc.), as well as non-visual conceits or long-range narrative devices (love, suspicion, betrayal, specific relationships between characters, the ring of power, etc.), are linked to short, immediately identifiable musical fragments, known as *leitmotivs*, which, once fixed in place, can have huge metonymic potential over the course of the film. Think Wilma's theme from *The Best Years of Our Lives* (William Wyler, 1946), or the Imperial March from *Star Wars*. The pairing of image/idea and musical figure can seem rote and clumsy, a blunt instrument with which to hammer the viewer into submission, or it can blossom into a multilayered, synesthetic language rich in reflection and allusion. Even at its best, however, it can still force us into one kind of relationship with the music, one in which every image, every dramatic subtext, has a specific musical analogue. The music, then, can only exist as a kind of surrogate for the visual diegesis, acting solely to intensify the image, but unable to shake free of it and forces us to reconsider the meaning of what we are seeing. In order to transcend this basic limitation it must exist in abundance, layering opposing *leitmotivs* in a manner that contradicts, or comments upon, the image through reference to things unseen, but remembered from previously in the film. The effect can be sublime (again, Friedhofer's score for *The Best Years of Our Lives* is one of the great touchstones here, with specific *leitmotivs* for each character and dramatic conceit, existing in shifting and often dense relationship both to each other and to the viewer),[4] but it requires far more music, in a far more assertive relationship to image, than Burwell prefers. Short of this level of genuinely operatic treatment, a score based in *leitmotiv* runs the risk of boxing a film into a one-dimensional musical programme.

It is this semantic shutdown that Burwell most strives to avoid in his film music, and so *leitmotiv*, as conventionally constructed, plays only a limited role in his work, with two or three closely related figures that engender varied, multiple linkages, with the image doing the job of a larger set of contrasting figures associated with specific characters and dramatic concerns. He is not fundamentally opposed to *leitmotiv*, and has spoken about the degree to which he conceives of the materials in his scores as connected in his imagination with certain characters and emotional states.⁵ But his is always a flexible, recombinant approach in which the highly specific materials are subjected to constant variation, in association with the full range of the film's visual and thematic content. The result is a music/image relationship that is free to redefine itself as the film progresses, giving the audience the freedom to construct the meaning of that relationship as they watch and listen. This is not to say that Burwell's sense of dramatic intention is vague or unformed, with nothing in mind as to what the music is telling us; on the contrary, his instinct for what lies at the heart of a scene and how it is best revealed in the music is uncanny, often extending far beyond what his collaborators have believed to be possible (Burwell has spoken of this, as have the Coens). Both Joel and Ethan Coen were, for example, apparently nonplussed by their first encounter with the musical material for *Miller's Crossing*, but became true believers as Burwell realized the score as a whole (Baldwin et al., *Art of the Score*).

What sets Burwell's relationship to *leitmotiv* apart is his interest in the big picture, and in getting at larger ideas lurking within narrative, ideas that are often most clearly illuminated cumulatively, over the length of the film, rather than in discreet, semantically fixed segments. His success in this stems, in large part, from the motivic identity of the different musical gestures employed in any given film. This is not unique to Burwell's music, of course; one reason the *leitmotivic* construction of *The Best Years of Our Lives* works so well is that all of the different themes can be played in counterpoint with each other, such that at any given moment we are hearing two or more motives at once. Going back to the putative source of *leitmotivic* construction, the same can be said of virtually all of Richard Wagner's output, as is well demonstrated by Nicholas Baragwanath.⁶ What Baragwanath demonstrates, however, which is immediately clear to anyone who has survived the *Ring,* is that in Wagner's approach, taken up and furthered by Alban Berg, among many others, underlying motivic unity is generally masked by gestural variety at the music's surface. It is the variety that gives each motive its own unique signature; it is the unity which gives the whole a sense of organic integrity and dramatic intelligibility. In a Burwell score the relationship is turned on its head: motivic unity is privileged over surface variety, with the result that each motive speaks to a larger whole, more than to one specific dramatic element.

This becomes clearer if we contrast Burwell's work with that of another excellent composer who, like Burwell, consistently renounces overcoded, and hence semantically reduced, means of expression in his music.

Mychael Danna's score for Ang Lee's *The Ice Storm* (1997) is wonderfully elliptical in its revelation of the emotional and cultural alienation central to the tragedy played out in the film. Seeming at first to have nothing to do with suburban Connecticut in the 1970s, the score takes as its primary sound source Indonesian gamelan, transposing its harmonic shimmer, and interlocking rhythmic patterns, onto the daily rituals of suburban life, of women shopping, and identically dressed 'company men' commuting into the city and back. One can read this weirdly effective juxtaposition on any number of levels. (One possibility that immediately comes to mind is the gamelan's primary role as the music of the *Wayang*, the shadow play that depicts the eternally balanced forces of dark and light, and the inevitable consequences their actions have across lifetimes of karmic repetition. It is this inexorability of consequence that drives the film's shattering climax and gives it its moral core.) But what is clear is that Danna wants to pull us out of the everyday, and into a more expansive, less personal view of the characters, and their wounded, imperfect lives. This suburban gamelan is sharply contrasted, however, with the clarinet theme associated with family, especially the Hoods (Tobey Maguire, Kevin Kline, Joan Allen and Christina Ricci). When that theme is fully realized in a powerfully affecting harmonization for clarinet and strings at the film's conclusion, there is no mistaking its role in deepening our experience of the Hoods' forced confrontation, both with the consequences of their own actions, and their resultant capacity for emotional growth. It is the stark contrast between musical images that makes this progression possible, and in Danna's hands it is unexpected and, at the same time, hugely effective. But this is not the way Burwell thinks. It's not a matter of better or worse here, but rather of what it is that the score seeks to accomplish. For Burwell, the long view, achieved through understated unity, is allowed to cut across divisions of tone and affect in the visual diegesis. The result is equally powerful, but rarely so clearly tied to one character, plot device, or dramatic revelation.

Generally renouncing extremes of *leitmotivic* contrast, Burwell pays particular attention in his work to evocations of *place*, of setting as character, with its own emotional agency. In traditional film music (as described by Aaron Copland in his excellent précis on the subject),[7] this would be accomplished with music evoking more or less the cultural tradition of the film's setting. That this practice in the past often took overtly jingoistic, and even racist, forms should not be surprising (consider, as just one deeply offensive example, the idealized minstrel show two-step that accompanies the appearance of the two young African-American messenger boys in the Technicolor biopic *John Paul Jones*, (John Farrow, 1959) starring a young and earnest Robert Stack and directed by none other than Mia Farrow's father); sometimes the results, while clearly stylized, were more dramatically effective, and less culturally insensitive, such as Max Steiner's main title music for *Casablanca* (Michel Curtiz, 1942). Still, even at its most ethnomusicologically pure, the approach is problematic, and runs the risk of sounding hilariously dated within ten years of a film's release. Burwell steers clear of this hazard altogether, dealing not with place as cultural landscape, but rather as the psychological terrain in which the action is played out.

The title music from *Fargo* illustrates this perfectly: the aforementioned conjunction of the hardanger fiddle style with the srangely mythic 'La Folia' reference ensures that, while we may semi-consciously connect the fiddle (actually two conventional violins played 'in the style of ...')[8] with the frozen Midwestern landscape, we are just as likely to sense a tragic dimension in the archaic harmonic patterns traced by the orchestra. This tragic weight seems outsized in comparison with the confused little lives we see colliding in the film's opening scene, and it is only in experiencing the film as a whole that it comes to make sense to us. Burwell has referenced this with regard to the tracking shot opening the film's second act that passes under the grotesque, leering statue of Paul Bunyan that stands in the town of Brainerd, Minnesota. The shot is bizarre, and seems to exist purely to throw into relief the film's already well-established feelings of alienation and claustrophobia, both personal and cultural. Burwell's music, however, unveils something entirely different in the image, something weirdly funny, but also fateful, impervious and terrifying, all of a piece with the gravity and scope of the opening music (Coleman, Carter Burwell Interview, 94–95).

Even when the music/image pairing is more obviously grounded in the action of a scene, Burwell's treatment of the relationship is fresh and unexpected, exploring the half-world between diegetic (scene-based) and non-diegetic (score-based) sound sources. For example, in *Fargo*, when Carl and Gaear, played by Steve Buscemi and Peter Stormare, are stopped by the ill-fated state trooper whom Gaear eventually kills, and when Gaear then gives chase to the two innocent passers-by whom he also dispatches, the music is marked by a subtle but persistent tattoo in the glockenspiel, not an instrument associated with chase scenes or gunplay. Its presence in the score becomes clear, however, when it dovetails with the open-door alarm of the overturned car in which Gaear's two accidental victims have tried to escape. This matching of non-diegetic glockenspiel with diegetic car alarm becomes a recurring signifier in the film. It reappears most forcefully in the showdown between Carl and Wade, played by Harve Presnell. Once again the open-door bell precedes the action, blending with the score such that the line between non-diegetic and diegetic becomes blurred. The incidental music here is harrowing, as the two-fiddle timbre that has defined the score is recast as low, processed sounds sliding away from each other in quarter-tone glissandi.

The effect of the door chime/glockenspiel pairing is almost *leitmotivic*, in that it seems to link the sound with the film's murders, but in a manner that surprises with the gentleness of the bell sounds, while at the same time activating a resonance of allusions that causes us to ask quite literally for whom the bell tolls. In this case, it tolls for all of Carl and Gaear's victims, as well as Jerry Lundegaard, the catastrophically incompetent locus of the destructive force that consumes the others (William H. Macy's performance here is truly one for the history books, so utterly does he embody obsessive, situational hubris). It tolls also for Wade, and eventually for Carol, and even for Marge (the great Frances McDormand), whose first encounter with the violence that disrupts her quiet existence is accompanied by the chiming of her own police cruiser; in Marge's case the bell is not a harbinger of death but rather of her own loss of innocence. Her cruiser's alarm acts as the final herald in this macabre procession, when at the film's climax its chiming announces the sound of the wood chipper, the most iconic sound in movies since the contrabasses at the onset of *Jaws* (Steven Spielberg, 1975).

In *Miller's Crossing* the principal materials, including the Scotch snap melody, are, unusually for Burwell, character-based. He has said that the main idea was inspired by Gabriel Byrne's face (Coleman, Carter Burwell Interview, 87–88), and there is something in the tune that seems to capture both the cheekiness and emotional isolation of his character, Tom Reagan, as the Scotch snap is both rhythmically active and intervallically confined. It is significant, however, that our first hearing of the theme pairs it not with Tom but with the title montage, set in the woods around what we will eventually learn is the place called Miller's Crossing; it also takes us into Tom's dream of losing his hat in the wind, a dream which comes to seem precognitive near the climax of the film, as he is led through the woods to what he believes to be his own demise.

Both of these readings of the woods montage come to us at different points in the film, and they reshape both our understanding of the opening sequence, and the music that accompanies it. And, like all of

Burwell's best work, the music itself is modular, seeming to express one thing, and then being put in the service of something completely different. This is most effective, and most puzzling, in the scene directly after the disowning of Tom by Leo, when both men's on-again off-again moll, Verna Birnbaum, played by Marcia Gay Harden, appears at Tom's door. The scene, up to this point, has played in silence, but at Verna's entrance the Irish tune strikes up, in the solo oboe; the connection seems to be with Verna, who is Jewish, and seems to contradict the culturally specific nature of the tune itself. Much is made in the film, however, of Verna's, and even more so of her brother Bernie's, Jewishness; the prevailing anti-semitism of both the Irish and Italian subcultures in which the film is set dictates that Bernie, who has been chiselling from the Italian boss Gianni Caspar, must be disposed of. He is saved from being whacked solely thanks to Leo's soft-hearted (and, from Tom's perspective, soft-*headed*) love for Verna. Bernie, as played with loopy intensity by John Turturro, is no saint; cheap, conniving, utterly not-to-be-trusted. Within the skewed moral universe of the film he probably 'deserves' to die. But, protected by Leo, he becomes a pending issue between Tom and Verna. Tom, whose own love for Verna is equally soft-headed, but whose sense of political and social reality is much keener than Leo's, is torn between his desire to be with Verna and his conviction that Bernie isn't worth protecting. This complex of emotional forces seems to be released by Verna's co-opting of the putatively 'Irish' music; associated with her, it seems no longer tied to anyone in particular, but rather to the various thwarted and illusory desires of all the principal characters. It is the force that, through the fuse of unspoken loyalties and apparent betrayals, drives the action of the film. Like the main material from *Fargo*, then, it migrates from one narrative position to another, now fuelling the narrative's progress, now stepping back to comment on it. Its ultimate position is mythic, and godlike; it toys with its creations even as it weeps for them.

If there is one salient *visual* image with which the main theme is connected, however, it is hats. We hear it first as we watch what we will learn is Tom's hat sailing away in the wind. We hear it again as Tom comes to fetch his hat from Verna, to whom he has lost it in a poker game. We hear it again at the end of the film, as both Tom and Leo affix their hats to their heads with great purpose and intention. If the theme is to be understood as *leitmotiv*, however, it is constructed in reverse, for the connection isn't firmly established until the film is over. Wagner himself, in *Opera and Drama*, laid out *leitmotiv*'s potential for foreshadowing, but in the case of his operas, and in more conventional film scores, once the connection with the narrative element is established the semantic range of the motif is severely constricted.[9] That this does not happen in *Miller's Crossing* is perfectly in keeping with the symbolic openness manifested by the music throughout: we can read the hat in any number of ways that seem germane to the world of the film. Physical protection, status, respectability, cultural assimilation, political power, control of one's destiny, and sense of place within the rituals of cultural order are just a few of the possible understandings of the various hats in the film. Tom's recurring question 'where's me hat'?, and Caspar's wounded sense of being given 'the high hat!', are far from idle concerns: they are at the heart of the immigrant experience of power, and the lack thereof, in turn of the century American society. The hat/music conjunction, then, forms a signifier of enormous expressive potential, condensing all of the film's semantic possibilities into one extraordinarily efficient construct, a perfect example of aural/visual metonymy.[10]

Place and acoustical space in *Miller's Crossing* are most fully explored in the magisterial set-piece in which Leo is attacked in his home, only to annihilate his would-be assassins. The sequence is introduced by music, a 78 RPM record of 'Danny Boy' (sounding for all the world like an old 78, but actually arranged and conducted for the film by Larry Wilcox, and featuring Irish tenor Frank Patterson),[11] to which Leo luxuriates as he reclines in bed, reading the paper and smoking a cigar. The music is firmly in the diegesis, as confirmed by our view of the Victrola on which it is playing. As the point of view shifts to the ground floor, the acoustical space of the music shifts with it, further locating the sound within Leo's upstairs bedroom. With the move downstairs, however, sounds that had been understood as part of the scratchiness of the disc are now recast as the graphic sounds of the butler's throat being cut, his gurgling and bleeding, and finally those of the cigarette he is holding setting fire to the newspaper that he, like Leo, had been reading. These sounds bleed, almost imperceptibly, back into the scratchy 78 as the view moves back upstairs to Leo, and to his dawning perception that something is not right in the house. At this point Leo springs into action, barely avoids being shot to pieces, gets the jump on his attackers and then blows them to bits in a fusillade of tommy-gun fire that is both weirdly compelling and deeply repulsive. Through it all Leo maintains his attitude of impervious grace, a kind of scrappy street nobility; he stands unbowed, raining down damnation on each new attacker, magically untouched by the hail of bullets coming in his direction.

This turnabout is matched by the migration of 'Danny Boy' from diegesis to non-diegesis: as Leo dispatches his foes the acoustical space of the music changes, the scratchiness disappears, and it enters the score position, giving voice to Leo's serene detachment as he sows mayhem on his quiet, respectable, residential street. We catch up with this process at the end of the sequence when we realize that Leo has now travelled half a block down the street in pursuit of Caspar's henchmen, and that the music, rather than fading from earshot as we move away from its source, is booming away louder than ever, in Dolby stereo, no less. The effect is masterful and, coming as it does in the context of a score that is constantly throwing off its moorings and reattaching itself to different dramatic elements at will, it has the effect of some of Godard's experiments with musical meta-diegesis, but in the service of dramatic and structural clarity as opposed to structural (and, for Godard, political) speculation. (As a classic example of diegetic migration of the sound source, the sequence is easily read, with great potential, in terms of Rick Altman's *ventriloquist effect*.)[12]

No such musical or dramatic tour de force exists in *True Grit*. By turns grim, picaresque, violent, and even more grim, the film is oddly affecting even as it turns an entirely jaundiced eye towards the human condition, or perhaps more accurately, towards the condition of the world as perpetrated by humans. Lacking the moral centre that Marge gave to Fargo, *True Grit* is left to find its humanity in the gradually dawning relationship between Jeff Bridges' dissolute Rooster Cogburn, and the exterminating angel that is Hailee Steinfeld's Mattie. Both Burwell and Ethan Coen were somewhat taken aback by the film's unrelenting bleakness, and came more or less together with Joel Coen to the idea of scoring it with hymns.[13] Primary among these is 'Leaning on the Everlasting Arms', which gives the film much of its motivic and gestural material. The other hymns that make up the score are 'The Glory Way', 'What a Friend We Have in Jesus' and 'Hold to God's Unchanging Hand', as well as the spiritual 'Talk About Suffering'. In a general sense, of course, nineteenth-century hymnody would seem to be well connected to the world of the film but, more than a reliable sense of place, the score imparts to the film a sense of time and of moral context. The lead character, Mattie, has one intention throughout the film, and that is to avenge the wrongful death of her father. So single-minded and righteous is she in this regard that the Coens have described her as an avenging Protestant (Ethan Coen having described the novel as 'hilariously Protestant').[14] The hymns, which in terms of place would have been more at home east of the Mississippi, do a fine job of expressing both the power and rigidity of Mattie's self-justifying moral obsession. Burwell has discussed this at length, saying that he 'tried to find something to say with the music that isn't already on the screen. I read the book *True Grit* when Joel Coen told me they were going to make it, and one of the things that is present in the book but not so present in the films is a sense of the girl's church background ... She just has this totally irrational sense of righteousness and justice, which is based upon her church learning.'[15]

Where the music does express place it turns from hymn to spiritual, and nowhere is this more effective than in the sequence in which Mattie, Rooster and LaBeouf venture onto Choctaw territory to search out the killer, Tom Chaney, played by Josh Brolin. The music swells from the attack of Rooster's pistol, settling into the aforementioned pentatonic ground-hum, suggestive of an old-fashioned parody of Native American music (replete with the parallel fifths that earlier composers would have used to evoke *the savage*), but the harmony quickly reveals itself through the clarinet melody that emerges from it to be that of the old spiritual 'Talk About Suffering'. Burwell manages a feat of musical and cultural allusion here that speaks to Mattie and Rooster's apprehensions around crossing on to Indian land, by referencing old Westerns and their outmoded approach to Native American musical materials, and at the same time exposing the common harmonic and melodic basis of both Native and Euro-American folk musics, the pentatonic scale. The point of view in the sequence is strictly Euro-American, but consciousness of the Native presence, both as imminent danger and a vanquished people, is palpable in the scene. This remarkable moment of seemingly stereotypical cultural difference leading to a powerful sense of cultural identity is made all the more effective by acting as one of the few passages in the film in which the music seems to reflect explicitly the scene's dramatic character. Thus the viewer is primed for a conventionally suspenseful treatment, with all the iconic sound imagery associated with *Cowboys and Indians*, only to find that, as usual, the music has something very much else on its mind, for it is soon after this beautiful and iconic transition that Mattie will finally come face to face with Tom Chaney.

All of the above examples have, in one way or another, been concerned with physical space. In *Gods and Monsters* the spaces are almost exclusively interior; most of the music in the film, aside from a few incidental and transitional passages, takes us into the internal world of James Whale. This is rich terrain, marked as it is both by lifelong conflicts around growing up gay in Edwardian England and then living as an openly gay artist in thirties

Hollywood, and by the stroke Whale has just suffered as the film begins, leaving him at the mercy of simultaneous, competing thoughts, shooting out in all directions. The three interior 'locations' Burwell maps for us, allowing us to experience Whale's multiplicity of thought, memory and advancing psychic terror, are personal memory, especially of childhood and of the First World War, dream, and the creative realm represented by his studio, where he paints and, most importantly, begins to project both his unchecked desire and his chaotic inner life on his young and beautiful yard man, Boone, played by Brendan Fraser.

The music we encounter in these inner landscapes is at once impressively tight motivically, all of it deriving from the half-step figures discussed earlier, and at the same time wildly varied, each episode taking its specific feeling tone from the visual world in which it moves. Thus, in the dream sequence where Boone, as Dr Frankenstein, removes Whale's brain and replaces it with another, suturing up the top of his skullcap and cutting the thread with his teeth, the music is all grand guignol, the tritone-to-fifth resolutions and major/minor shifts cast as orchestral bombast, with massed, ponderous low brass making a hallucinatory nod to the scores of the old Universal horror films. Upon entering his studio, on the other hand, Whale 'hears' a musical place of imagination and relative serenity, in which the pair of motives already laid out start to assemble themselves into the haunted, at times sardonic, waltz that eventually flowers in Whale's dream memories of the war, and the lover he left in the trenches. The childhood memories are often sparked by an external stimulus, such as the cloud of exhaust belched out by Boone's lawnmower; this morphs into a smokestack, and the accompanying factory whistle, with which the young Whale is fascinated, seeming to hover between diegesis and non-diegesis, in one of Burwell's most fascinating constructions of an interior, aural space. When the memory is sparked again in the next scene it progresses further, with young James hectored by his abusive father, the whistle now replaced with high, sustained violins. In this way the setting of the memory merges with its place in Whale's psyche. Interior and exterior conjoin just as sound design and score become momentarily interchangeable.

In a similar but still more subtle, and virtually unprecedented, way, the score itself migrates across narrative dimensions to move from the non-diegetic to the diegetic at the film's conclusion. The waltz that grows from the music's motivic seeds and reaches its apogee in the final dream sequence leaps from Whale's internal world and is grafted on to the violin played by the blind hermit, displacing Schubert's 'Ave Maria', in Whale's

The Bride of Frankenstein. It is only after finding ourselves here, in the hermit's cabin, and believing ourselves still to be deep in Whale's unconscious, that we realize we are watching the film on television, through the eyes of Boone's young son, and that we have now advanced several years into Boone's life after finding the old master post-suicide in his swimming pool. Whale had called Boone one of his 'monsters', and now Boone clearly finds some measure of healing from the sexually charged Oedipal relationship into which Whale had pulled him, in sharing the one-time director's most personal and visionary work with his son. The music now takes its place in the older film, occupying the specific acoustical space of the TV set. As the movie ends and the boy is sent to bed the spell is broken. There is something deeply sad about this moment; for all the domestic satisfaction and putting to rest of old demons the scene seems to be enacting, the leaving behind of the world of dreams and the dissipation of the music into the everyday comes as a terrible loss. Burwell's music and its ingenious straddling of film and film-within-a-film allow us to feel these conflicting emotions simultaneously, with no need to come down on one side or the other.

Narrative Disconnect to Emotional Synchrony: Motive, Image and Affect

One of the hallmarks of the Coen brothers' style is, of course, a mordantly ironic point of view that borders, at times, on a kind of visual nihilism. This has been much discussed, and need not be rehashed here, but it is worth noting that their films are, against all Hollywood odds, successful on many levels, including commercial. There is something here that transcends any kind of college-boy sneering, or easy postmodern posturing. Their films are, by turns, disturbing, confounding, nightmarish, hilarious and moving, and more often than not all of the above at once. It is perhaps this quality, quite apart from their visual and literary brilliance, this multifarious expressive dimension in which conflicting psychological and emotional states are conveyed simultaneously, that makes the films so powerfully effective. Not surprisingly, Burwell's music has a significant role to play here.

Burwell himself has said that he enjoys confusion, and that he finds films in which sound and image seem to be contradicting each other to be richer and more satisfying than the more conventional alternative (Baldwin et al., *Art of the Score*). That this is the case is apparent to anyone who has seen any of his work, particularly with the Coens. More than anything else it has to do with the motivic unity of the material, and with Burwell's rejection of the more typical *leitmotivic* approach. As we've seen, *leitmotiv* does operate in his work, but as part of a structural process that far transcends the cartoonish matching of specific images with specific sound. In fact, the motivic unity that defines Burwell's work ensures that the range of musical referents is small, and that in being recycled and varied over the course of the film they come to take on multiple and increasingly complex and resonant meanings. Put another way, Burwell denies us the luxury of associating different themes with different characters because, for the most part, different themes do not exist: there is one musical image, presented at the outset, that shape-shifts as the narrative progresses.

In *Fargo*, the Hardanger music is present almost throughout the film. With the exception of a few passages in which the score merely intensifies a dramatic climax, the main melodic/harmonic motive is in operation. Burwell communicates changes in emotional tone and setting not through new material, but through changes in orchestration and textural density. Thus, after the first act, and the initial high point around the kidnapping and the first two murders, the fiddle music returns as we track across what we will come to know is Marge and Norm's bedroom, the couple asleep, Norm's snoring in rhythmic counterpoint to the music. The scoring here is intimate, chamber—rather than orchestral-based, for solo violin, harp and gently ringing crotales—and matches the hushed stasis of the image. The musical substance, however, is unchanged. There is no 'Marge's Theme' to signal a new and central character. It is difficult at first to say with certainty what the music is telling us, but the feeling tone is unmistakable: whoever these people are, whoever this woman is who is unsurprised by a phone call at 4:00 a.m. summoning her from her bed, their narrative world is the same as that of Carl, Gaear and Jerry, and their fates are intertwined. There is a mythic strength in this, a pulling back of the music from the level of individual character, up to a narrative position that is beyond the reach of personal concerns. Everyone in *Fargo* is subject to the same fate, the same uncanny and uncontrollable forces that tear lives to pieces. At the same time, there is in this neutral position the capacity for tremendous pathos: when we are lifted from the personal into the collective and hear the struggles with darkness and desire in the film as elemental, atemporal and cyclic, we recognize them as being universal, and that we, far as we may be from northern Minnesota, are in the grip of the same incomprehensible fate. This is what we call Tragedy, and is what lifts *Fargo* far above the level of self-referential nineties *noir*.

The same can be said of *Miller's Crossing*. The peregrinations of the theme nominally associated with Tom, or his hat, engender multiple significations throughout the film. There is no 'Italian' music to signal the temporary rise of Gianni Caspar to the level of political boss. If the music in *Fargo* seems Olympian in its gaze, then perhaps in *Miller's Crossing* it is a leprechaun's-eye view we have of the proceedings. There is a lightness of touch here consistent with the film's stylized evocation of the period. However we choose to think of it, the music is pulling us away from easy characterization, away from aural stereotype, into an impersonal position that allows us to hear all of the conflicting agents in the film as entwined and interdependent. There is one nice moment of cultural identification in the film that acts as a counterweight to the 'Danny Boy' set-piece, in which one of Caspar's goons begins to sing an Italian folk song in a mellifluous tenor, all as Tom is marched out to the Crossing to certain death. The music here is diegetic, however, and does nothing to disrupt the overall tone and unanimity of the score.

Of all the Coen/Burwell films after *Fargo*, *True Grit* is easily the most disturbing in its dogged refusal to match image with corresponding music; it seems deliberately to confound expectations with regard to how a Western 'sounds'. Even in comparison with seventies 'anti-Westerns', such as *McCabe and Mrs Miller* (Robert Altman, 1971), it is dogged in its refusal to bend to convention. It is also possibly the most affecting of their recent films (not to mention the most brilliant), even though the film as a whole is, as aforementioned, flinty to say the least. The key to this strange expressive power lies both in Burwell's settings of the hymns, which are ultra-simple, usually starting with solo piano and building from there to include solo strings, rarely achieving anything close to orchestral density, and more importantly their cyclic recombinations over the film's narrative arc. As with *Fargo* and *Miller's Crossing*, each repetition brings a new level of resonance, as the characters' physical and emotional journey becomes increasingly confused and violent. No matter how depraved the image, with few exceptions the music retains its stolid, impassive serenity. Even in the aforementioned sequence based on 'Talk About Suffering', the sense of menace that the music seems at first to be communicating gives way to something more generalized, less concerned with the potential for violence than with an encompassing sadness.

Even where music does ape image, it does so in a way that brings emotional complexity to a visual action that seems straightforward. Consider, for example, the scene in which Mattie finally realizes her desire and kills Tom Chaney. As we've already seen, both Burwell and Ethan Coen were uneasy with the film's unrelenting starkness (Coleman, Carter Burwell Interview, 95–96). Coen, for his part, set about recutting the climax of the film, intercutting long shots with close-ups and thus locating Rooster and Mattie as human figures in the implacable Western landscape. Burwell turned his attention to Chaney's killing; he was uncomfortable with how matter-of-fact the scene seemed to him. He wanted to feel more of a sense of conflict, of moral crisis, on the part of this 14-year-old child who has come to gun a man down with malice and forethought. He decided that the incidental music accompanying the scene would, as the shot rings out, take on an extra layer of dissonance, a major seventh above the bass that would, at least for him, signal some degree of disquiet on Mattie's part, if only internal and unconscious. The effect is brilliant, acting on us as unconsciously as the pang of conscience it seeks to illuminate. We don't reflect on it, we're barely aware of it. We know only that, in contradiction of the genre convention to which it responds, this is not a cynically triumphal Hollywood killing.

Absolute asynchrony between score and image reaches its apex in the climactic race to save Mattie from the snake bite that will surely kill her if help isn't reached in time. While the visual construction is frantic, with the aforementioned montage cutting from close-up to long shot as Little Blackie, Mattie's smallish horse, is raced literally to death in the effort to save her, the music reaches its most intimate and fully voiced expression, first of the material based on 'The Everlasting Arms', and then, as Rooster picks Mattie up and carries her on foot, of 'Hold to God's Unchanging Hand'. At first the effect is jarring, seeming willfully to contradict the image in the most extreme terms possible, but after a moment it settles, and we settle with it, into an entirely different experience of the chase and its meaning, for it forces us to see that it is Rooster, whom we have come to know as a fiercely mercenary, amoral being, who is desperately racing Mattie to safety. As Rooster drives Little Blackie past his breaking point, and while Mattie quietly ponders the stars that look down on this seemingly hopeless pair, the music takes us directly into the quiet, resolute desire for grace that has forced Mattie and Rooster suddenly into real human relationship. And yet, as in *Fargo*, there is an imperviousness to the music which tells us also that, no matter how far Rooster carries her, and no matter how moved Mattie is by his gesture of sacrifice on her behalf, she may well die. There are no guarantees here, but only the quiet turning of fate. Indeed, when we see the grown Mattie in the film's epilogue we see that she has in fact survived the ordeal, but at the cost of her arm, lost to the creeping venom of the snake. Mattie, in full agreement with the stoic affect of the hymns, accepts this outcome without question. What matters to her at this point is finding Rooster; this she does, but too late to thank him. So she does the next best thing and has his body disinterred and moved to her family plot. Hard-boiled and uncompromising in all things, she carries the relationship forged over the course of that race against death well beyond the grave. This peroration is important, because it tells us that the affective depth we experienced as Rooster carried Mattie to the strains of 'The Everlasting Arms' was real; no passing dramatic device, it both provided strong narrative closure and revealed to us a powerful human connection acting as the heart of this otherwise heartless film.

Conclusion: Film as Music

Carter Burwell is an unusual composer, not just by the woefully low and cynical standards of contemporary Hollywood, but in the context of film writ large. He was extraordinarily lucky when, in 1984, he received a call from the Coens to write the music for their first feature *Blood Simple* (1984); through that ongoing and singularly fruitful relationship he has found his way to a conception of film music that, while it privileges silence, understatement and narrative complexity, comes perhaps closer than any other body of work to achieving Sergei Eisenstein's vision of a total integration of sound and image. In Burwell's case this is not accomplished through the *leitmotivic* saturation of the image with accompanying sound, but rather through a sound/image relationship in which semantic openness and multiplicity results in a kind of *visual music*, a *gesamtkunstwerk* in which both levels of the discourse work together, and against, each other to move past narrative specificity towards an experience of structure that is multisensory, and cognitively, as well as emotionally, rich.

This is not to say that plot is irrelevant in a Burwell film, either with the Coens, or any of the other first-rate directors with whom he has worked. This is not some deconstructionist attempt to deprive the filmic 'text' of its capacity for storytelling. As we've seen with each example under consideration, issues of plot, character, dramatic conceit and long-range psychological theme, or visual metaphor, are central to Burwell's compositional choices. The essential thing here is that, while those choices intensify the dramatic intention, they also free it from any reductionist reading that would rob it of semantic and emotional possibility. We care deeply about Marge, Mattie and Tom, as indeed we do about poor James Whale, but we care precisely because we are never told *exactly why we should*. In this way the experience of a Burwell-scored film comes closer to the experience of music than it does film as traditionally conceived: powerful emotional clarity, free from any imposed or literal signification, that works over time to reveal an emotional arc that must be taken as a whole in order for it to work its magic upon us. This is true, to varying degrees, of all great time-based art, of course, but it is especially so in Burwell's work, as it is in that of the Coens.[16]

There have been many fine examples of imaginative music/image juxtapositions over the course of film's short history, particularly where the music is in the foreground. Think of Toru Takemitsu's astonishing battle-ballet in Kurosawa's *Ran* (1985), or of John Corigliano's musical hallucinations in Ken Russell's *Altered States* (1980). There is also, more recently, Alexandre Desplat's score and Erik Aadahl, Craig Berkey and Will Files' deeply affecting sound design for Terrence Malick's *The Tree of Life* (2011). Further back, there are, to name just two, Georges Delerue's music, and Godard's discombobulating treatment of it, in *Le Mépris* (1963), and Gato Barbieri's haunted, dimension-crossing saxophone melody in Bertolucci's *Last Tango in Paris* (1972). But in Burwell's best work, both with and without the Coens, the music intensifies not only isolated dramatic moments, but makes audible the whole structure of the film. And, as we have seen, it does this often by hovering in the background, just out of reach. In speaking softly it renders the entire experience more inherently musical.

It is tantalizing to consider the possibility that Burwell's approach, as revealed in his now considerable oeuvre, might form the basis for a renewal of imagination and creative integrity in film composition. That seems unlikely for now. When it comes it will most likely sprout first in any number of the different television formats that have upended the traditional hierarchy of film over TV. There are signs, in fact, that that is already happening, with distinctive, risk-taking scores being composed for shows like *Breaking Bad* (2008–2013), *Hannibal* (2013–2015) and even *The Walking Dead* (2010–), thanks to composers like Dave Porter and Bear McCreary, among others. But for now Burwell remains unique, an artist blessed with extraordinary collaborators, who thus has had the freedom to pursue a bracing, personal and revelatory creative vision.

NOTES

1. By 'gesture' we mean simply a self-contained musical idea that has an immediately recognizable character and a strong sense of motion, akin to a physical gesture, but heard rather than seen.
2. Lindsay Coleman, Carter Burwell Interview, this book, Chapter 6, 89.
3. Burwell has stated, 'I wanted to suggest with the music that his actual motivation was his love for Finney, and I proposed doing this with a sappy Irish melody arranged for orchestra' (carterburwell.com).
4. For a perceptive analysis of the *leitmotiv* technique in *The Best Years of Our Lives*, see Frederick Sternfeld, 'Music and the Feature Films', *Musical Quarterly*, Vol. 33, No. 4 (Oct., 1947), 517–32.
5. In both his interview with Lindsay Coleman and in the NY Phil presentation *Art of the Score*, Burwell describes the genesis of the principal music from *Miller's Crossing* as arising directly from the actor Gabriel Byrne's face. A. Baldwin, C. Burwell, et al.: *Art of the Score*.
6. Nicholas Baragwanath, 'Alban Berg, Richard Wagner, and Leitmotivs of Symmetry', *19th-Century Music*, Vol. 23, No. 1 (Summer, 1999), 62–83.
7. Aaron Copland, 'Music in the Films', in *Our New Music* (New York: McGrawHill, 1941), 260–75.
8. Coleman, Carter Burwell Interview, 91.
9. For Wagner's notion of 'Ahnung', see Richard Wagner, *Opera and Drama* (Lincoln: University of Nebraska Press, 1995), 336.
10. For a first-rate introduction to metonymic substitution, see Christian Metz, *The Imaginary Signifier: Psychoanalysis and the Cinema* (Bloomington: Indiana University Press, 1982).
11. David Morgan, *Knowing the Score: Film Composers Talk About the Art, Craft, Blood, Sweat, and Tears of Writing for Cinema* (New York: HarperEntertainment, 2000), 66.
12. Rick Altman, 'Moving Lips: Cinema as Ventriloquism', *Yale French Studies*, No. 60 (1980), 67–79.
13. Justin Craig, 'Burwell Serves Up Homily and *Grit*', *Film Score Monthly Online*, Vol. 15, No. 1 (December 2010).
14. A. Baldwin, C. Burwell, et al.: *Art of the Score*.
15. Craig, 'Burwell Serves Up Homily and *Grit*'.
16. Beyond the scope of this article is an experiment that one can easily perform at home: match any sequence from a Burwell/Coen film

with music more stereotypically associated with the film's putative genre and experience the results: often shocking, always hilarious. It is almost chilling, the degree to which even the Coens' most breathtaking visual constructions can be undone with conventional non-diegetic music.

Bibliography

Altman, Rick. 1980. Moving Lips: Cinema as Ventriloquism. *Yale French Studies* 60: 67–79.

Baldwin, Alec, Carter Burwell Ethan, Joel Coen, and Aniruddh Patel. 2013. *Art of the Score*. A Co-Presentation of World Science Festival and the New York Philharmonic. https://www.youtube.com/watch?v=u8TqjA-iMD0. Accessed 13 October 2015.

Baragwanath, Nicholas. 1999. Alban Berg, Richard Wagner, and Leitmotivs of Symmetry. *19th-Century Music* 23(1): 62–83.

Copland, Aaron. 1941. Music in the Films. In *Our New Music*, 260–275. New York: McGrawHill.

Craig, Justin. 2010. Burwell Serves Up Homily and Grit. *Film Score Monthly Online*, Vol. 15, No. 1, December.

Metz, Christian. 1982. *The Imaginary Signifier: Psychoanalysis and the Cinema*. Trans. Celia Britton. Bloomington: Indiana University Press.

Morgan, David. 2000. *Knowing the Score: Film Composers Talk About the Art, Craft, Blood, Sweat, and Tears of Writing for Cinema*. New York: HarperEntertainment.

Sternfeld, Frederick. 1947. Music and the Feature Films. *The Musical Quarterly* 33(4): 517–532.

Wagner, Richard. 1995. *Opera and Drama*. Trans. William Ashton Ellis. Lincoln: University of Nebraska Press. Reprinted from the 1893 translation of volume 2 (Opera and Drama) of *Richard Wagner's Prose Works*, published by Kegan Paul, Trench, Trübner & Co., Ltd., London.

CHAPTER 8

Rachel Portman Interview

Lindsay Coleman

Rachel Portman is equally comfortable scoring frothy comedies and intense dramas, her style clearly recognizable irrespective of genre. Winning the Academy Award for Best Musical or Comedy Score for her work on the 1996 film *Emma*, Portman's music is often used outside of the films she has scored, on television series, commercials, and thus widely recognized. Major films in her career include *The Cider House Rules* (Lasse Hallström, 1999), *The Duchess* (Saul Dibb, 2008), *Beloved* (Jonathan Demme, 1998), *The Manchurian Candidate* (Jonathan Demme, 2004), and *Never Let Me Go* (Mark Romanek, 2010).

The following interview was conducted via Skype in mid-2013. Lindsay Coleman conducted the interview.

Q: Carter Burwell, when I spoke with him, noted that he liked his music to stand separate from, and observe, the story.
A: I would say yes, I definitely favour a counter-intuitive approach. I think those are the most fun films to do. When you can stand back. I did that on *The Human Stain* (Robert Benton, 2003). I felt like the music was just one step removed from the characters. It was in the same movie. But there was no reason for it to be *that* music. When

---

L. Coleman (✉)
Nunawading, Australia

© The Author(s) 2017
L. Coleman, J. Tillman (eds.), *Contemporary Film Music*,
DOI 10.1057/978-1-137-57375-9_8

I am allowed to do that it is very exciting. I don't really know where that music comes from, it just kind of happens. It is exciting because it is not the expected thing which somebody would have written there, and is just one step removed. That can add a lot to a film. It adds a different kind of level, it takes you out of it. For many people it can be completely unconscious to the experience of watching the film. It adds a richer layer.

Q: In the book of *Emma* Austen offers the character up for ridicule. The degree to which we, the audience, ridicule Emma is somewhat relative. Did you feel your music on the film was offering a commentary on the character which would be comparable to that of Austen? Or was it serving a separate purpose?

A: That's a complicated question. I would say the film version isn't exactly the book. It's a much lighter version. I knew the book *really* well. To me it seemed that it just skimmed across the top. I just forgot all that and treated it as it was. There's a lot of lightness of touch in there. There's a lot of light irony. The music is playing along with the same tone as that. For example, when she's engaged in archery with Mr Knightley the music is having fun there. It's also having fun in the sewing scene with Harriet. The music is full of comic irony. The music is sincere when Emma is sincere, and when she learns her lessons.

Q: Even though you are quite varied in your output, you yourself agreed in an interview for BAFTA that there was such a thing as the Rachel Portman style of composition.

A: Yes, absolutely, we as composers have a natural affinity for certain kinds of composition. I think it's like if you have a friend, or person you know really well. You'll know how they're going to respond to certain things because you know their character. I think the same thing is true for the character of what I write in that it comes from my world, from who I am. I am going to have a reaction, which means that there is a big part of me in everything. I think that's why it sounds like I have a style, because that is *me* speaking. You do develop a style, just as you develop a character within yourself.

Q: Did you have a time this style came into focus for you?

A: No. I look back sometimes and I think, when I started off, my style on *Oranges Are Not the Only Fruit* (Beeban Kidron, 1990), where my music was quite dark and bold, was not necessarily just used in a describing way. I think as I've matured my music has become simpler, and perhaps more sophisticated. I have changed, as I've grown up. I've become more subtle, as I've come to understand drama more. I'd still love to be unsubtle, and to be offered more wacky stuff. I love comedy, sort of emotional comedy. I also love really *sad* dramas. I often get given things with a lot of heart. I don't seem to get offered Wild West adventures, horror, that sort of thing.

Q: Would you want to score a blockbuster?
A: Hmm... No, not really. I don't really go to see blockbusters. Assuming it would be something fun to go and see, that I'd want to go and see, then yes, I'd consider it. It would be fun to do an animated feature. Not really a blockbuster, or something violent.
Q: You've said Rachmaninov was too romantic, and you have repudiated that kind of romanticism. But listening to your score for *The Duchess* it is *quite* romantic in sections.
A: I probably said that many years before I wrote *The Duchess*. I don't like *saccharine* music. I don't listen to music that is too sweet. That is not to say that I haven't written music which is itself accused of being too *sweet*, but I tend to try *not* to. I think I might have changed my views about Rachmaninov; he's a brilliant composer. But that kind of *gushing* music I try to steer away from. My taste of what is sweet won't be the same as someone else's. I try to temper the sweet stuff I write with some bitterness, so they are not just sweet.
Q: Does the bitterness come through with particular instruments?
A: No, the bitterness comes through in the harmonies. It's never resting on one thing or the other. Really, broadly speaking, I'll counter something sad with a bit of hope, I'll counter something which could be considered sweeter with something bitter.
Q: Would you say that your score for *Never Let Me Go* has that characteristic?
A: That's really hard. It is such a sad film. I don't think it's sweet. I think it is *really* sad. But definitely I put hope in there. Definitely! Not in all the themes, but I believe there are some which contain what sounds like hope to my ears.
Q: *The Cider House Rules* features a central relationship between Homer and Candy which has a question mark over it. Did that come through in how you chose to score it?
A: Do you mean that the relationship was tinged with sorrow? Well, it wouldn't have been a conscious choice, but the overall film is quite sad, even though it is wonderful when Homer comes back at the end of the film. But it wouldn't have made sense to have a theme which

was all completely light between Candy and Homer. That's not the spine of the story. The spine of the story is Homer, and his coming back, and his connection to his roots.

Q: In *Only You* (Norman Jewison, 1994), the Robert Downey Jr. character is revealed not to be the typical romantic lead, which he nevertheless becomes in the end. Do you feel that irony works its way into your score?

A: I can't answer that question because it was so long ago. I can say that that is a really *sweet* melody. I was told to write the most 'falling in love' music I possibly could. That is an example of something which completely goes against the grain of what I normally do.

Q: In line with your comments on Rachmaninov, do you feel it is possible to question the canon of great composers?

A: Absolutely it is. But I think our tastes change as we go through life. Sometimes it's worth going back to composers you had dismissed. I always used to think I didn't like Mahler. But, you are going to be drawn to some composers over others, just because of the harmonic language they use. You won't know why. It's like someone plays your song. But I think it's fine. Anyone should be free to like or dislike anything. Even if it's the greatest composer in the world, you can have an argument with someone about it.

Q: I'm a big fan of the third movement of the Fifth Symphony of Beethoven, very specific parts of the Ninth—not the Ode to Joy—but do you have given moments from scores which really resonate with you? Or is it the piece as a whole?

A: Definitely given moments. There's a lot of Beethoven I'm not particularly in love with, and there are other parts which I find incredibly beautiful. I just heard part of the Moonlight Sonata, not the well-known bit, on the radio today, and it was *so beautiful*. There are parts of him I really love. There are other things, the first movement of the Fifth Symphony, I could really take it or leave it. I think that is normal. Nearly all of Mozart is incredible. All of Bach! I love *all* of Bach! I love his whole canon. The same would be true of Rachmaninov, where much of it is wonderful, but the bits which are really famous I would not really respond to. I think it is normal to respond that way.

Q: Do you visualize the music before you write it?

A: It's a strange process. You become really drawn into the film, drawn into the performances. Usually, three or four days after watching a film I'll be drawn into a little chord sequence, a little melody. It will be a little piece of the jigsaw. For me it's a feeling, a tonality, a key. Usually, I keep going back to put it in A minor, for instance. I find that a lot of the score of a particular film is in D minor, or G major. I keep working in those tonalities. I find that as you let things settle, you sleep on it, then things begin to gel. It's kind of about a process of forgetting, and then things begin to happen. It like ... not forcing something. Then you realize 'ah, that might work'.

Q: A.R. Rahman says he is hearing music at all times. Is this true for you as well?

A: Yes. Often. I find it distracting having other music on because it distracts me from what is in my head. Yes, I have music in my head the whole time.

Q: Physically, composition can be very taxing.

A: No, I think I'm fine. It feeds me, if anything. It is exhausting. But really it is the deadlines which are exhausting. The music itself, the writing of it, is easy.

Q: Mychael Danna believes the music he makes is only meant to go with the images of the film it was composed for.

A: I agree that the music should serve the film, be it as a bold part or a subtle part. Whether it has a life outside, most film music doesn't. Every now and then there is a piece which does rise up. It is surprising how much film music *is* listened to. A lot of it plays in the concert hall. It really depends on how interesting the music is, taken away from the images of the film. If people like it, who is anyone to say it should be experienced only with a film? Lots of music written for film deserves a place in the concert hall. The thing about film music is that people believe it is a soundtrack to their lives just as it is a soundtrack to a film. There is something very easy about them which pulls you in. It's really interesting.

Q: The theme for *The Cider House Rules* is used a *lot*.

A: I'm amazed. I hear it is played a lot in the States. It was cut into the UK *X Factor* the other day! I was really startled to hear that. People who don't know what that piece of music is, don't realize what it is from, are exposed to it often. It's a piece which has developed completely on its own. There is no reason for it to have that life. It's *lovely*! Depending on what it's used for.

Q: On *One Day* (Lone Scherfig, 2011) you weren't asked to do a large amount of score. Was that what appealed on that film?

A: There wasn't a heavy reliance on music in the film. Sometimes directors say 'I want music here, here, here' and you feel 'oh, I love writing music but I wish I wasn't filling in in this way!' *One Day* wasn't like that at all. I thought it was a great film. It seemed to me that there was a great balance of music in the film, just lots of little pieces as opposed to long, lyrical bits.

Q: Lots of the composers I've spoken with have had scores rejected. Have you had a similar experience?

A: It happens. I had one recently. I hadn't yet recorded the score. It makes you feel like shit. You've done everything you can. Ninety-nine per cent of the time I'm doing my absolute best, putting myself in. It can be very soul-destroying, and shocking, shocking in the way it's done. But the stakes are high, working in film. You can't take it personally. It could be the director wants green music, and you can only write blue music. So even though it is personal to you, it just doesn't match up.

CHAPTER 9

Eero Tarasti and the Narratological Construction of Rachel Portman's *Emma*

Lindsay Coleman

Music and narrative have always seemed to be close to one another, tied. Certainly, in the imagination of audiences, a theme might represent 'heroism', or 'the pain of loss'. Think perhaps of Elgar's Cello Concerto in E minor, as performed by Jacqueline Du Pré. The emotional shifts in the famous piece engender such passionate identification from almost everyone who hears it that a narrative is perhaps inadvertently assembled around it to house the powerful emotions it provokes. There are also, of course, ballets and operas, in which the music performed articulates the emotions, and often the events, of the scenarios depicted. However, in formal terms, less emotional ones, the relationship between 'story' and music is not necessarily as close as we might want to believe, certainly in the case of purely instrumental music. Jean-Jacques Nattiez has argued that 'in itself, and as opposed to a great many linguistic utterances, music is not a narrative, and that any description of its formal structures in terms of narrativity is nothing but superfluous metaphor'.[1] What this means is that a desire to attach narrative significance, or power, to a piece of performed music does not automatically enable said fusion.

And yet, as can be seen from the history of the cinema, the musical accompaniment of moving images has always been seen as an essential

L. Coleman (✉)
Nunawading, Australia

© The Author(s) 2017
L. Coleman, J. Tillman (eds.), *Contemporary Film Music*,
DOI 10.1057/978-1-137-57375-9_9

part of an evolving visual scenario. Clearly, the view of certain theorists on the plausibility of instrumental music evoking narrative are only part of a more heterogenous view, context-dependent on music's potential for narrativity. A theorist who may help elucidate further this heterogeneity is musicologist Eero Tarasti, who suggests, 'As a general rule, the minimal condition of narrativity is the transformation of an object or state of affairs into something else through a process that requires a certain amount of time.'[2] Given this broad definition, he argues that music is fundamentally a narrative art, different musical forms and structures outlining different narrative approaches. Tarasti elaborates on what is best described as the anthropomorphic side of music, otherwise known as 'actoriality'. Within this view on music the attribution of human emotions, events and characteristics is natural. Coherence in music, he argues, comes from the sense of a deeper meaning to the music, what would be classified as an actoriality, which in turn is normally identified with a theme and with thematicism, but in the broadest possible sense represents the spark of emotional identification by which the listener projects themselves into the work of music, very much as one might Du Pré's fine work on the cello. In the Elgar concerto there is nothing 'sad' inherent to the music, other than that it is identified as a 'sad' theme, and in turn one rendered 'sad' by the near universal consensus of all who hear the piece.[3] In the following passage Tarasti describes how, via his interpretive lens, a case may successfully be made for musical narrativity:

> For example, the aforementioned Dante sonata by Liszt represents music where the narrative model functions and where 'despair' and the powers of hell at the beginning are later replaced by the principle of 'hope' and the light of paradise. This simple narrative program in music could be described using the categories mentioned above: the actantial category of 'personage' appears in the way how Liszt's theme serves as a sort of musical fictive subject, a musical actant, personage and hero with which the listener can identify himself; the temporal category contributes to the time-shape of this actant-theme: first, in the restless, jerking and panting alternation of pairs of sixteenth notes in the 'despair' section, and particularly in the absence of a clearly marked verse boundary in the 'despair' section, and again in the rhythmic expansion when it expresses 'hope'; the spatial category is manifested by the way the 'despair' motif dwells in a low register, erring back and forth chromatically with minor harmonies; in the 'hope' motif the music moves into the luminous upper register and a major key. The way musical narrativity precisely emerges from a series of emotions (caused by the music itself)...[4]

What Tarasti's description allows for is the manner in which, through the testimony of concert-goers and music lovers alike, it is well known that a work may take an audience on an emotional journey. Tarasti both posits that the said journey is reflective of a sequence of emotions, and that the belief in said emotions also constitutes a belief in a symbolic hero, imaginatively placed within the score, who is in turn the eager proxy for the audience's own emotional projections onto the performance of the score. How is this possible?

The term Tarasti also uses to describe these notions is that a piece of music may contain a variety of 'passions'. Tarasti believes that the piece of music 'does not consist of presenting only one passion, one state of mind, but that music in particular is a temporal continuum of several passions, and that a composition may contain several passions successively and even in a certain, precisely planned order'.[5] This sequence in turn, in communicating a series of experiences the listener may empathize with, creates the notion of a living soul whispering of experience within the music. He even goes so far as to posit that a musical work is, metaphorically, a 'living organism', a sort of 'body'.[6]

The question of how any composed work, for film or stage, attains fluent narrativity is a vast one, likely beyond the scope of this chapter to answer with ease. However, as a specific case study, the compositional work of Rachel Portman on the 1996 film *Emma* may be offered up as a strong practical and aesthetic instance of music achieving storytelling through thematic and formal necessity. In turn, when viewed through the prism of Tarasti's theoretical work, more than necessity, it likewise attains conceptual viability. Beyond the subjective claims of the audience believing Portman's score complements and enhances the narrative of *Emma*, Tarasti offers a conceptual paradigm where such claims may find validation. Within this paradigm discussed above, that of the passions, there is no standardized point of view. So, too, it is possible that the music, in a situation such as aiding in the adaptation of narratively complex source material such as *Emma*, might transition easily between multiple narrative points of view, yet all the while maintaining its emotional hold on the passion of the listener.

As source material, Jane Austen's *Emma* is innately concerned with character and event. Essentially an epic character study set in the minutiae of domestic life in early nineteenth century England, the book's ongoing relevance stems from its commitment to a fulsome exploration of the quirks, failings, and belated evolution of its title character. The reader of the book, or indeed the viewer of the film, must engage with the title character, her actions, her psychology, her misdeeds, their feelings for her, or be precluded from any particular engagement with the story at all. Without the focus being on Emma, there is no *Emma*. This creates, with the form of novel's storytelling, great amplitude in which to explore the character, given that all of the resources at Austen's disposal are in service of the exploration of the title character's standing on the precipice of adulthood. In being a narrative of such a particular quality, it also offers up a character both well-rounded, and sufficiently open to interpretation and reconfiguration, as to slip its own conventional bounds of characterization, adding a tonal ambiguity to its themes and plot equally.

Austen's greatest problem in constructing Emma is said to be the control of our response to its 'flawed' subject, and the critic's greatest problem in defending Emma to be justifying Austen's exercise of that control. Emma is flawed as a person but not as a character, the defence goes, because her pride, snobbery, gullibility and self-deception are what enable the comedy and, indeed, the plot—such as it is. But because comedy, or at least this comedy, also requires our sympathy, our desire for the heroine's reform and reward, Austen must simultaneously shield us from those very flaws.[7]

Ironically, the narrative's comedy, its satirical digs at the heroine and her society, invests its structure with an instability. Emma, the character, is a unique personality, and also a servant to the comedy her presence produces. This element of the narrative's construction is further complicated by what some critics note in its delivery, the narrator's voice, and that of Emma herself, arguably at odds with one another.

The importance of separating the narrative voice from Emma's voice is evident in the following passage, in which Emma declares her intention to become more like Harriet, for the sake of her own happiness: 'It was rather too late in the day to set about being simple-minded and ignorant; but she left her with every previous resolution confirmed of being humble and discreet, and repressing imagination all the rest of her life' (*Emma*, p. 142). When this passage is read as narrative statement, there is an ugly harshness in Emma's opening thoughts ('It was rather too late in the day to set about being simple-minded and ignorant') but, seen as part of Emma's narrated monologue, it forms a comic beginning to Emma's attempt at self-reform. There are moments when it is unclear whose opinion is being given, Emma's or the narrator's, and this lack of clarity subtly undermines the reader's confidence in the objective value of statements.[8]

In short the reader is forced into a place of both great enjoyment of the narrative, and similarly a subliminal mistrust of it, of whose perspective they are engaging with. This is again compounded by a technique wherein, through the periodic investiture of bifurcated third person perspective, the narrative perspective is further problematized:

> Judging primarily on the basis of content, we can divide the novel's third person narration into two types: first, that which might represent a transcript of a character's conscious thoughts during the action; and, second, the so called 'exposition,' which constitutes reports of settings and action, and which is usually felt to be the product of the narrator.[9]

In turn the scenario may be judged to be presented in two separate voices, voices in turn which are interrupting one another throughout the course of the narrative. In short, the storytelling of *Emma* is flighty, whimsical, and unpredictable, just like its heroine.

Douglas McGrath's 1996 adaptation of *Emma* is itself a further iteration of said narrative. While its preoccupations may be more those of a typical nineties heroine, coming as it did only a year after *Clueless* (Amy Heckerling, 1995), itself an adaptation of *Emma*, the essential elements of the story remain. Emma, spoiled and not quite so clever as she imagines, spends the film learning about the ways of adulthood, and the mysteries of the human heart. And yet, arguably, it is not Austen's *Emma*. To writer Anna Despotopolou McGrath's Emma

> is the protagonist of a broadly amusing film which abounds in verbal and physical comedy arising from superficial conversation (e.g. the merits of celery root or the horrors of a sore throat), which is amusing only because it is dated. The director treats the novel as a series of slapstick-inspired gaffes which provide him with the facile opportunity of filming an entertaining comedy centred around the heroine's hilarious blunders. He accentuates the humour in a prosaic way, comfortably ignoring the more serious concerns of the novel.[10]

The comedy, noted above, is still present, and indeed the review presented here would seem to subscribe to the notion that Emma is both a clown and an ingénue. Yet, also, as a film, and a light film comedy at that, the piece cannot become bogged down by the duelling perspectives of an off-screen narrator and the heroine herself. And yet, as an unstable narrative, prone to sudden shifts in narrative and thematic perspective, I would argue it is highly dependent upon music to bolster and clarify said ambiguities. In short, what would otherwise be missing in a screen adaptation is supplemented by the oscillations in its score, between the overtly comical, ironic and romantic, by the composer Rachel Portman.

There is yet another intriguing dimension to the potential of narrativity in forms of music. Nobel Laureate Romain Rolland notes that music may be naturally tied to event, in the analysis of the work of a given composer. In fact it is seen as 'a direct continuation of the inner and outer events of the composer's life'.[11] In short, Rolland represents the vibrant discourse that, given the emotions stirred by music, it is a natural default to inscribe into the music, both the events of the composer's life, and also our passionate desire to identify with said events. Music tells both *a* story, as well as *the* story of the composer themselves. Examine the following excerpt from his book on Beethoven:

> We had become so accustomed to living in our Beethoven, to sharing with him from our infancy the bed of his dreams, that we had failed to perceive to what degree the tissue of his dreams was exceptional. Today, when we see a new generation detaching itself from this music that was the voice of our inner world, we perceive that that world was only one of the continents of the spirit. It is none the less beautiful for that, none the less dear to us; nay, it is dearer still. For only now do our eyes clearly perceive its delimiting lines, the definite contours of the Imperial figure that was our *Ecce homo*. Each great epoch of humanity has its own, its Son of God, its human archetype, whose glance, whose gestures, and whose Word are the common possession of millions of the living. The whole being of a Beethoven, his sensibility, his conception of the world, the form of his intelligence and of his will, the laws of his construction, his ideology, as well as the substance of his body and his temperament, everything is representative of a certain European epoch.[12]

What Rolland's words represent is, in their very insistence on pinning the vagaries of composition to the precision of his lyrical descriptions, a desire that the relation of the composer, to their music, and in turn to their audience, take on the more axiomatic form of a literal, or even literary, text. Audiences love Beethoven's music, identify with it. In so doing, they insist on identifying with the events of Beethoven's own life, and in turn the fluctuations of his emotional life. We, the audience, posit in Beethoven's work a figure which Carolyn Abbate calls the 'narrating survivor of the tale who speaks of it in the past tense'.[13] If Beethoven suffered, we imagine, according to Rolland's account, his own voice is whispering to us through the music of said suffering:

> The misfortune that descends on him between 1800 and 1802 ... like the storm in the Pastoral [Symphony] though in his case the sky never clears again smites him in all his being at once; in his social life, in love, in art. Everything is attacked: nothing escapes.[14]

While the poetic nature of Rolland's project perhaps defies easy empirical, or even musicological, analysis, it nevertheless opens the door to a wider field of possibilities when it comes to the place of narrative within music.

This kind of biographical criticism, where works of art are interpreted as direct expressions of what was going on in the artist's life, was a widespread phenomenon in the nineteenth and early twentieth centuries. But, it fell out of fashion during the twentieth century, especially after 1950, because of the influence of New Criticism. Today, after the critique of formalism and autonomy, earlier biographical readings of, not the least, Beethoven's music are viewed as important elements in a 'Wirkungs', and reception history, that again are considered important and relevant in shaping the understanding of his works. In the chapter 'Life and Work' in Carl Dahlhaus's *Ludwig van Beethoven: Approaches to His Music* the author notes:

> The image of Beethoven that survives in the mind of posterity is a diffuse compilation of impressions emanating from music and biographical fragments that consist to a great extent of legends and anecdotes. Indeed, the relationship between the works and the life apply all the closer if we place our faith in the revelatory power of anecdotes in which the truth is more symbolic than empirical, instead of relying on documentary testimony that stands up to historical criticism.[15]

What Dahlhaus is suggesting, marvellously, is that there can be a strong argument made for the validity of emotional biography buried in music, a testimony provoked by the events of life, yet eternally comingled with the emotion and subjectivity of the artist-composer.

Jean-Jacques Nattiez, a theorist who might be classified as a naysayer on the possibility of narratology and music coinciding, complains that the requisite specificity of narrative can never be captured by music, and writes:

> When I hear a march in Mahler's second symphony, I imagine that it's got something to do with a band of people, but I don't know which people … The responsibility for joining character-phantoms with action-shadows lies with me, the listener, since it does not lie within *music's* semiological capacities to join subject and predicate.[16]

Conversely, musicologist Anthony Newcomb argues that 'formal and expressive interpretation are in fact two complementary ways of understanding the same phenomena. Neither is intrinsically closer than the other to the object.'[17] To Carolyn Abbate the quest for a narrative in music is foiled by music's inability to present the narrator whispering out their experience, the narrator Rolland hears, or more importantly imagines he hears, in Beethoven. Nattiez believes such claims fall apart in the details. We can hear a note, trace its relationship to our life in the broadest sense, based on the cultural and historical context in which we receive the music, yet a note is not precisely a colour, nor is the opening of a given orchestral movement the roar of a precise crowd in a precise place. Yet Newcomb, like Rolland, is saying that our 'feeling' that a narrative movement is manifesting in a strain of music can and should be sufficient to claim that it is, in fact, a component of the narrative's effective development. Emotional biography/autobiography must originate, by very definition, from a source, a human imagination. This awareness of some hypothetical point of origination in actual experience, then generating the music, for an audience, or for writers such as Dahlhaus and Rolland, is sufficient to build a complex architecture of identification within a larger piece of work. In this paradigm the prime emotional fuel and shorthand of a given composition, ironically irrespective of the broader subject matter of the work in which it appears (i.e. a commercial period comedy such as *Emma*), is the composer themselves. Their 'voice', the voice of their emotional autobiography, is the voice we wish to hear, regardless of the song they are singing. Indeed, just as Portman knows the book *Emma*, she equally knows herself as a composer:

> Yes, absolutely, we as composers have a natural affinity for certain kinds of composition. I think it's like if you have a friend or person you know really well. You'll know how they're going to respond to certain things because you know their character. I think the same thing is true for the character of what I write in that it comes from my world, from who I am. I am going to have a reaction which means that there is a big part of me in everything. I think that's why it sounds like I have a style, because that is *me* speaking. You do develop a style, just as you develop a character within yourself.[18]

What, in essence, this represents, is the possibility that Rolland's musical biography of Beethoven, while itself based on his own empathic imagination—given that the work was written a century after the composer died, it would be impossible for his insights into the composer's emotional life to be based on anything other than his own powerful imagination—nevertheless was formulated on a basis which not only the audience believes to be valid, but also the composer themself, and certainly Portman, by her own admission. This raises an obvious, but still intriguing, possibility. If narration is a bedrock of narrative, composers are in turn cognizant of communicating said experience in their music. The experience recedes into the past, and in turn is recounted in the present act of composition. Surely the case might be made for, at the very least, music constituting a variant on storytelling in its more conventional forms, a manifestation of character formed by experience, then reorganized in a chosen artform, music. The signature style noted in Portman by Christian Clemmensen can be found throughout *Emma*. There is Portman's trademark bed of lightly chopping strings, with the use of cellos found in the more serious moments, and the comedy cues then transitioning back to violins. Clarinet and oboe carry the melody lines.[19] What this represents, remarkably, is the possibility that, without being explicitly 'narratological' in character, a musical accompaniment to a story may be so personally derived as to virtually represent the composer singing along to the story, divorced from the characterization, and yet still capable of expressing sympathy for the narrative to the point of virtual synchronicity, an illusion that the sound of the music, the feeling of the music, and the rigidity of a scenario may coincide with one another. Jerrold Levinson talks about additive film music, another kind of non-diegetic music which has other functions than narrative film music: 'Such music, which can be labelled additive film music, is generally a vehicle of commentary on a film's fictional world, rather than a device for delineating that world; additive music must thus be ascribed directly to the implied filmmaker or author.'[20] A more extensive presentation of these ideas can be found in Levinson article 'Film Music and Narrative Agency':

> It will turn out that there is a rough coincidence between film music to which we intuitively accord narrative significance and film music for which we implicitly hold an internal cinematic narrator accountable, and between film music to which we do not accord narrative significance and film music that we implicitly assign directly to the implied filmmaker.[21]

In this instance, naturally, the filmmaker is Portman herself, and, equally, it is Portman's insight into the character, as refracted through the musical prism of her own character, which produces the richest vein of commentary in the film of *Emma*.

The critical consensus holds that the reception of the narrative of *Emma*, to be effective, must possess a strain of irony, a counterpoint of critique of our heroine. It might equally be argued that this strain, while not specific to a given character, a given place, is *very* specific to the story of Emma. The film's composer would seem to admit as much:

> I would say the film version isn't exactly the book. It's a much lighter version. I knew the book *really* well. I read it first at school. To me it seemed that it just skimmed across the top. I just forgot all that and treated it as it was. There's a lot of lightness of touch in there. There's a lot of light irony. The music is playing along with the same tone as that. For example, when she's engaged in archery with Mr Knightley the music is having fun there. It's also having fun in the sewing scene with Harriet. The music is full of comic irony. The music is sincere when Emma is sincere, and when she learns her lessons.[22]

What Portman's score thus allows for is the sense of a teasing doubleness in the film, a sense of irony which actually further enriches the more obvious moments of indecorous behaviour. However, I would argue, if an attempt were made to claim that the music, which might otherwise stand in for a narrator slightly at odds with our heroine, surely the musical tone which accompanies so much of the arch dialogue for which Austen is famous might be argued to add 'to posit a narrating survivor of the tale',[23] confounding Abbate's claims. How else might Portman, who knows the source material so well, present her own musical 'voice' in the piece but as an accompaniment in tune with the source material, and also as her own honed appreciation and absorption of the source material. Just as she was formed by the book in her youth, so to could she form the film *Emma*.

Concluding his essay on the possibility of musical narratology Lawrence Kramer states:

> Of the possible conclusions to be drawn from [music], the one I would single out as primary is that narrative elements in music represent, not forces of structure, but forces of meaning.[24]

Stories may have beginning, middles and ends, a three-act structure. A piece of music cannot echo said three-act structure, but may invest proceedings with a resonance, both from the composer themselves, and through the use of the composer as the audience's proxy, one producing a narratology of a kind, yet perhaps less of a kind described by the more rigid parameters set by the theorists at this chapter's beginning.

This is perhaps especially pertinent when considering that the comic nature of Austen's scenario—the comic form, of course, a prime exemplar of the strictures of narrative structure—can and must be reinforced by the presence of an appropriate score. Portman offers, over the course of the film, two primary themes. The first represents the main character, and is found at the film's opening, and the second often manifests in the comedy of the story. The first half of the end titles is a variation of Emma's theme. These are, true to the irony found within Portman's composition, themes for Emma's schemings, activities which are dead serious for Emma herself, but which the comic tone of the theme puts in a different light.

So, what does all of this toing and froing add up to? Naturally, the score of *Emma* is not the literal score to Portman's own life. However, in using her compositional language, Portman falls into a natural expressive pattern representing a sensibility honed from the experiences of her life, and in turn reflecting the specificity of said life, a specificity Nattiez claims is absent in music. As the key of C minor holds significance in Beethoven's canon, so, too, does Portman's affinity for particular arrangements of strings represent her own musical fingerprint. In turn, this specific character to Portman's composition reflects on her own fondness and emotional connection to *Emma* the book, and Emma the character, through her composition. In aiding in the telling of Emma's story, Portman is expressing her own sensibility, one defined by Emma the character, and doubtless many other works of music, art and literature. The score, in turn, so specific to Portman herself, to her relationship to *Emma* the text, allows for a specific 'knowingness' within the film itself, a sense of the book's irony which adds an essential component to the film without which the tone of the film, so essential to the successful delivery of its themes and central character, would not be achieved.

The questions asked in this chapter provide no simple answers. To claim that music itself is analogous to a narrative would be misleading at best. It certainly would not address the simple point that there is ample space typically for interpretation on the part of the listener of a piece of music. Yet, equally, the extent to which music may accompany and enhance a detailed narrative suggests that it does not possess anti-narrative qualities. Equally, the belief of writers such as Rolland, and composers such as Portman, that the self of the composer may be constituted in their music, and in turn the faith of audiences that some kind of report of lived experience is found within music, suggest the potential for a new narratological category to which music might apply. Tarasti, as a musicologist, goes some way to assembling, broadly, a group of complementary aesthetic models which help us to understand what would essentially be qualified as the faith of the audience that music, despite superficial indications to the contrary, is a medium of pure storytelling. Certainly, Tarasti's theories deserve greater investigation, just as do the statements of composers such as Portman to the effect that their music is literal self-expression, and as such become an easy vessel for the tale of life's experience. In effect, any song they sing, regardless of whether it is *Emma*, or some other tale, will inevitably be sung in their own voice.

Notes

1. Jean-Jacques Nattiez, 'Can One Speak of Narrativity in Music?', *Journal of the Royal Musical Association*, Vol. 115, No. 2 (1990), 257.
2. Eero Tarasti, 'Music as a Narrative Art', in Marie-Lauren Ryan (ed.), *Narrative Across Media: The Languages of Storytelling* (Lincoln: University of Nebraska Press, 2004), 283.
3. Eero Tarasti, 'Music as a Narrative Art', 295.
4. Eero Tarasti, 'Music Models Through Ages: A Semiotic Interpretation', *International Review of the Aesthetics and Sociology of Music*, Vol. 17, No. 1 (June, 1986), 11–12.
5. Tarasti, 'Music Models Through Ages', 11.
6. Eero Tarasti, 'The Emancipation of the Sign: On the Corporeal and Gestural Meanings in Music', *AS/SA*, No. 4 (1997), 186.
7. Adena Rosmarin, '"Misreading" *Emma*: The Powers and Perfidies of Interpretive History', *ELH*, Vol. 51, No. 2 (Summer, 1984), 318.
8. Rachel Provenzano Oberman, 'Fused Voices: Narrated Monologue in Jane Austen's *Emma*', *Nineteenth-Century Literature*, Vol. 64, No. 1 (June 2009), 3.
9. Helen Dry, 'Syntax and Point of View in Jane Austen's *Emma*', *Studies in Romanticism*, Vol. 16, No. 1, Romanticism and Language (Winter, 1977), 88.

10. Anna Despotopoulou, 'Girls on Film: Postmodern Renderings of Jane Austen and Henry James', *The Yearbook of English Studies*, Vol. 36, No. 1, Translation (2006), 120.
11. Tarasti, 'Music Models Through Ages', 21.
12. Romain Rolland, *Beethoven the Creator: The Great Creative Epochs; I. From the Eroica to the Appassionata*, 8th ed., trans. Ernest Newman (New York: Garden City Publishing, 1937), 21.
13. Carolyn Abbate, 'What the Sorcerer Said', *19th-Century Music*, Vol. 12, No. 3 (Spring, 1989), 230.
14. Rolland, *Beethoven the Creator*, 48.
15. Carl Dahlhaus, *Ludwig van Beethoven: Approaches to His Music*, trans. Mary Whittall (Oxford: Clarendon Press, 1991), 1.
16. Jean-Jacques Nattiez, *Music and Discourse: Toward a Semiology of Music*, trans. Carolyn Abbate (Princeton: Princeton University Press, 1990), 128.
17. Anthony Newcomb, 'Sound and Feeling', *Critical Inquiry*, 10(4) (June 1984), 638.
18. Lindsay Coleman, Rachel Portman Interview, this book, Chapter 8, 120.
19. Christian Clemmensen, 'Emma', editorial review of the soundtrack CD, *Filmtracks*, 24 September 1996 (rev. 23 April 2006), http://www.filmtracks.com/titles/emma.html, accessed 25 June 2016.
20. Jerrold Levinson, 'Soundtrack', in *Routledge Encyclopedia of Narrative Theory*, ed. David Herman, Manfred Jahn, and Marie-Laure Ryan (London: Routledge, 2005), 550.
21. Jerrold Levinson, 'Film Music and Narrative Agency', in *Post-Theory: Reconstructing Film Studies*, eds David Bordwell and Noël Carroll (Madison: University of Wisconsin Press, 1996), 257.
22. Coleman, Rachel Portman Interview, 120.
23. Abbate, 'What the Sorcerer Said', 230.
24. Lawrence Kramer, 'Musical Narratology: A Theoretical Outline', *Indiana Theory Review*, Vol. 12 (SPRING and FALL 1991), 161.

Bibliography

Abbate, Carolyn. 1989. What the Sorcerer Said. *19th-Century Music* 12(3): 221–230.

Clemmensen, Christian. 1996/2006. 'Emma,' Editorial Review of the Soundtrack CD. *Filmtracks*, 24 September 1996 (rev. 23 April 2006). http://www.filmtracks.com/titles/emma.html. Accessed 25 June 2016.

Dahlhaus, Carl. 1991. *Ludwig van Beethoven: Approaches to His Music*. Trans. Mary Whittall. Oxford: Clarendon Press.
Despotopoulou, Anna. 2006. Girls on Film: Postmodern Renderings of Jane Austen and Henry James. *The Yearbook of English Studies* 36(1): 115–130. Translation.
Dry, Helen. 1977. Syntax and Point of View in Jane Austen's *Emma*. *Studies in Romanticism* 16(1): 87–99. Romanticism and Language.
Kramer, Lawrence. 1991. Musical Narratology: A Theoretical Outline. *Indiana Theory Review* 12(Spring and Fall): 141–162.
Levinson, Jerrold. 1996. Film Music and Narrative Agency. In *Post-Theory: Reconstructing Film Studies*, ed. David Bordwell and Noël Carroll, 248–282. Madison: University of Wisconsin Press.
———. 2005. Soundtrack. In *Routledge Encyclopedia of Narrative Theory*, ed. David Herman, Manfred Jahn, and Marie-Laure Ryan, 550–551. London: Routledge.
Nattiez, Jean-Jacques. 1990a. Can One Speak of Narrativity in Music? *Journal of the Royal Musical Association* 115(2): 240–257.
———. 1990b. *Music and Discourse: Toward a Semiology of Music*. Trans. Carolyn Abbate. Princeton: Princeton University Press.
Newcomb, Anthony. 1984. Sound and Feeling. *Critical Inquiry* 10(4): 614–643.
Oberman, Rachel Provenzano. 2009. Fused Voices: Narrated Monologue in Jane Austen's *Emma*. *Nineteenth-Century Literature* 64(1): 1–15.
Rolland, Romain. 1937. *Beethoven the Creator: The Great Creative Epochs*, I. *From the Eroica to the Appassionata*, 8th ed. Trans. Ernest Newman. New York: Garden City Publishing.
Rosmarin, Adena. 1984. 'Misreading' *Emma*: The Powers and Perfidies of Interpretive History. *ELH* 51(2): 315–342.
Tarasti, Eero. 1986. Music Models Through Ages: A Semiotic Interpretation. *International Review of the Aesthetics and Sociology of Music* 17(1): 3–28.
———. 1997. The Emancipation of the Sign: On the Corporeal and Gestural Meanings in Music. *AS/SA* 4: 180–190.
———. 2004. Music as a Narrative Art. In *Narrative Across Media: The Languages of Storytelling*, ed. Marie-Lauren Ryan, 283–305. Lincoln: University of Nebraska Press.

CHAPTER 10

Dario Marianelli Interview

Lindsay Coleman

Dario Marianelli is presently perhaps the pre-eminent composer of dramatic and period scores in mainstream cinema. His collaborations with Joe Wright have produced evocative, romantic scores for films such as *Pride & Prejudice* (2005), *Anna Karenina* (2012) and *Atonement* (2007). The latter garnered him an Academy Award in 2008 for Best Original Score. Marianelli has also composed driving scores for films such as *V for Vendetta* (James McTeigue, 2005), and spare compositions for the most recent adaptation of *Jane Eyre* (Cary Joji Fukunaga, 2011).

The following is an e-mail interview conducted with Dario Marianelli in late 2012, by Lindsay Coleman.

Q: You use string and cello to communicate great melancholy in 'Elegy for Dunkirk'. Morricone famously used woodwinds to communicate a similar scene of desolation in *The Mission* (Roland Joffé, 1986). What leads you to choose a cello over an oboe? What do you feel is the specific emotional quality of each instrument?

A: The oboe in *The Mission* is actually a character, present in sound and body as one of the elements of the story. I cannot say my use of the cello in *Atonement* comes from the same kind of thinking. I have

---

L. Coleman (✉)
Nunawading, Australia

© The Author(s) 2017
L. Coleman, J. Tillman (eds.), *Contemporary Film Music*,
DOI 10.1057/978-1-137-57375-9_10

an ongoing love affair with the cello. I think it started in *Pride & Prejudice*, with a few pieces where the cello solo was quite prominent. I suppose I am attracted by the vocal quality of that instrument; I find its sound very close to a (male) human voice. My love for the cello might go back even further, as I remember as if it was yesterday being blown away by hearing Rostropovich, playing live the six Bach suites for unaccompanied cello, almost 30 years ago. But, for whatever reason, I found myself using it more and more to underline moments of solitude, where the emotional focus of a scene is on one single character.

I do not use the oboe very often. Perhaps for similar reasons, I am more drawn to the sound of the cor anglais [English horn], which plays in a lower register than the oboe—although it has a similar sound, I find its sound closer to my heartstrings. But I make it a rule not to have rules when I write music, so I won't be a bit surprised if at some point I start writing a lot of oboe music!

Q: Seamus McGarvey's Steadicam shot for the Dunkirk scene is now famed. What do you see as the specific interplay between your music and his imagery, the movement of his camera?

A: That scene was for a long time without any music, during the post-production, while the movie was being edited. I kept raising the question as to whether we should attempt to score that moment, but Joe seemed to resist the idea, as he found (as I did, mind you) the singing soldiers moving enough in their own right. However, I kept feeling there might be a way to amplify the emotional space of that scene. I think what struck me to start with was the sense of alienation that Seamus had been able to create, a combination of the pace and the fluid quality of the camera movement. It is a huge space, crowded with what feels like thousands of people, but at the same time the camera is fixed on one character, who is taking in the enormity of the situation he's in. So I wanted the music to reflect that, and I tried to slow down even further the sense of time passing with the music. The pace of the beginning of the piece is very different from the pace of the singing soldiers, and since at some point they had to merge, I had to find some trick that allowed me to do that. It took a while, just to find something that could run, slowly, under a faster choir. Only as the camera briefly abandons Robbie, our main character, to show us the soldiers singing away, does the music allow itself to become truly a support for them. But, very quickly, as the camera abandons the soldiers to go back to Robbie walking, the music returns to its original elegiac mode, to accompany him to his destination.

Q: Ideally, what qualities should a character's theme possess? I am thinking specifically of Briony, especially given that the theme appears quite early in the film when the character is new to the audience.

A: I have never been very fond of 'characters' themes': they usually end up forcing me to be more literal then I wish to be. On occasion, however, I've found them useful, if anything to create some kind of shortcut into the less visible side of one of the characters. In the case of Briony, in *Atonement*, you have a novel that dedicates several pages to the inner workings of her mind, and as a reader it is easy to become party to some obvious turns of mind. What struck me as obvious, reading the book, was that Briony is a very obsessive kind of girl, among other things. She is highly intelligent, but there is a vague hint of malady, I find, in the way she obsesses about herself. I had my own nickname for her: she was 'the girl without brakes' for me; she could go down a mental path and not be able to stop easily. The 'theme' that came out of these thoughts was a fast, minimal, quite repetitive one, which starts its life as a single repeated note on a piano. It walks a tightrope between minor and major keys, and I wanted it to feel full of driving motivation, but unstable, precarious. Sometimes it gets stuck, and then it frees itself, rushing around a little unpredictably. All that, which was on my mind as I was trying to give a sound to some of the less obvious qualities of her mind, came together with the sound of the typewriter, with which I was also experimenting. Initially the experiments were confined to the sound of the typewriter 'solo'. It wasn't long, though, before I realized that the mechanical, clunky quality of its sound could serve to reinforce even further the slightly mechanical workings of Briony's mental cogs. It also fitted perfectly with her aspiration as a writer, and with a number of other moments in the movie.

Q: One of your first scores was for *I Went Down* (Paddy Breathnach, 1997), a tale very much in the Irish idiom. What do you believe is music's power to transcend cultural differences? Correspondingly, what do you feel places certain scores very much within a given time and place?

A: I am not sure how Irish is the idiom of the score on *I Went Down*. I did not use any of the instruments you would normally associate with Ireland; there are no tin whistles, or Irish harp, or bodhráns, no obvious references to Irish folk tunes, no Irish fiddle. Perhaps it feels Irish because you know it's for an Irish movie, but I would venture that if you gave the CD to someone to listen to, without saying what it is for, they could not place the music easily. I had the same approach on my previous, also Irish, movie, my first, called *Ailsa* (Paddy Breathnach, 1994). I have always been extremely suspicious of the 'ethnic' placement of the music, although I have relaxed a little in recent years. My feeling is that 'style', meaning a recognizable idiom that can place a piece of music in time and geography, can be detrimental to the deeper understanding of the characters' motivations. If we assume (let's say) that music has the power to throw light on some hidden aspects of a story—and not simply comment on what is already visible on the screen, or serve as atmospheric background—I think it is a mistake to divert that power away from what is invisible, and towards what is already well represented on-screen. If you are obviously in Ireland, and all characters speak with an Irish accent, do you really need the music to do the same? Well, that is a question I ask myself every time I score a movie that would have an obvious geographical interest. I think the answer is that if one can succeed in maintaining a connection with the specific characters of a particular movie, of that particular story, with those unique sets of motivations, destinies, aspirations, then it's okay to have some gentle inflections, here and there—as long as they do not swamp the general feel in a geographically, or historically, accurate pastiche. It is very easy, otherwise, to end up with music that is 'generic', for lack of a better word. It might sound Irish, or, I don't know, 'Jazzy' or 'Classical', but it remains superficial, and it could just as well have been taken from some music library.

Q: What are instances where you feel a score has far surpassed in brilliance the film it appears in?

A: You are asking me to pass judgement on directors! I don't think I want to: ask me again after I have retired…

Q: In a discussion with a composer acquaintance I noted how often major composers seem to 'borrow' from themselves, perhaps changing the arrangement, or dynamics of a score slightly, but maintaining a given harmony, often played on the same instruments. He said this was an unavoidable reality of composition. Do you feel this is a tendency that you, and other composers, share in?

A: Maybe there is a bit of that, but I think it is hard to divide the 'borrowing' from what is one's own 'brushstroke'. You would expect to recognize a Francis Bacon painting, even if you have never seen it before, just from the colours, the subject, the way to apply paint on the canvas (assuming you have seen enough Bacons before). Equally, when you become familiar with the music of a certain composer you start recognizing common traits in his or her music. I prefer to think, unlike your acquaintance, that what we are, our very life and experience, our way to move and be in the world, ends up invariably in what we do, whether it is a painting or a piece of music, and as such it gives what we do consistency, almost by definition. If for a painter it might be the brushstroke, then for a composer it might be a certain harmonic inclination, or a taste for some orchestral or instrumental combination, or a way to move inner parts in the polyphony, or what function the bass line is fulfilling. They are important elements of the composition, and composers, I think, each have their own individual way about it.

Q: In *The Soloist* (Joe Wright, 2009) you have a major character who is a classical musician. He plays the cello in a number of scenes. The soundtrack itself features some classical music. How much did these elements of story and production influence your approach to composition on *The Soloist*?

A: It would be easier to say that my approach to the composition influenced the production, in this case. I was involved very early with the script, and I chose all the pieces that Nathaniel, the main character, had to play, or hear in his head. The original script had references to a lot of other composers besides Beethoven, but I thought the movie would be stronger, in the end, if we turned Nathaniel's obsession with music into an obsession with Beethoven. I tried very hard not to butt in with my own music, and derived the entire score from Beethoven's work: the 'Eroica', a couple of late quartets, the triple concerto, a cello sonata. It felt, at the time, quite a responsibility, to 'edit' perfect music to make it fit our story, but I was convinced that the film would have been stronger by doing that. So I am proud to say there's very little me in *The Soloist*, and a lot of Ludwig.

Q: *Shooting Dogs* (Michael Caton-Jones, 2005) is a film which, unlike its counterpart *Hotel Rwanda* (Terry George, 2004), directly confronts the reality of genocide. Musically, in terms of the specific key you chose for compositions, also in terms of changes in the dynamic of the music, how did you, as a composer, approach such a monumental theme?

A: It was quite a challenging movie, exactly because it portrays quite realistically events that did happen. It is a huge dilemma, always, how to deal with 'truth', with real events, without fictionalizing them by smothering that truth with music—or with acting, and lighting, and editing, for that matter. My own way, on that occasion, was to find the strongest available musical connection to the Rwandan genocide. I discovered that, at the time of the genocide, there was a hugely popular Tutsi singer in Rwanda, Cecile Kayirebwa, who had become a strong voice for the plight of the Tutsi people, who were at the receiving end of one of the most brutal mass killings in history. I found her, living in Brussels, and travelled there to try to convince her to sing for this movie. It wasn't completely easy, as she was not sure about the rationale of the story. Also, she wanted to sing songs *about* the genocide, that she had composed herself. This was the last thing I wanted, and eventually I managed to convince her to sing some very ancient rural songs and lullabies, songs that had been around possibly for centuries. I was particularly interested in the lullabies, because they encapsulate something very tender and often very sad. I had this idea, that if a mother sang to her baby during the killings that happened outside her front door, it would be to make the baby fall asleep so she couldn't hear or, even worse, see what was happening.

That was my ticket to attempting to doing something that had some truth, something that could connect deeply with Rwanda, with Tutsi people, and with the tragedy.

Q: Julia Roberts is a talented actress who is also very much a star, and *Eat Pray Love* (Ryan Murphy, 2010) is definitely a Julia Roberts vehicle. How did such a brief affect your approach to composing the score?

A: I am not sure the result of the score would have been any different if another actress had played the part. I try not to see the 'actress', and instead I concentrate on the 'character'—which is made easier by working with such good performers.

In truth, there was no brief on Eat Pray Love—I felt a little disconnected from the cutting room in Los Angeles, as I was working away in London. Communication with the director was intermittent, as he was very busy with a number of things, so I ended up working closely with the editor of the movie, Brad Buecker, and being reminded once again how a brilliant editor is totally essential to my own work. This is an experience I've had on many movies, where the dialogue with the editor becomes just as important as the communication with the director. Ideally it is a three-way conversation, but that is not always the case, unfortunately.

Q: Both *Goodbye Bafana* (Bille August, 2007) and *The Soloist* represent some of the finer aspects of the human condition: Love, Forgiveness, Friendship, Respect. How can a composer, through the mechanics of composition, go about expressing such a blend of redemptive emotion? Can you give examples from specific scenes from either of these films?

A: Fortunately, we don't always have to express the very same emotions that are already expressed by the actors, and the script, and everything else. Music has a very strange placement in a movie, and does not occupy the same emotional space as the other elements in the storytelling. In fact, it doesn't even have to occupy an emotional space—it can address pace, structure, rhythm, direction (in the sense of an arrow pointing somewhere), punctuation, and many other aspects of filmmaking. In *The Soloist* I would say we got lucky, in that the music of Beethoven is the very (aural) embodiment of those ideals you refer to, all with their capital letters: Love, Friendship ... It might be difficult to 'use' it within a movie, because it is music which contains a very strong narrative of its own, and would often clash with the changing narrative of the movie. The tricky part was to use it without losing the inbuilt 'ethics' (the finer aspects of the human condition) which are intrinsic to Beethoven's work, and reshape the pieces so they could accompany some scenes—or plan, shoot and edit scenes *to* existing music.

In *Goodbye Bafana* I struggled a little to find a strong musical hook to the narrative. I spent long hours in the British Library, listening to field recordings of old rural settlements, trying to find something that had not been touched by Western music. I travelled to South Africa, and started going around with the idea of finding some music, some performer, or some instruments, that could link to Mandela's childhood. Eventually, I got to understand a few things about the music of South Africa. It is extremely hard, now, to find any music that is free of Western influences, but there are still singers and players that would use the ancient five-tone, and even more ancient six-tone, scales coupled with a very interesting polyphony, not one that was imported by missionaries and slave traders from the sixteenth century onward. I tried to find some of it, and stumbled upon Madosini, a very old woman who lives just outside Cape Town. She has a voice that seemed to come from a thousand years ago, and she played some very ancient instruments. I recorded her and brought some of her tunes into the score, and tried to model some of the rest to the simple harmony I heard in what she was doing. As always, the effort is to end up with something individual enough that can live within the boundaries of the movie without being generic.

Q: Recently I was listening to the Thomas Newman scores for *Wall-E* (Andrew Stanton, 2008), *Finding Nemo* (Andrew Stanton, 2003) and *The Shawshank Redemption* (Frank Darabont, 1994). I was struck by how distinct the themes were for *The Shawshank Redemption* as 'whole' pieces of music, featuring clear structure and dynamic rise and fall, whereas for the Pixar films each piece of music was clearly a cue for a given scene, and in turn was very much dependent on the scene, and the scene's beats. At which point in your process of composing a score do you determine which approach is best for the film?

A: I generally strive to continue a musical idea, rather than interrupt it in response to some event in the movie, if I can. This reflects my aspiration (and aesthetics) that the music should as much as possible go under the visible skin of the movie, and address deeper layers of narrative. This is not obviously possible all the time, or even desirable, and on more event-driven movies it can become very difficult to do. But, for example, even in a movie like *Wall-E* there is a very extended first chapter where Thomas Newman did use a more organic and fluid type of approach. For me it is a matter of trial and error: I always try the 'organic' first, and once I get a musical idea going I will keep it running as long as I possibly can. There comes a moment when it is very clear that I need to change, or introduce a new musical idea, and that, I guess, is a decision partly dictated by instinct, partly by individual taste, partly by experience, and to some extent discussed with the director. But, it is very much subjective: I am always struck by movie scores that don't pay too much attention to the detail of what happens locally in a given scene: I am thinking of European, and perhaps even more French, Italian and Spanish movies, as opposed to American movies. One has only to think of Morricone, or Rota, or Delerue, or Alberto Iglesias. Whenever I find myself working with a director that asks for the music to twist and turn in step with the movie—it happens on occasion—I know I am in trouble.

Q: Artists occasionally complain that their work, even when it is successful, is being misinterpreted. What attitude do you take to an audience's appreciation of your music?

A: I am not sure: misinterpreted by which audience? By the critics who review it, or by the public who might pass comment, or 'rate' it online? My audience is also the directors, the producers, the financiers, the distributors, the editor of the movie, who will judge my work before it is allowed in.

But, I think the best answer I can give to this is that I do not feel, or think, I am an 'artist'. I am not even sure what that really means. I try to make music that has some function, locally, within a movie (or a ballet, or a piece of theatre) and I try to fulfil that function in the most interesting way I can think of. In that respect I feel more like a problem-solver, a helper, a team-mate. I work with sounds that connect to ideas in order to tell stories. The 'success' of film music is measured by how well the storytelling is helped by it, not by how beautifully the music stands on its own. I think now, for example, of the very distinctive music Rota wrote for Fellini—quite different from what he would write, say, for Coppola—. It is music in each case designed to live within the confines of a world put together for a particular movie, and not another. In fact, one could say that this job of building boundaries for a movie is what music is really good at: to put in place the borders beyond which characters will not go, and enforce them. Or, if you like, to light the lay of the land, to provide reference points helping the story from getting lost.

Q: You have worked with Joe Wright on a number of films, yet not on *Hanna* (2011), which was scored by The Chemical Brothers. Does a part of you, when watching the images from that film, following along with the emotions of the story, imagine how you might have composed for the same scenes, the same story?

A: Not really—I watched *Hanna* and enjoyed it for what it was, without trying to imagine too much what it could have been.

Q: 'Briony' as a theme is played over a scene which feels very deliberate in terms of its editing. How much of how that sequence in the film was cut was in place at the time you were composing, and conversely, how much did you adapt any composition to the final cut of the scene?

A: The opening piece in the movie, as I mentioned, started life long before the film was shot. I wrote it simply on the basis of the script, and of the novel, and Joe liked it straight away. So much so, in fact, that he had it playing on the soundstage while the initial scene was being shot. The piece was, at that point, about three-and-a-half minutes long: Saoirse Ronan tried very purposely to walk in step with it, while she rushed through the house. After shooting, as I got the first assembly of the movie, I had to start thinking how to readjust the overlong piece to the edited sequence. This was a long process, as editing went on for months, and every time I would get a new cut of that scene I would find that some further adjustments were needed in order to keep the lines of dialogue clear, and have the music supporting the structure of the scene. Eventually, the scene settled at about one-and-a-half minutes. One of the trickier problems was that I wanted it to be quite a forceful, driving piece, but I didn't want to obscure the dialogue. I remember fiddling with the piece for a while before I found a structure that could run through the scene and do that.

Quite a lot of work went into the typewriter sound as well: I had a good working sound through the editing period, but eventually I went back into a studio and rerecorded the final typewriter with several stereo pairs of microphones. We had the typewriter on a desk, and we put close mikes, ambient mikes, a stereo pair inside one of the desk drawers, and I think a contact mike on the desk, too. This allowed the sound mixer to play with the perspective of the sound, so that when, for example, Briony is galloping down the staircase we could change the typewriter sound to amplify the knocking, echoing steps. This work on the sound didn't go into the album, but it is quite evident in the movie.

Q: There is a fair amount of intercutting between sequences in *V for Vendetta*. How did you approach composition when your score would be taking place beneath intercut scenes in which the quality of the action, or tone of the dialogue, might be quite distinct from one another?

A: Dealing with the type of editing you describe can be quite difficult. You are reminding me of one very amusing occasion, when I was asked to improvise to a 1930 silent movie I had never seen before (it was *Earth* by Alexander Dovzhenko), and found myself in that very predicament, literally on the spot. I was playing piano looking at the screen, and doing my best to anticipate what might be the tone of the next section. But, some scenes would cut between a very solemn funeral procession for a shot farmer, and his very naked widow trashing a bedroom in a fit of utter madness. No matter how I tried to accommodate the two intercut scenes, musically, I would always be wrong on the next cut, by having funeral music on a naked, mad woman, or by having mad music on a slow funeral.

In *V for Vendetta* I had the leisure to work it all out in my studio. I think what I discovered is that if you have an 'epic' storytelling idiom, you can use it without too much jumping around, as long as the music is not obviously trying to comment on specific events. By 'epic' I don't mean grandiose, I simply mean the style of a storyteller who uses a consistent voice to narrate disparate events and dialogues happening in a kind of 'mythical' time. In *V for Vendetta* there is an extended section which exemplifies this approach: at one point Detective Finch (played by Stephen Rea) pieces together Everything that has happened so far, and that will happen in the immediate future. Intercut with his narrative we see what he is describing, and there is a massive build-up to the point where V flicks the first tile of a domino construction, triggering the fall of all the other tiles in a spectacular cascade. All these are also intercut with scenes of street violence and riots. The way I dealt with this, and with similar scenes, was to have a very simple chord structure, that would repeat over and over. I called them my 'freedom chords'. The chords were familiar, by this point in the movie, as they had been heard several times prior to this scene, every time the ideal of Freedom was talked about, or implied in the story. I tried to build a piece that inexorably would grow to a very massive statement towards the end, and tried to do so by following only loosely the structure of the extended scene. I would punctuate important moments, but never derail the rhythm and the chord sequence. In this way I did not have to jump between different types of music every time the scene cut from Finch's face to a clash between people and the riot police, or anything else that might happen.

Q: You spoke of working to integrate Beethoven into *The Soloist*. What of Tchaikovsky in *V for Vendetta*?

A: Tchaikovsky was only a passing reference in *V for Vendetta*, but it provided me with a way into the very beginning of the movie, where I quoted one of the opening motifs in the *1812 Overture*. The very end also had the *1812 Overture* written in the script, and it was a matter of rearranging it to fit the scene, with a couple of simple cuts. But, apart from bringing some fun into the recording studio, when we had to rerecord the finale of the *1812*, and then put cannons and explosions on top of it for the album track, Tchaikovsky does not really figure in the score elsewhere.

Q: The composition 'Your Hands Are Cold' in *Pride & Prejudice* involves a quite celebrated piano piece complemented by a throbbing string section. What attracted you to the piano for such a romantic piece and scene?

How, in your view, does the composition found in 'Your Hands Are Cold' illuminate the very specific emotional details of the romance between Darcy and Elizabeth?

A: The whole of the *Pride & Prejudice* score has a very important piano presence. It evolved in a slightly unusual manner, in that for the first time I found myself writing some music before the film was shot—something I have repeated in every subsequent collaboration with Joe Wright. Joe fell in love with my early piano pieces, and for a while he thought that the whole of the score for the movie should be played simply on a piano. Many of the pieces were written originally for piano solo, and eventually got orchestrated at a later stage, after Joe realized that confining the score to using just piano was unnecessarily restrictive. But, in all the pieces that do have piano, the orchestra is there mainly as support and amplification, more than as a dialoguing partner.

The scene you refer to was written quite late in the process, and by then I had found all my themes already. It starts with a motif that recalls the letter Darcy had written to Elizabeth to explain his apparently arrogant behaviour, long before. Then it shifts into a variation of the music we had heard with Elizabeth perched high on top of a cliff, in a scene that might have been perhaps imagined by her, or dreamt, as she realizes she is in love with Darcy. So these two pieces meet, right at the point when Lizzie has lost any hope of being happy, and finds herself alone at sunrise, in a meadow. I wanted the shift from the more introspective first section, to the more expansive second, to somehow introduce the feeling of weak knees, or butterflies in the stomach, that I imagined Elizabeth would feel as Darcy emerges from the mist, walking sure-footed towards her. In the last part of this piece, which gently underscores the lovers' dialogue, my main concern was to avoid the music expressing any feeling, not to hurry them towards what would have been a premature kiss. The music segues into the next scene with a reprise of the very first piece we heard when Elizabeth was introduced at the beginning of the movie, perhaps a theme that reflects her strong, passionate and caring character.

In all this, I think, there was never an explicit desire to be 'romantic', and I must say I am consistently confused by what that means.

Q: How, in turn, is the emotional tone/romantic tone of *Jane Eyre* complemented by its music, and your choices in orchestration?

A: I saw *Jane Eyre* as an essentially dark story, only briefly interrupted by a moment of pure happiness. It has the elements of a ghost story, which I tried to address using some disembodied voices. But, perhaps most of all, it is a story about coming of age, and how Jane's strength gradually helps her to become a woman, in spite of her awful childhood.

I started to think about instrumentation from the very beginning, mainly concentrating on the ghost story and the childhood elements. A very simple Jamaican lullaby, which we then discover to be the connection with Bertha, the hidden mad wife locked up in the mansion, is the basis for several musical ideas that establish the tone within Thornfield Hall. Eventually, it became clear to me that I needed some focus for the emerging character of Jane as an adult. In one very important piece, 'The End of Childhood', which plants the germ for what then becomes, very much, Jane's theme later, we hear a childish recorder gently disappearing in the distance, to leave space for the solo violin. In a very naive manner, I think, I used those two instruments to represent Jane's childhood, and adult self. Once I arrived at the idea of the solo violin as the voice of Jane's inner strength, trying to become free of the shackles imposed by upbringing and social status, the score took on a life of its own, and it was fun to follow the chopped-up time structure of the movie.

But, I think if you listen to the album, in comparison with how the music is represented in the movie itself, you probably would have two distinct experiences: of all the movies I've worked on, I think *Jane Eyre* is the one that has most mistreated my music, in the final dub, stripping away layers, and rearranging elements of several pieces. Unfortunately, this happens, now and then.

Q: There is often discussion of the need for film music to cover a multitude of sins. An actor's performance might be hollow, the sound mix might be tinny, the editing itself might be awkward. What are some specific instances when you feel your score has salvaged technical or artistic problems in a given scene?

A: I am not that big-headed, and besides, I wouldn't pass judgement on my fellow filmmakers. I also think music is unlikely to salvage anything that is bad, although it can, I believe, enhance what is good. But, for sure, I do think music has the power to change the way film is perceived (not necessarily to make it 'better'), and I have often wondered where that power comes from. At its best I think music has the ability to give voice to unspoken and unseen emotions, and to introduce into the storytelling an 'ethical' depth, lighting moral points, or providing a spiritual compass. But, it is possible that, often, it functions at a much more basic and instinctive level, perhaps simply interfering with the analytical faculties of the spectator, so that the more emotive faculties are able to grasp the story by a more visceral handle (you know, right brain, left brain ...). But, I doubt good music can cure bad acting or a weak story.

Q: Do you feel typecast ever as a composer? Would you score a big summer blockbuster like *Men in Black* (Barry Sonnenfeld, 1997), for instance, or *The Avengers* (Joss Whedon, 2012)?

A: Sometimes it feels a little like that, an unavoidable consequence of having scored a couple of successful 'period' dramas. Generally, I try to get myself out of my comfort zone, if I can, and of course I would score any movie that would get me to do new things, or in a different way from what I have done before. But, I think, more than a type of movie, I seem to attract a certain type of director, and that's fine by me. I have been blessed with very stimulating collaborations with some very inspiring and creative people.

Q: How would you describe your own film education, in terms of composers, directors, films? Do you watch contemporary films often? Which scores from recent years have impressed you?

A: To paraphrase Antonio Machado, I always feel burdened by an encyclopaedic ignorance. I have an extremely busy life, which doesn't leave a huge amount of space for watching movies. But, I have picked up bits and pieces over the years, and I think by working in films, now for almost 20 years, I have developed some sense of how the various parts that make up a movie feed off each other. There are a few movies that have stayed in my mind for a particular way the music was used, and I am sure this has some bearing on the way I go about writing my own music. In recent years I have been constantly impressed by how varied the film music landscape has become, and how much it has expanded in terms of instrumental colour, and purpose. There still seems to be a great divide between independent movies, which often have very interesting and quirky scores, and larger, especially

American, productions, that often rely on a somewhat tired, big and bombastic sound. But, as I always remind myself, the rule of film is that there are no rules, and there's plenty of new inspiration coming from fresh talents coming into the industry. My own inspiration, when I was starting, came from people like Gabriel Yared and Alberto Iglesias, among many others, who seemed to have a distinctly 'European' approach to scoring. I have admired immensely how especially Iglesias has developed his own very personal idiom, which serves him on scores for completely different types of movies.

Q: What are your thoughts on electronic scores? What do you see as the relationship between traditional scores and electronic scores? It is worth noting, for example, that Trent Reznor's 'Hand Covers Bruise' is dominated by an incredibly simple piano melody.

A: I think there haven't been many composers that have been truly successful writing completely electronic scores, but Trent Reznor, together with Hans Zimmer, and perhaps Clint Mansell (I am thinking, for example, of the very interesting score he did for *Pi* (Darren Aronofsky, 1998)) have definitely made their mark. Zimmer, who pioneered electronics in movies 30 years ago, moved on to more grandiose orchestrations later in his career, but I think he remains a huge reference point for the use of synthesizers and computers. My own approach has always been to use whatever I can think of in my orchestration: often the film dictates what can go in, and what can't, at least for me. Electronics have the tendency to make the score colder, in my view, and so they are not always the best thing to use—but it really depends on the story, and what side of the narrative is addressed by the music. The great challenge of using electronic and sampled sounds is, for me, to allow a human, and humane, element in the performance, even when the sound is mediated by a computer.

CHAPTER 11

Solo Instruments and Internal Focalization in Dario Marianelli's *Pride & Prejudice* and *Atonement*

Joakim Tillman

The important role played by solo instruments is a subject that is mentioned several times by Dario Marianelli in Lindsay Coleman's interview (this book, Chapter 10, 139–140, 150, 151): the solo cello in *Atonement* (Joe Wright, 2007), the piano in *Pride & Prejudice* (Joe Wright, 2005), and the recorder and solo violin in *Jane Eyre* (2011). According to Marianelli the two instruments in *Jane Eyre* (Cary Joji Fukunaga, 2011) represent Jane's childhood and adult self, respectively. The use of solo instruments to represent individual characters has a long history in opera and programme music. Notable examples are the solo viola in Hector Berlioz's *Harold en Italie* (1834), and the solo cello in Richard Strauss's *Don Quixote* (1897). There are also many precedents in the history of film music. For instance, Fred Karlin mentions Michael Kamen's *Lethal Weapon* (Richard Donner, 1987) score where the guitar represents Martin Riggs (Mel Gibson), and the alto saxophone Roger Murthaugh (Danny Glover).[1]

J. Tillman (✉)
Stockholm, Sweden

© The Author(s) 2017
L. Coleman, J. Tillman (eds.), *Contemporary Film Music*,
DOI 10.1057/978-1-137-57375-9_11

In representing characters, solo instruments most often speak *for-* and not just *about-* those characters. As Marianelli points out, the solo violin in *Jane Eyre* is 'the voice of Jane's inner strength, trying to become free of the shackles imposed by upbringing and social status',[2] and in *Pride & Prejudice* 'the piano is the inner voice of Elizabeth'.[3] In this way, solo instruments are used for what French literary theorist Gérard Genette calls internal focalization, that is, the narrator presents information from the point of view of a character. Internal focalization is one of three main types in Genette's model. The other two are non-focalization (or zero-focalization) where an omniscient narrator knows more than any of the characters, and external focalization, the 'objective' or 'behaviourist' narrative, where the narrator knows less than the characters.[4] Film music scholar Guido Heldt, in consideration of later refinements by other narratologists, has made a useful account of how Genette's model may be applied to the analysis of film music.[5] In his discussion of internal focalization, Heldt applies Edward Branigan's distinction between internal focalization (surface) and internal focalization (depth). The former concerns what a character sees or hears, for instance a point-of-view shot, and the latter the character's internal mental states. According to Heldt (126–128), there are two ways in which music can represent subjectivity in internal focalization (depth). The first is focalization 'of music through a character's internal experience or imagination of it'. Following Claudia Gorbman, most film music studies use the term meta-diegetic to designate this kind of music, but 'internal diegetic music' is also used. The second is the use of non-diegetic music 'as representation or intimation of a character's mental states or processes'. Heldt argues that this is a problematic and ambiguous category. Of course, as Heldt points out, ambiguities are possible in literature as well:

> 'She was tired and distracted' could be understood as saying, 'She *felt* tired and distracted': the narrator informs us of the inner state of the character (internal focalization). But it could also be understood as saying, 'She *seemed* tired and distracted': the narrator describes the impression the character makes on her, judged by external appearance (external focalization). While the ambiguity inherent in the neutral 'was' can be used consciously, it would be easy to avoid by choosing either 'felt' or 'seemed'.
>
> Film has other options and other problems. A film could show us an actress that seems tired and distracted—external focalization is the default setting of most narrative fiction films. If the film wanted to switch to internal focalization, it could use a homodiegetic voice-over—the inner voice of a character telling us that she is tired and distracted. Or the film might use nondiegetic music to imply the character's inner state. But in film and its use

of music, precision is difficult to achieve, and there often is a vague position between being a voice *about* and a voice speaking *for*. Music cannot achieve the precision of narrative perspective achievable in language ...[6]

Even though I agree with Heldt that music cannot achieve the precision of language, the thesis of this essay is that the use of solo instruments is a method Marianelli exploits in order to achieve precision of narrative perspective. An examination of the roles of solo instruments in *Pride & Prejudice* and *Atonement* will demonstrate how these are used to convey the inner states of Elizabeth Bennet and Robbie Turner, but also how the internal focalization in the latter film is made ambiguous by its denouement.

Pride & Prejudice

Deborah Moggach, the writer of the screenplay, wanted to emphasize that *Pride & Prejudice* is Elizabeth Bennet's story, and her first decision was that 'she would be in every scene and it would be viewed through her eyes'.[7] Even though other scenes eventually were added, Joe Wright embraced this concept completely when he was hired as director:

> I think it's terrible the way people say 'the Laurence Olivier version,' or 'the Colin Firth version,' do you know what I mean? It's a story about a young woman falling in love. Why do you always call it the 'male-lead version'? So this is the 'Keira Knightley version.' And we're very careful to put Keira, to put Lizzy, at the center of the film. It's a story told from her point of view.[8]

As Marianelli states in Coleman's interview (150), the piano has a very important presence in *Pride & Prejudice*, and in other sources he makes clear that the instrument is associated with Lizzie, and her perspective.

> For Pride and Prejudice the piano was the inner voice of Elizabeth. There was a direct connection between a character and the sound of the piano.[9]

> Lizzie's piano piece became one of the main themes of the score, and the piano became very much her voice, or perhaps the voice of her feisty and independent soul, strong minded and passionate, but also gentle and caring.[10]

Thus, the piano plays an important role in realizing Wright's idea to make the film 'as subjective as possible'.[11] There are a few exceptions to this, but these concern scenes not seen through Lizzie's eyes. For instance, the scene where Bingley practises making a marriage proposal to Darcy, so he can work up the courage to do it for real, is accompanied by a non-diegetic rendition of the piano piece earlier played by Georgiana, Darcy's sister, now with the full orchestra supporting the piano. Consequently, this non-subjective scene is scored with one of the few pieces not associated with Lizzie.

Lizzie's Theme

There are many different themes in the score, but two are more important, and frequently used, than the others—about half of the cues in the film are based on them. In Coleman's interview (141), Marianelli states that he is not fond of character themes, but in another interview he refers to one of those themes as 'Elizabeth Bennet's theme'.[12] However, the two themes are not used to characterize Lizzie from an external point of view, but are used to convey different mental states from her perspective. Elizabeth Bennet's theme (or Lizzie's theme for short) is the first music heard in the film, and it starts just before Lizzie appears, and follows her when we are introduced to her home and family. In their very first conversation, Wright and Marianelli discussed Beethoven's early piano sonatas, and 'their spirit' was the starting point for the piano piece that became Lizzie's theme.[13] The narrative significance of this is not just to indicate the time period when the film is set; according to Marianelli, 'Beethoven was one of the most innovative composers of Jane Austen's time, so he's suited to Elizabeth's forward-thinking character'.[14] It is true that the music does not feature any of the early Beethoven's more progressive traits; for instance, Lizzie's theme is harmonically very simple, but this may be considered appropriate as the more experimental elements of a style aimed at the connoisseurs of Viennese high nobility would be too out of place in the late-eighteenth-century English countryside.

Deborah Cartmell claims that the first presentation of Lizzie's theme is revealed to be diegetic when we see Mary, one of Lizzie's sisters, playing the piano.[15] Two circumstances render this claim less convincing. First, as the camera moves into the house and approaches Mary, the source music she plays is heard simultaneously with Lizzie's theme, and Mary is clearly not playing Lizzie's theme. Second, the quality of the piano-playing in the first cue is far above the capacity of Mary, both as described in the novel, and depicted in the film. Despite these objections, it is of significance that this music indeed fits into the world the characters are occupying, and in two important scenes Lizzie's theme does appear as diegetic music. First, it is played by Lizzie herself at Rosings. Therefore, this theme is not just non-diegetic music expressing her emotions, but also music that is part of the fictive world, music that she herself uses to give expression to her feelings (even though she plays it badly). The second diegetic use occurs when Lizzie visits Pemberley, Darcy's estate. After the tour in the sculpture gallery, Lizzie stands alone by the window in the drawing room and realizes that someone is playing the melody she herself played at Rosings (but now played exquisitely). Lizzie gets curious, approaches the open door and discreetly looks into the room. In a point-of-view shot the piece is revealed to be played by Darcy's sister, Georgiana. Just a moment later the playing stops when a man arrives, and, frozen with surprise, Lizzie realizes that it is Darcy, who was not supposed to arrive until the next day. Wright's comment about this scene is:

> And then the music that starts at the window, you'll recognize as being the piece of music that we first hear when we enter Longbourn at the very beginning of the film. And the reason why I used the same piece of music, also by Dario, the composer. I had him compose it before we ever started filming. And the reason why I used the same piece of music is because it would remind her of home. In a way finding the person that you're supposed to be with is like coming home. And that even though this house is so completely different from her house, it's the same spirit, the same music moves here.[16]

I would argue that Wright's statement about 'finding the person that you're supposed to be with is like coming home' is a key to the significance of the theme. During the first presentation of the theme in the opening of the film, Lizzie is reading the last page of a book, which she then closes. In the film we don't see the title of the book, but according to the screenplay the novel is entitled *First Impressions*,[17] that is, the title of the first unpublished version of *Pride and Prejudice* written in 1796–7. Even though Lizzie's theme is influenced by the classical style of early Beethoven, it is hard for me to hear the rising chromatic line with its yearning appoggiaturas without being reminded of Richard Wagner's *Tristan und Isolde*.[18] In Coleman's interview Marianelli states that this theme perhaps 'reflects her strong, passionate and caring character' (150). Passion seems to be the keyword here, and the theme can be interpreted as an expression of Lizzie's desire to find true love in the same way as the heroine of the book she is reading.

Besides the opening cue ('Dawn') and the two diegetic renderings, there are four other cues, all non-diegetic, based on Lizzie's theme, and they all occur in scenes which involve this concern for true love and marriage. These four cues present one or the other of the three different statements of the theme in the 'Dawn' cue. The first statement is slow and dreamy, and the melody is accompanied by broken triads. The second statement is faster and livelier, but is registrally constricted, and the accompaniment is dominated by an obstinately repeated tone. These features lend this statement an impatient character, and create a tension that is released in the outburst of the third statement. The third statement is slightly slower than the second, but the register is widened and the texture is richer, with the left hand playing broken triads extended over three octaves, and the right hand playing both the melody and accompanying patterns.

A reprise of the third statement underlines the excitement of the Bennet sisters after learning from their father that Mr Bingley will attend the ball the next day. When the music starts, attention is not focused exclusively on Lizzie, but the final part of the scene shows a smiling Lizzie looking at her exhilarated sisters. The reason for their joy is of course the hope that the new tenant of Netherfield Park will marry one of them. The marriage issue is explicitly addressed after the ball when Lizzie and Jane are too excited to sleep, and talk under the bed covers. When provoked by Lizzie's teasing remark that Mr Bingley is 'conveniently rich', Jane protests and states that she does 'not believe marriage should be driven by thoughts of money'. Lizzie agrees entirely: 'only the deepest love will persuade me into matrimony, which is why I will end up an old maid'. After discussing Mr Darcy's disagreeable behaviour, the good humour returns as the two girls start to giggle. At this moment the first dreamy version of Lizzie's theme, now supported by the orchestra, starts and continues as the camera moves away from the bed and out through the window to show the full moon. Because she does not believe in finding true love herself in this scene, the theme here may be understood as conveying Lizzie's hopes on her sister's behalf, and not for herself.[19]

After this scene between the two sisters, Lizzie's theme does not reappear as non-diegetic music until the very end of the film. The second, impatient version from the 'Dawn' cue is rendered by the solo piano as Lizzie paces outside the door of the library, waiting while Darcy speaks to her father. Eventually Darcy emerges, Lizzie walks in and the music stops as she closes the door. Lizzie talks to her father and, when he understands that she really loves Darcy, he heartily gives his consent to their marriage. At this moment the second version of Lizzie's theme starts again, now supported by the orchestra, and is succeeded by the rich third version as the end credits start to roll. Thus, Lizzie's theme has come full circle. The music accompanying the happy ending of the novel Lizzie was reading in the opening of the film returns when this ending becomes a reality in her own life. The meaning of Lizzie's theme suggested here is a reasonable interpretation when the theme is considered in the context of the whole film, but is not something the music wears on its sleeve. The way it is used rather seems to reflect Marianelli's aspiration and aesthetics that 'the music should as much as possible go under the visible skin of the movie, and address deeper layers of narrative' (Coleman, Dario Marianelli Interview, 146).

The Secret Life of Daydreams

The second theme, with its melody floating freely over a repetitive and harmonically static accompaniment, gives voice to another side of Lizzie's character. It is used before the two visits to Netherfield, when she sits on the swing, and then travels to visit Charlotte and Mr Collins, when she is 'on top of the world', and finally when Darcy appears in the morning mist. In Coleman's interview (150), Marianelli comments on this last use of the theme:

> Then it shifts into a variation of the music we had heard with Elizabeth perched high on top of a cliff, in a scene that might have been perhaps imagined by her, or dreamt, as she realizes she is in love with Darcy. So these two pieces meet, right at the point when Lizzie has lost any hope of being happy, and finds herself alone at sunrise, in a meadow. I wanted the shift from the more introspective first section, to the more expansive second, to somehow introduce the feeling of weak knees, or butterflies in the stomach, that I imagined Elizabeth would feel as Darcy emerges from the mist, walking sure-footed towards her.

It is revealing that Marianelli understands the sequence with Elizabeth on top of the cliff as a moment of her imagination, or a dream. The previous cue featuring this theme is labelled 'The Secret Life of Daydreams', and my interpretation would be that this theme is about Lizzie's dreams and wishes, even though the actual content of these daydreams is left unspecified by the music. And the last statement of the theme in the film, when Darcy emerges in the morning mist is about dreams coming true, about wish-fulfilment.[20] Aptly this daydream music has the character of a berceuse. As Kenneth Hamilton points out, the defining work of the genre is Chopin's Berceuse in D-flat major op. 57,[21] and many of the most notable characteristics of this piece mentioned by Hamilton are shared by Marianelli's theme: compound time, a quiet dynamic level, a simple melody over a tonic pedal bass, and a 'rocking' accompaniment oscillating between two chords (I and IV in *Pride & Prejudice* instead of Chopin's I and V). In contrast to Chopin, though, Marianelli never varies the melody 'with a profusion of filigree passagework'.[22]

The first presentation of the Daydreams theme, rendered by the solo piano, accompanies Lizzie's walk to, and arrival at, Netherfield to attend the sick Jane.[23] Cartmell claims that 'we see from her point of view', even when Lizzie is not present.[24] It is to a large extent Marianelli's score which makes this effect possible, and this cue demonstrates how the music in *Pride & Prejudice* stays with Lizzie also during intervening shots of other characters. Even though the theme itself is new, the piano has already been established as Lizzie's instrument, and when the music begins with a shot of Lizzie as she stomps out of the room at Longbourn, after declaring her intention to go to Netherfield at once, it is clearly established that the music gives voice to her thoughts and emotions; that is, internal focalization (depth). The cue continues during the outdoors long shot where she strides across a vast, muddy field, but then there is a cut to the grand dining room at Netherfield where Caroline Bingley and Darcy are having breakfast. However, there is no change in the music, which continues to convey Lizzie's mental state despite her absence. After a while the footman announces Lizzie's arrival and she comes in dirty and warm after the walk. In the following point-of-view shot the astonished Darcy and Caroline are seen through her eyes, and the music comes to an abrupt end when Darcy quickly rises to his feet and pulls Lizzie out of her reverie.

The next presentation of the Daydreams theme, also in the solo piano, again starts at the end of a scene, now with a medium close-up of Lizzie as she gazes at Mr Wickham, with sympathy, after his disclosure of how Darcy had mistreated him out of jealousy and pride. After the cut, the theme continues as the Bennet sisters prepare for the Netherfield ball, and the camera pans through the bedrooms at Longbourn. The music ends when the camera reaches Lizzie. In the previous sequence featuring the Daydreams theme, the camera only leaves Lizzie's perspective for a short time. In this sequence, though, only the beginning and ending of the cue are explicitly attached to Lizzie. But because of the connection between the piano and the character, and the earlier use of the Daydreams theme, this way of beginning and ending the cue is enough to facilitate an understanding of the music as her voice during the whole sequence.

A different version of the Daydreams theme is heard at the end of the Netherfield ball. Lizzie, having escaped Mr Collins, stands alone on the terrace and breathes a deep sigh. At this moment an unaccompanied solo clarinet starts to play the theme, and it continues while the Bennet family, as the last of all the guests, leave Netherfield. In this sequence the theme is not so much about Lizzie's dreams and wishes, but rather about the shattering of those dreams. The music conveys her shame, vexation and pain over her family's embarrassing and ill-mannered behaviour at the ball. This cue shows that the piano is not the only solo instrument used to create internal focalization in *Pride & Prejudice*, a circumstance that will be further explored in the next section.

The Solo Cello in Pride & Prejudice

In Coleman's interview, Marianelli states that he thinks his love affair with the cello 'started in *Pride & Prejudice*, with a few pieces where the cello solo was quite prominent' (139–140). There are three scenes in which the solo cello appears. The first is when Darcy delivers his letter to Lizzie, which the audience hears in his voice-over. The second is when Lizzie informs the Gardiners and Darcy of Lydia's elopement with Wickham. The solo cello starts on a medium close-up of Darcy, and accompanies the last lines of the dialogue where the resigned Lizzie states that nothing can be done. When Darcy offers his help, she answers that it is too late, and Darcy leaves after attesting that the situation indeed is grave. Finally, the solo cello appears in the scene on the meadow towards the end of the film.

Marianelli states that he finds the sound of the cello very close to the male human voice (Coleman, Dario Marianelli Interview, 140). Thus, it would seem obvious to interpret the solo cello in those three scenes as giving voice to Darcy's emotions. If the first introduction of the solo cello had coincided with Darcy's entrance in the letter delivery scene, this interpretation would have been perfectly reasonable. However, the instrument is first heard before Darcy's arrival, when Lizzie is alone in the drawing room at Hunsford. The cue, 'Darcy's Letter', begins with Lizzie's instrument, the solo piano, which has an important role throughout the scene. The solo cello is introduced at the moment Lizzie picks up the book on the table, *Fordyce's Sermons*.[25] For the first two measures the cello plays the same melody as the piano (but two octaves lower). Thus, the cello grows out of the piano, and is not established as an independent entity. As Lizzie puts down the book and walks to the window, the solo cello continues the melody alone, accompanied by broken chords on the piano; but when she moves to the mirror and looks at herself the cello temporarily stops playing, and the piano takes over the melody (now discreetly supported by the strings). After a short while the solo cello returns as the door opens and Darcy enters.

The question, though, is: does this really happen, or is it Lizzie's memory of the event we see? In the novel Lizzie reads Darcy's letter many times until knowing it by heart, and gradually changes her opinion of Darcy, but also her own self-image. In the film this process is compressed and portrayed in a non-realistic way. In a point-of-view shot, Lizzie looks at herself in a mirror as daylight fades into night in a time-lapse. Suddenly, Darcy is reflected in the mirror as he enters the room. After a short but awkward silence, he says, 'I came to leave you this,' places a letter on the table behind her, and continues, 'I shall not renew the sentiments which were so disgusting to you, but if I may, I will address the two offences you have laid against me.' During all this Lizzie does not turn, but watches him through the mirror. Darcy starts to read the letter, but we do not see him, and when Lizzie finally turns she realizes that he has gone. The voice-over of Darcy continues to read the letter, but Lizzie does not actually open the envelope and start reading the letter until some moments later. Joe Wright has said that he doesn't know why he did the letter scene in the way he did, but 'poetically, it just seemed right that he should start speaking the letter and then disappear'. And he adds: 'then she's lost him just when she realized she wanted him'. Thus, in contrast to the novel, this is the decisive moment when Lizzie realizes that she is in love with Darcy, but also that this love is impossible.

Consequently, the solo cello may be interpreted in different ways in this scene. It can be understood as an expression of Darcy's feelings, but it would also be plausible to read it as an expression of Lizzie's emotions for him. Two small details support the second interpretation. First, the crescendo and rising line in the cello in the middle of the cue is not related to the content of the letter as conveyed by Darcy's voice-over, but is a build-up to Lizzie's action of opening the letter. Second, the cue stops abruptly when Charlotte walks in, and the effect is that Lizzie is interrupted in her sad contemplation of the letter.

In the scene in the meadow towards the end of the film, the solo cello starts right after Darcy's line, 'If your feelings are still what they were last April, tell me so at once. My affections and wishes have not changed, but one word from you will silence me forever.' It then accompanies his following declaration of love: 'If however, your feelings have changed, I would have to tell you, you have bewitched me, body and soul, and I love … I love … I love you. I never wish to be parted from you from this day on.' Again the narrative perspective of the cello is ambiguous. Is it expressing his feelings, or is it expressing her emotions for him, revealing that her feelings indeed have changed, the music creating a connection to the moment when this happened in the letter scene?

The Role of the Orchestra

Marianelli wrote some of the piano pieces before the film was shot, and for a while Wright 'thought that the whole of the score for the movie should be played simply on a piano'. Eventually, it was realized that this would be unnecessarily restrictive, but Marianelli claims that 'in all the pieces that do have piano, the orchestra is there mainly as support and amplification, more than as a dialoguing partner' (Coleman, Dario Marianelli Interview, 150). However, there are some cues where the orchestra does play a more significant role than suggested by this statement, especially in the second half of the film. This is a change that has an important narrative function in the trajectory of Lizzie's development. Lizzie's instrument, the piano, was the domestic and female instrument par excellence during the long nineteenth century. The style of her music, as remarked earlier, emphasizes that she transcends the constrictions of her immediate surroundings. But it is the entrance of the orchestra that underscores the widening of Lizzie's world, and her growing self-consciousness. The cues featuring the solo cello are part of this process, but this section will focus on three other cues.

The first cue where the orchestra plays a more important role is the festive music—with horns, trumpets and timpani—which accompanies the arrival at the Netherfield ball. When compared to the earlier Meryton Village ball it is obvious that this is a far grander occasion, a spectacle of elegance and splendour not previously experienced by Lizzie and the local gentry. During much of this sequence Lizzie is not seen, but, as in several cues discussed earlier, the music starts on a shot of her, and ends when she in vain looks for Wickham among the assembled officers. Therefore, even if the music also creates an appropriate general atmosphere, it primarily gives voice to Lizzie's impressions of the magnificent event, and the more subordinate role of the piano might suggest that she is overwhelmed by the pomp and circumstance.

Another important cue in this trajectory is 'Liz on Top of the World', which starts in the solo piano with music related to Lizzie's theme as sunlight flickers through the leaves of trees. After a cut to an extreme close-up of Lizzie's eyes, this is revealed to have been a point-of-view shot. The extreme close-up is abruptly followed by an extreme wide-shot with Lizzie alone on top of a peak with her arms outstretched. It is at this cut that the Daydreams theme enters in the orchestra. The cinematic context here clearly supports Marianelli's view of the shot as imagined, or dreamt, by Lizzie (Coleman, Dario Marianelli Interview, 150). Furthermore, the shot is highly symbolic, conveying that her horizons have widened, and that her dreams of true love and happiness are even more intense, but also more impossible, than before Darcy's proposal.

The next cue, 'The Living Sculptures of Pemberley', which accompanies Lizzie's visit to Darcy's estate, Pemberley, also begins with the solo piano. The music is again introduced in a way that aligns it with Lizzie's perspective. It starts after her aunt and uncle have passed out of the picture and she has fallen back, and then continues during the following point-of-view shot where Lizzie admires the magnificent ceiling paintings. In the novel, Lizzie thinks about the fact that she might have been the mistress of Pemberley, but is saved 'from something very like regret' by the recollection that her uncle and aunt would have been lost to her, as she would not have been allowed to invite them (chapter 43). Marianelli's music, though, gives expression to grief and sadness, and this difference is justified by the circumstance that, in the film, Lizzie has realized by this point that she loves Darcy, something which is not the case in the novel. The orchestra enters discreetly when the scene changes to the sculpture gallery and Lizzie is seen deeply affected by a marble statue. The orchestra gradually grows in importance, and the piano is reduced to a purely accompanying function, doubling the harp, and eventually disappears completely. The importance of this scene in Lizzie's development is emphasized by Joe Wright:

> I also like the idea that this is about sex, this place, as well, that it's about her discovering sensuality, that it's about bodies ... And also that she's not just admiring Darcy's wealth, but she's admiring his culture, she's admiring his appreciation of beauty. That he has a sensitive soul and that she loves him for his sensitivity.[26]

Besides the use of the orchestra, it should also be noted that the music in this cue has left the classical style of early Beethoven far behind. As

Marianelli points out, later on in the score he 'abandoned historical correctness for a more intimate and emotional treatment of the story'.[27]

The effect of the orchestra in 'The Living Sculptures of Pemberley' is evident when a slightly varied version of this cue later is rendered by the solo piano. This cue starts when Lizzie, deep in thought, sits alone under an old oak tree after Bingley's proposal to Jane. During the proposal Lizzie stands apart from the rest of the family and suddenly can't bear to be there and walks away. According to Joe Wright, 'it's difficult for Lizzie here 'cause she's happy for her sister, but, at the same time, she's wishing it was her…'[28] The absence of orchestral colours underscores her emotions about being back where she started, confined to a grey, domestic and local everyday life after experiencing a bigger world, and realizing that she has found true love at the same moment she lost it.

ATONEMENT

The author of *Atonement*, Ian McEwan, points out that it is a novel with particular difficulties for the screenwriter:

> It's a very interior novel. It moves inside the consciousness of several of the characters. With the movie, you only have what people say and do, and you've got to find, with this, some way of getting that interior feeling across.[29]

In an article about the use of opera in *Atonement*, Alexandra Wilson argues that music is often overlooked in adaptation studies, and she demonstrates 'the vital contribution music can make to the adaptation process' through a close reading of Puccini's *La Bohème* in Robbie's letter-writing scene.[30] Marianelli's score also plays an important role in this adaptation process. Prior to the letter-writing scene, as Wilson notes,[31] the music is almost entirely associated with Briony, and after this scene it continues to be from her perspective for the rest of the first part of the film. In Coleman's interview Marianelli states that, with the theme he created for Briony, he was 'trying to give a sound to some of the less obvious qualities of her mind', and the typewriter sound even further reinforces 'the slightly mechanical workings of Briony's mental cogs' (141). Thus, the music is a crucial element in conveying the interior aspects of a novel where internal focalization is of the utmost importance.

As in *Pride & Prejudice* the piano is an important instrument in *Atonement*, and again it is played by renowned French pianist Jean-Yves Thibaudet. In the earlier film there was a direct connection between a character, Lizzie, and the piano, but according to Marianelli that is not the case in *Atonement*:

> It's mainly an orchestral score, but the piano and the cello have a dialog. I didn't think in the terms of an instrument for a character in *Atonement*, but I did like the idea of a dialog between two prominent instruments.[32]

Despite this statement, and even though solo instruments are not used as consistently as the piano in *Pride & Prejudice*, the harmonica, English horn, clarinet, and solo cello are used to convey inner mental states of Robbie in the second part of the film (which in the novel is mostly narrated from Robbie's point of view; that is, he is the focalizer).

'Elegy for Dunkirk' and the Solo Cello

In Coleman's interview Marianelli states that he has found himself using the solo cello 'more and more to underline moments of solitude, where the emotional focus of a scene is on one single character' (140). Therefore, it may appear strange that, in *Atonement*, the solo cello plays the greatest role in the Dunkirk scene, the most spectacular scene in the film, where a mere thousand extras give the impression of a beach teeming with soldiers engaged in a wide variety of activities. But at the same time, Marianelli points out, 'the camera is fixed on one character, who is taking in the enormity of the situation he's in'.

At first Joe Wright did not want any non-diegetic music in the scene, but Marianelli felt there might be a way to amplify the emotional space of the scene (Coleman, Dario Marianelli Interview, 140). Wright eventually allowed him to give it a try, and on the Blu-ray commentary he admits that the emotion is largely carried by the score. According to Wright, the overriding theme of the scene is the wastage of war[33], and the music starts just after Robbie has observed the killing of the horses. Mace is the first of the three soldiers to realize what the gun shots, first heard off-screen, mean, but, significantly, the music does not begin with his reaction, 'That's not right.' From the beginning of the cue the music is presented from Robbie's perspective, and while Mace remains behind, the music continues as Robbie and Nettle move on and round a stranded whaler. The camera then pans up, following the paper blowing into the air, before it pans down to a close-up of Robbie. It is at this moment that the solo cello is introduced, and starts presenting the complete Elegy theme. Thus, the music becomes even more clearly attached to Robbie, but after just a few seconds he disappears out of the picture to the left. According to Wright, the shot is 'kind of turned into a point-of-view shot here'.[34] Even though it is not a strict point-of-view shot, Marianelli also understands this element of the sequence as being from Robbie's perspective:

> ...it's almost like Robbie walks through it and he's our eyes, we're witnessing the mayhem, the chaos, and the pity of war through his eyes and it's quite hard to comprehend. He's not completely able to comprehend it, he happens to be very ill and feverish at that point, so it has this dreamy, ghostly quality to it, but at the same time it introduces a sense of attachment where you see things in front of you happening. It had to be moving at the same time, emphatic, it had to express some empathy of the war for the pity of the war in front of us.[35]

As the camera approaches the bandstand, the chorus of the singing soldiers gradually grows stronger. The hymn used, 'Dear Lord and Father of Mankind', was chosen by the film's co-producer, Jane Frazier.[36] Therefore the hymn was a given element, and it was a challenge for Marianelli to bring the singing soldiers into his own music. As he points out, his Elegy theme is quite independent from the tune of the psalm,[37] but despite this he wanted the two elements to merge completely seamlessly.[38] The hymn starts barely audible, midway through the Elegy melody. When the first words can be discerned (the fourth line of the fourth verse; the first three verses are not used in the film), the chorus is still heard faintly in the distance, but the cello melody now becomes less active, even though the long, slowly rising notes still constitute the primary voice of the music. After the culmination with the highest tone of the Elegy theme, the crescendo of the chorus becomes more prominent. At the same time the solo cello decreases in importance, and as the fifth verse of the hymn begins the solo cello stops playing. In this way, the score gradually turns into the accompaniment for the chorus.

As Marianelli points out in Coleman's interview (140), the pace of the singing soldiers is very different from the slow pace at the beginning of the 'Elegy for Dunkirk'. Therefore, he had 'to find some trick' that allowed him to compose 'something that could run, slowly, under a faster choir'. In the interview he does not state what the trick is, but a study of the music reveals that the solution is fourth species counterpoint,[39] which is used in the accompaniment both to the Elegy theme in the solo cello and the hymn. This counterpoint behind the chorus brings a new harmonization to the hymn which is Marianelli's own. The whole cue is almost entirely diatonic, and is based on a natural B minor scale (however, it hovers between B minor and D major). The exception to this diatonicism is the C major chord that appears in the eighth measure of every verse of the hymn and/or the highest note in the Elegy theme. This C major chord, a Neapolitan sixth chord in root-position, is an old topic for grief and lament. But the suspensions which are an important feature of fourth species counterpoint also contribute greatly to the expressive character of the music. Furthermore, the fourth species counterpoint also adds sacred connotations to Marianelli's music, which enhances the symbolism of the hymn. The religious dimension of the scene is also established by other elements. For instance, when Robbie and his two companions reach Dunkirk, and in amazement look down on all the soldiers and activity on the beach, Mace exclaims, 'Fuck me, it's like something out the Bible.'

Marianelli points out that the camera briefly abandons Robbie when it shows us the singing soldiers, and during the hymn the string orchestra becomes a support for them (Coleman, Dario Marianelli Interview, 140–141). But when the camera goes back to Robbie, 'the music returns to its original elegiac mode, to accompany him to his destination.' At this close-up of Robbie, the solo cello returns, coinciding with the ending of the sixth verse of the hymn, and leads to a varied reprise of the beginning of the cue. As Nettle reappears, Robbie temporarily disappears out of the picture, but then joins Nettle and Mace with the line, 'Come on. I have to get something to drink.' Here a reprise of the Elegy theme in the solo cello begins and accompanies Robbie and his two comrades as they make their way towards the bar and cinema. Thus, three times in this long Steadicam shot, the solo cello starts to play when Robbie reappears in the picture and becomes the centre of attention, and the association of the instrument with Robbie's perspective is established in an unmistakable way.

Before entering the cinema Robbie takes one last look out across the beach, and then the camera pans around to show what he has seen. Joe Wright states that he used Robbie looking out to motivate this camera move,[40] but when the camera pans around Robbie has already disappeared into the cinema. Therefore, this part of the shot cannot be understood as a kind of point of view. The solo cello does not disappear, but becomes a secondary voice in the texture, and to underscore that this is not Robbie's direct impression of the raucous inferno of the beach, a solo violin, very softly, and as if from a distance (*lontano*), plays the Elegy theme as an echo of his emotional reaction to the sight.

The Love Theme

The 'Elegy for Dunkirk', though, is not the first cue in *Atonement* to feature the solo cello. The instrument is introduced earlier when Robbie remembers his last encounter with Cecilia. The first part of the flashback is set in a café, and the music starts when Cecilia reaches out and puts her hand on Robbie's cheek. This is followed by a cut back to 1940 in France, where Robbie is composing a love letter in his mind. The letter is heard in voice-over, and after the first 'Dearest Cecilia' the solo cello starts to play the Love theme. Thus, as in *Pride & Prejudice*, the solo cello is used to accompany the voice-over of the male protagonist reading a letter to the woman he loves. The earlier film, though, is subjective from Lizzie's point of view and, as argued above, the solo cello is more plausibly interpreted as expressing her emotions for Darcy, and not his for her. In contrast to this, the second part of *Atonement* is narrated from Robbie's perspective, and the solo cello here clearly conveys his feelings. However, Marianelli emphasizes that the Love theme does not belong to a specific character; it is neither just for Robbie nor Cecilia, but was meant to take the weight of the tragic love story between them.[41] The origin of the Love theme was Marianelli's idea to compose a spurious wartime song that also could function as diegetic music:

> Initially I was considering writing a spoof wartime song, which would have played from a gramophone in the dormitory of the hospital where the older Briony has became [sic] a nurse. I was looking for a theme that could belong to both worlds, within the space of the film, where the characters might be able to hear it but which would also function as a main romantic idea.[42]

Even though a real wartime song was eventually used for the dormitory scene, the idea that the Love theme could belong to 'both worlds' is exploited in the film. At the very beginning of the second part of the film, the Love theme is introduced diegetically, played by Mace on his harmonica, and in the epilogue it is again played on the harmonica by a man (not Mace) in the Balham tube station sequence. The second harmonica rendition of the Love theme, though, can be construed in several different ways. It starts after the flashback of Robbie's last meeting with Cecilia, and is played as he stands outside the barn in early dawn and looks at the photograph of the cottage which Cecilia gave him. Because Mace has been seen playing the theme in the earlier scene, the music can be understood as off-screen diegetic music. But it may also be read as meta-diegetic, Robbie mentally hearing the love song as the photograph revokes the hope of his being reunited with Cecilia in the cottage when he returns to England. Or it can be read as non-diegetic music, giving voice to Robbie's inner state, conveying his love and yearning for Cecilia. The third and fourth presentations of the Love theme by the harmonica are also ambiguous as to whether the music is meta-diegetic, or non-diegetic, but now the theme is clearly not diegetic. During the third rendition Mace is seen walking behind Robbie with his arms at his sides, and the fourth rendition is played as Robbie and Nettle search for Mace, calling out his name. If they actually had heard Mace playing his harmonica, they obviously would have found him. This kind of ambiguity is also exploited elsewhere in the film. For instance, in the cinema at Bray Dunes, Robbie suddenly finds himself at the foot of a giant screen where the French film *Le Quai des brumes* (Marcel Carné, 1938) is playing. Wright's commentary on this situation is: 'Are we in his head, or is this reality? I'm not sure. I kind of like to think it's in his head, really.'[43]

In addition to the solo cello and the harmonica, the Love theme is also played by two other solo instruments, the English horn and the clarinet, both instruments rich in extra-musical connotations. In his treatise on orchestration, Hector Berlioz writes about the English horn that it 'is a melancholy, dreamy voice, dignified too, with a retiring, remote quality which makes it superior to every other instrument when it comes to arousing images and feelings of the past, or when the composer wants to pluck the secret string of memory'.[44] And about the clarinet Berlioz writes that its medium register (the one used in *Atonement*) has a feminine quality of tone, and that its voice is that of heroic love.[45] Of course, as Richard Strauss points out, in his revised and enlarged edition of Berlioz's treatise, the character of the music 'is determined not only by the timbre of the instrument, but also by the form of the theme and by the rhythm, harmony and melody'.[46] The Love theme appears in two different versions, one in major and one in minor. The latter is not just a transposition of the former into minor, though. The first half of both versions is similar, with a presentation of a basic idea that is sequentially repeated. But the continuation, the second half of the theme, displays more marked differences.[47]

The major version is the one most similar to a spoof wartime song, and it is the beginning of this version that is played by Mace on his harmonica. The harmonica always plays the major version, and, with one exception, so does the clarinet. The cello and English horn, though, only play the minor version, which begins with a prominent 6-5 appoggiatura, an old topic for grief and anguish, and ends with a sighing appoggiatura over a major chord (the dominant chord of the key). This ending is almost identical to the most prevalent conclusion of the Love theme in *The English Patient* (1996), another film about doomed love during World War II, and the intertextual reference is underlined by the fact that Anthony Minghella, the director of the earlier film, plays the interviewer in the epilogue of *Atonement*.[48]

There is no complete consistency in the use of the different solo instruments, but as the following discussion will demonstrate, there is a certain tendency in how they convey different nuances of Robbie's emotions in the renderings of the Love theme. For instance, the solo cello appears to give expression to his strong yearning to be reunited with Cecilia, the English horn speaks of regret and sadness when he thinks of the past, and the clarinet represents his most sensual memories of Cecilia.

After the diegetic introduction of the Love theme, the next appearance is an unaccompanied rendition by the solo clarinet. The first phrase starts on a close-up of Robbie in France 1940 as he closes his eyes and gets lost in thought. By beginning the cue this way, as in *Pride & Prejudice*, the subjective perspective of the music is established. A cut to Robbie's flashback of his last meeting with Cecilia follows. According to Edward Branigan, flashbacks of a character's memories is a filmic example of internal focalization (depth).[49] Furthermore, the subjectivity of the sequence is enhanced by the almost complete absence of sound effects. The clarinet continues with the second phrase of the theme as Robbie sees Cecilia in her nurse's uniform at a table in the café on the other side of the glass. Robbie is then overcome with fear and turns away. As the second half of the theme begins, he regains his courage and returns to the glass wall, and Cecilia, 'lit by a shaft of sunlight, is standing by her table, looking at him'.[50] When the door opens, and Robbie enters the café, the music stops, and the entry of sound effects, the noisy chattering in the café, has a startling effect.

The first rendition of the minor version is the one played by the solo cello which has already been mentioned. The solo cello plays the first half of the theme, and the clarinet then continues. This is the only time the minor version involves the clarinet, but it is worth pointing out that the clarinet plays the second half of the theme, and not the beginning with the 6-5 appoggiatura. The clarinet here accompanies Cecilia's words about the cottage by the sea, which they will be able to use during Robbie's next leave. When Robbie kisses Cecilia, the Love theme begins anew, now for the first time rendered by the English horn. A more conventional musical solution for this long, deep kiss would have been to pull out all the stops and let the whole orchestra play the major version of the Love theme. In the novel the kiss in Whitehall is described as one of Robbie's most sensual memories of Cecilia, but in the film the music makes another reading of this moment. Due to the cultural connotations of the English horn, Robbie's recollection of the kiss is tinged with regret and sadness. Robbie's emotions when remembering the kiss could be expressed by the words of Francesca da Rimini in Dante's *Divina Comedia*: 'There is no greater pain than to remember happy days in days of misery' (*Inferno Canto V*). The full orchestra then enters with the second half of the theme when Robbie starts to run after the bus, giving expression to his despair and grief.

Another sequence that juxtaposes the clarinet and the English horn playing the Love theme is the last cue in the second part of the film. Robbie falls asleep in the cellar at Bray Dunes, and a montage replays key moments from his past, many of them running backwards to indicate the feverish status of his dreams. The first shots, which involve the fountain scene and Robbie's letter, are accompanied by the major version (second half) played by the clarinet, which thus again is used to underscore sensual memories of Cecilia. After the soldiers singing 'The White Cliffs of Dover' (another instance of meta-diegetic music), the English horn starts to play the minor version of the Love theme as the last part of the montage shows Robbie's arrest (played backwards).

The actual Love theme is only presented once by the solo cello in the second part of the film. However, in two other scenes the instrument plays important counter-themes. When, after the night in the barn, Robbie and the two corporals move across a field as the sun rises, the English horn first plays the Love theme (first half). Just before this shot, Robbie has been looking at the picture of the cottage (accompanied by the harmonica), and the Love theme again may be interpreted as exciting regret in the revival of images and sentiments of the past. The Love theme then starts anew (in a new key) in the violins and at the same time the solo cello starts to play an expressive counter-theme. Midway through the first phrase Cecilia's voice-over is heard, and is immediately followed by a cut back in time to Cecilia who is seen walking with a letter in her hand. Her voice-over conveys the content of the letter, that she has been contacted by Briony who 'says she's beginning to get the full grasp of what she did and what it meant'. As the novel makes clear, this letter evokes Robbie's hope of being acquitted of the crime he was convicted for, giving him an opportunity to be reunited with Cecilia. The most frequently used counter-theme is introduced during the kiss in the 'Farewell' cue. In a later scene, where Robbie has a vision of his mother washing his feet, this counter-theme in the solo cello gives expression to Robbie's intense yearning to be reunited with Cecilia before and during his lines: 'I have to get back. I promised her. To put things right. And she loves me. She's waiting for me.'

The most puzzling appearance of the Love theme, at least without knowledge of the denouement of the film's epilogue, occurs in the scene where Robbie discovers the dead girls in an orchard, and then remembers how Briony, eight years earlier, dived into the river and forced him to save her life. The unaccompanied solo clarinet starts to play the major version of the Love theme (second half) when Robbie stops and the camera slowly begins to track backwards to reveal the corpses of the girls. At the cut to the close-up of Robbie, showing his reaction, the accompaniment to the minor version of the Love theme follows, but the theme itself remains absent. Instead, the most frequently used counter-theme is heard as the primary voice. As the second half of the counter-theme begins there is a cut back in to the river at the estates of the Tallis house. Robbie is dressing after teaching Briony to swim, but she is still in her swimsuit, and asks Robbie if he would save her if she fell in the river. 'Of course,' Robbie answers, and as a splash is heard the Love theme begins in the strings, and continues during Robbie's rescue of Briony.

The question is what role these different versions of the Love theme play in this scene? Why is this clarinet version, earlier heard when Robbie looks at Cecilia in the café, used when he discovers the dead girls? And why does a passionate rendering of the minor version accompany Briony's jump into the river? In order to make sense of this scene it is important to realize that the flashback again is from Robbie's perspective. Joe Wright emphasizes this in his commentary:

> This scene is a difficult one. It's important that the audience are aware, and I'm not sure if they are aware enough, that this is Robbie's version of this scene. He's remembering this scene, and he's trying to figure out why

Briony did what she did, why Briony accused him of the rape. And he's decided in his mind that it's because she was jealous of his love of Cecilia, that, in fact, Briony was in love with him.[51]

Thus, the scene is, after all, about Robbie and Cecilia's love, and the use of the Love theme underscores that this love was the cause of Briony's jealousy, at least according to Robbie's understanding, when she discovered that Robbie was in love with Cecilia after reading his note and discovering the pair just after having sex in the library. The scene with the dead girls is not in the novel, and the flashback where Robbie tries to understand Briony's behaviour is introduced in a different way. According to the screenplay, all the dead girls are supposed to be around 13, and are dressed in the uniform of a convent school; that is, they are schoolgirls of the same age as Briony when she falsely accused Robbie of the rape in 1935. Therefore, the girls remind Robbie of Briony, and motivate the flashback. But why does the major version of the Love theme begin the cue? The use of the Love theme in this cue remains ambiguous, at least until the denouement changes the assumptions on which the interpretation is based.

Denouement and a Change of Narrative Perspective

In the postscript of *Atonement*, which switches to first person, it is revealed that Briony is the author of the previous parts of the novel. Joe Wright was trying to find a cinematic equivalent to first person and his solution was to make the epilogue an interview. He wanted as little barrier and artifice between the character and the audience as possible, and in a full-screen close-up Briony is talking directly to the audience.[52] Alexandra Wilson argues that this revelation has repercussions for our understanding of the diegetic Puccini music in the letter-writing scene in the first part of the film:

> Thus, on a first viewing of the film, we naturally assume that Robbie actually hears Puccini's music, whereas on a second viewing we are led to consider whether Briony hears it as she imagines Robbie writing the letter.[53]

A similar question might be asked of the music in the second part of the film. Is the music that this essay has interpreted as a medium for the focalization of Robbie's inner state revealed to be a voice speaking *about* rather than *for* Robbie? Is there a change of narrative perspective from Robbie to Briony, at least on a second viewing, also when it comes to the music?

The first minutes of the epilogue are without music, and the score starts at the crucial moment when Briony decides to take the interview in an unexpected direction, what Wright calls the 'truth moment'.[54] It then accompanies her disclosure of what really happened, a truth so pitiless that she 'couldn't any longer imagine what purpose would be served by it'. So far in the film, in the first and third parts, Briony has almost always been associated with the Briony theme. This cue, though, is based on the Elegy and Love themes. The music during the first part of Briony's account, leading up to the revelation that Robbie died in Bray Dunes during the last day of the evacuation, is a slightly varied reprise of the 'Elegy for Dunkirk' cue, again prominently featuring the solo cello. Briony then relates the fate of Cecilia. After the cut to the Balham tube station the music continues with the Love theme played by the harmonica. For the first time in the film a harmonica rendition of the Love theme is harmonized, and the initial A minor chord makes the start identical to the minor version. However, the continuation makes clear that, as in all the previous harmonica presentations, it is the major version that is played. In this scene the harmonica is seen being played by a man in the tube station. Thus, the melody, though not the accompaniment, is diegetic. However, we do not see Cecilia's death the way it actually happened; what we see is Briony's conception of the event, perhaps as it was told in an earlier, more truthful version of her novel. But if this is the case, is it reasonable to interpret the music as also being a part of Briony's vision? Wilson raises this question in connection with the Puccini music in the letter-writing scene, and I agree with her conclusion:

> One might observe, of course, that Briony is a writer rather than a filmmaker, and that there is a tension between the idea of Briony as the author of a novel when we are reading a novel and Briony as the author of a novel when we are watching a film of a novel. However, there is no reason why music should be any less a part of Briony's re-conceptualisation of events than the stylised shots we see on screen.[55]

It is only the first half of the Love theme that is used in this scene, and after Briony's revelation that Cecilia was killed that night, when the cascading water floods the station, the music continues with an orchestral version of the Elegy theme. Thus, the music creates a connection between the deaths of Robbie and Cecilia, a connection that is further underlined by the culmination of the music in the Neapolitan sixth chord at the cuts to Robbie lying dead in the cellar, and Cecilia's body drifting through the tube tunnel. After revealing the true fates of Robbie and Cecilia, Briony states that, because of her actions, they 'never had the time together they both so longed for and deserved'. But she could not see what sense of hope or satisfaction a reader would derive from an ending like that, so in the book she wanted to give Robbie and Cecilia their happiness. During this last part of the revelation, the solo cello plays the Love theme simultaneously with the Elegy theme in the orchestra. In this cue the Elegy and Love themes are used to express Briony's feelings of remorse, compassion and empathy for Robbie and Cecilia, and their doomed love. The solo cello is obviously no longer a voice for Robbie's inner states. But given the close connection between the instrument and Robbie in the second part of the film, it is hard to ignore this association in the denouement music. Furthermore, the solo cello is not used in the section of the revelation which exclusively deals with Cecilia. Thus, the instrument may now more reasonably be interpreted as a voice *about* Robbie from Briony's perspective rather than a voice *for* Robbie.

In the last lines of the film Briony tells the interviewer that, in her book, as a final act of kindness, she wanted to give Cecilia and Robbie what they lost out on in life: 'I gave them their happiness.' In his commentary, Joe Wright discusses the purpose and role of happy endings, and asks whether *Atonement* has a happy ending. He is not sure himself and thinks it is up to the audience.[56] Wright does not mention the music, which contributes to making the ending more ambiguous. The culminating Neapolitan chord of the Elegy theme follows Briony's last word, 'happiness', undermining the meaning of the word. The chord is held during the cut to a beach below white cliffs. Robbie and Cecilia appear and 'crunch across the pebbles and splash gleefully through the waves, below the towering white cliffs on their way back to their white clapboard cottage'.[57] This last sequence in the film is accompanied by the minor version of the Love theme played by the English horn. The music does not underline the happiness seen on the screen. On the contrary, it seems to render Briony's regret, remorse and grief that Robbie and Cecilia never got to experience this happiness in real life.

In the last music played during the end credits (track 14, 'Atonement', on the soundtrack recording) the English horn plays a new version of Briony's theme that is not heard earlier in the film. According to

Marianelli, this version of the theme was 'drafted for the part starting with Briony finally revealing what really happened all those years earlier'. But, as the epilogue was restructured, the score was changed and it was 'decided to use the piece written for the last scene at the end of the credit roller'.[58] These late uses of the English horn in the film seem to suggest that this instrument could also retrospectively be reinterpreted as expressing Briony's emotions. But then the Love theme itself could be read as speaking *for* the lovers from Briony's point of view all the time. As Wilson does concerning the Puccini music during the letter-writing scene, we may ask if the music interpreted as focalizing Robbie's inner state during a first viewing of the film may be understood as an expression of Briony's emotions during a second viewing.[59] It is revealing that Marianelli considered writing the spoof wartime song which became the Love theme for use as diegetic music in the dormitory in the hospital, a scene featuring Briony and not Robbie and Cecilia. If a song based on the Love theme had been used in that scene, this would have been a clue that the events shown in the second part of the film could be open to reinterpretation even before the epilogue. An understanding of the Love theme as being from Briony's perspective may above all reframe the scene where Robbie 'remembers' Briony expressing her love for him. In the third part of the film, Briony tells fellow nurse Fiona that she had a crush once when she was ten or eleven. She states that she jumped in the river to see if he would save her from drowning, which he did: 'But as soon as I told him I loved him the feeling sort of disappeared.' Joe Wright considers this the true version, and he does not believe in the jealousy theory suggested by Robbie's flashback.[60] However, it has to be remembered that both versions are written by Briony, and both are equally trustworthy or untrustworthy. If Wright takes the position of the second version, Marianelli's use of the Love theme appears to take a stand for the first version.

As noted above, Alexandra Wilson convincingly argues that, on a second viewing, the diegetic Puccini music can be understood as 'part of Briony's re-conceptualisation of events',[61] and that also goes for the diegetic uses of the Love theme. But, is it equally convincing to reinterpret the non-diegetic uses of the Love theme (and the Elegy theme) in the second part of the film as being part of Briony's storytelling, or an expression of her emotions when telling the story? When rereading the novel, the internal focalization of the second part is not affected; Robbie remains the focalizer, and the story is still narrated from his perspective. What changes is that there is a new link added to the chain real author

(Ian McEwan)-implied author-narrator, which after the epilogue becomes real author (Ian McEwan)-fictive author (Briony Tallis)-implied author-narrator. At first reading, *Atonement* is a novel in which the narrative has an unmediated character—the real author, implied author, and the narrator are all virtually absent. On a second reading, though, it is hard to ignore the fictional author.

In the film, the focalization and agency of the non-diegetic music in the second part becomes more complex and ambiguous at later viewings.[62] As in the novel it can still be understood as internal focalization from Robbie's perspective, but it could also be construed as internal focalization from the old Briony's point of view. A more radical reading is to assign the agency of the music to Briony. Alexandra Wilson mentions the obvious objection to such an idea: 'Briony is a writer rather than a filmmaker,' and, of course, nor is she a composer. But in his commentary, Joe Wright talks about the storyteller as God, and when the full-screen close-up of the old Briony appears in the epilogue he says, 'So there's the face of God. The God of this story.'[63] And the storyteller as God may plausibly be assumed to have greater creative powers than just typing the words.[64]

Conclusion

This essay has demonstrated how Marianelli uses solo instruments for internal focalization in *Pride & Prejudice* and *Atonement*, for conveying the inner states of Elizabeth Bennet and Robbie Turner. Several factors work together to create this effect. First, because of the tradition in opera, programme music and film music to use solo instruments to represent individual characters, there is a convention that facilitates a reading of solo instruments as speaking for individual characters. Even in a non-programmatic genre like the solo concerto, the solo instrument is often metaphorically described as representing the individual against the mass, collective or society. Second, the solo instruments play associative themes which accumulate meaning by the way they are used, but also through different style topics and intertextual references. Third, as Kathryn Kalinak points out, the musical codes and conventions in film music are 'always dependent on a coexistence with the visual image'.[65] The solo instruments in *Pride & Prejudice* and the second part of *Atonement* work in tandem with filmic techniques for internal focalization like point-of-view shots, voice-over, and flashbacks or dreams. And even when these techniques are absent, the music frequently begins and ends at shots where Lizzie and Robbie are the centre of attention. In this way music and image collaborate and there is a mutual dependency between them. Neither the appearance of a solo instrument in itself, nor orchestral music accompanying a close-up of a character or a point-of-view shot, entails the music being from a specific character's perspective; there are numerous counter-examples, or vague positions 'between the music being a voice *about* and a voice speaking *for*'.[66] But in *Pride & Prejudice* and *Atonement* Marianelli and Wright show that music and image can indeed collaborate to achieve a precision of narrative perspective; that the music can be a voice speaking *for* Lizzie and Robbie, making internal focalization possible.

Notes

1. Fred Karlin, *Listening to Movies: The Film Lover's Guide to Film Music* (New York: Schirmer, 1994), 19.
2. Lindsay Coleman, Dario Marianelli Interview, this book, Chapter 10, 151.
3. Rudy Koppl, 'Atonement: A Twist of Mind', http://www.musicfromthemovies.com/index5.php?option=com_content&view=article&id='. (2743), accessed 1 June 2015.
4. Gérard Genette, *Narrative Discourse* (Oxford: Blackwell, 1980), 188–9.
5. Guido Heldt, *Music and Levels of Narration in Film: Steps Across the Border* (Bristol: Intellect, 2013), 119–33.
6. Heldt, *Music and Levels of Narration in Film*, 128.
7. Adam Spunberg, 'Scripting Pride & Prejudice with Deborah Moggach Pt. II', *ScreenPicks*, 5 April 2011, http://screenpicks.com/2011/04/scripting-pride-prejudice-with-deborah--moggach-pt-ii/, accessed 12 June 2016.
8. Annie Wagner, 'Weeping into a Pint of Lager: Joe Wright on the Making of "Pride & Prejudice"', *the Stranger*, 10 November 2005, http://www.thestranger.com/seattle/Content?oid=25183, accessed 5 June 2016.
9. Koppl, 'Atonement: A Twist of Mind'.
10. Dario Marianelli, 'Note from the Composer, Dario Marianelli', *Music from the Motion Picture 'Pride & Prejudice'*. Decca B000AD1NXK, 2005.
11. Joe Wright, 'Commentary', *Pride & Prejudice*, directed by Joe Wright (Universal Studios, 2010), Blu-ray Disc.

12. Bryan Reesman, 'Dario Marianelli', *Mixonline*, 1 June 2006, http://www.mixonline.com/news/films-tv/dario-marianelli/369137, accessed 24 May 2016.
13. Dan Goldwasser, 'A Musical Vendetta', *Soundtrack.Net*, 15 March 2006, http://www.soundtrack.net/content/article/?id=187, accessed 3 June 2015.
14. Anon., 'Pride And Prejudice By Dario Marianelli', http://www.classicfm.com/composers/marianelli/guides/film-score-focus-dario-marianelli/#SPkXdaXraeUt1fhk.97, accessed 15 September 2015.
15. Deborah Cartmell, *Jane Austen's Pride and Prejudice: The Relationship between Text and Film* (London: Methuen Drama, 2010), 89–90.
16. Wright, 'Commentary'.
17. Deborah Moggach, *Pride and Prejudice*, The Internet Movie Script Database (IMSDb), http://www.imsdb.com/scripts/Pride-and-Prejudice.html, accessed 21 May 2016.
18. See Michael L. Klein, *Intertextuality in Western Art Music* (Bloomington, Ind.: Indiana University Press 2005), for a discussion of this type of ahistorical intertextuality, which Klein designates transhistorical intertextuality.
19. In interpretation it is often easy to read too much significance into small details. But it is still worth pointing out that this G major statement is the only occurrence of Lizzie's theme in a key other than C major.
20. In the alternate US ending it is the Daydreams theme that accompanies the last scene, showing Lizzie happily married to Mr Darcy.
21. Kenneth L. Hamilton, 'Berceuse', *Grove Music Online. Oxford Music Online* (Oxford University Press), http://www.oxfordmusiconline.com.ezp.sub.su.se/subscriber/article/grove/music/02749, accessed 7 June 2016.
22. Hamilton, 'Berceuse'.
23. Whether significant or not, this cue is in the same key, D-flat major, as Chopin's Berceuse, a key that is not otherwise used in the *Pride & Prejudice* score.
24. Cartmell, *Jane Austen's Pride and Prejudice*, 86.
25. According to Wright, this should indicate that she's thinking about the absurdity of Mr Collins. Wright, 'Commentary'.
26. Wright, 'Commentary'.
27. Goldwasser, 'A Musical Vendetta'.
28. Wright, 'Commentary'.

29. 'From Novel to Screen: Adapting a Classic', Extras on *Atonement* Blu-ray Disc (Universal Studios, 2010).
30. Alexandra Wilson, 'Unreliable Authors, Unreliable History: Opera in Joe Wright's Adaptation of *Atonement*', *Cambridge Opera Journal*, Vol. 27, No. 2 (July 2015), 155.
31. Wilson, 'Unreliable Authors', 160.
32. Koppl, 'Atonement: A Twist of Mind'.
33. Joe Wright, 'Feature Commentary', *Atonement*, directed by Joe Wright (Universal Studios, 2010), Blu-ray Disc.
34. Wright, 'Feature Commentary'.
35. Koppl, 'Atonement: A Twist of Mind'.
36. Wright, 'Feature Commentary'.
37. Jon & Al Kaplan and Tim Curran, 'Nothing to Atone For: Dario Marianelli's Atonement score, boldly front and center', *Film Score Monthly Online*, Vol. 13, No. 1 (January 2008), http://www.filmscoremonthly.com/fsmonline/story.cfm?maid=1193, accessed 31 May 2016.
38. Koppl, 'Atonement: A Twist of Mind'.
39. 'In fourth-species counterpoint, the counterpoint line and cantus firmus both move once per bar, but they are rhythmically offset from each other by a half note. (Think syncopation on the bar level.) The counterpoint line will be notated in half notes, with each weak-beat half note tied across the bar line to the following strong beat. This arrangement means that in pure fourth-species counterpoint, the two lines always move in oblique motion. It also introduces a new kind of dissonance: the *suspension*.' *Open Music Theory*, http://openmusictheory.com/fourthSpecies.html, accessed 15 July 2016. This website presents a short and simple, but very informative, explanation of fourth-species counterpoint.
40. Wright, 'Feature Commentary'.
41. Kaplan et al., 'Nothing to Atone For', and Scott Macauly, 'Dario Marianelli. Playing to Type: Scoring Atonement', 30 November 2007, www.focusfeatures.com/article/dario_marianelli, accessed 8 June 2015.
42. Macauly, 'Dario Marianelli. Playing to Type'.
43. Wright, 'Feature Commentary'.
44. Hugh Macdonald, *Berlioz' Orchestration Treatise: A Translation and Commentary* (Cambridge: Cambridge University Press, 2002), 109.
45. Macdonald, *Berlioz' Orchestration Treatise*, 125.

46. Hector Berlioz, *Treatise on Instrumentation*, enlarged and revised by Richard Strauss, trans. Theodore Front (New York: Kalmus, 1948), 210.
47. The Love theme is structured as a sentence. For more information on this theme type, see Konstantinos Zacharopoulos's article in this book.
48. For an excellent analysis of the Love theme and its narrative functions in *The English Patient*, see Heather Laing, *Gabriel Yared's The English Patient: A Film Score Guide* (Lanham, MD: Scarecrow Press, 2004), 122–5 and 144–56.
49. Edward Branigan, *Narrative Comprehension and Film* (London: Routledge, 1992), 103.
50. Christopher Hampton, *Atonement: The Shooting Script*, based on the novel by Ian McEwan (New York: Newmarket Press, 2007), 48.
51. Wright, 'Feature Commentary'.
52. Wright, 'Feature Commentary'.
53. Wilson, 'Unreliable Authors', 173.
54. Wright, 'Feature Commentary'.
55. Wilson, 'Unreliable Authors', 173–4.
56. Wright, 'Feature Commentary'.
57. Hampton, 2007, 92.
58. Kaplan et al., 'Nothing to Atone For'.
59. In the epilogue interview Briony states that she got first-hand accounts of the events she didn't personally witness, for instance the evacuation of Dunkirk (in the novel it is revealed that Nettle wrote her several letters, and also that Robbie and Cecilia's love letters are in the Imperial War Museum). Therefore, it is established that Briony could have knowledge of all the events depicted in the second part of the film.
60. Wright, 'Feature Commentary'.
61. Wilson, 'Unreliable Authors', 173–4.
62. The issue of film music and narrative agency is discussed by Jerrold Levinson, 'Film Music and Narrative Agency', in *Post-Theory: Reconstructing Film Studies*, eds David Bordwell and Noël Carroll (Madison: University of Wisconsin Press, 1996), 248–82, and Heldt, *Music and Levels of Narration in Film*, 69–89.
63. Wright, 'Feature Commentary'.
64. It is beyond the scope of the present essay, though, to pursue this intriguing issue of narrative agency in *Atonement* any further.

65. Kathryn Kalinak, *Settling the Score: Music and the Classical Hollywood Film* (Madison, Wis.: University of Wisconsin Press, 1992), 15.
66. Heldt, *Music and Levels of Narration in Film*, 128.

Bibliography

Anon. n.d. Pride And Prejudice By Dario Marianelli. http://www.classicfm.com/composers/marianelli/guides/film-score-focus-dario-marianelli/#SPkXdaXraeUt1fhk.97. Accessed 15 September 2015.

Berlioz, Hector. 1948. *Treatise on Instrumentation*. Enlarged and revised by Richard Strauss, trans. Theodore Front. New York: Kalmus.

Branigan, Edward. 1992. *Narrative Comprehension and Film*. London: Routledge.

Cartmell, Deborah. 2010. *Jane Austen's Pride and Prejudice: The Relationship Between Text and Film*. London: Methuen Drama.

From Novel to Screen: Adapting a Classic. 2010. *Atonement*, extras on Blu-ray Disc. Directed by Joe Wright. Universal Studios.

Genette, Gérard. 1980. *Narrative Discourse*. Trans. Jane E. Lewin. Oxford: Blackwell.

Goldwasser, Dan. 2006. A Musical Vendetta. *Soundtrack.Net*, 15 March. http://www.soundtrack.net/content/article/?id=187. Accessed 3 June 2015.

Hamilton, Kenneth L. 2001. Berceuse. *Grove Music Online. Oxford Music Online*, Oxford University Press. http://www.oxfordmusiconline.com.ezp.sub.su.se/subscriber/article/grove/music/02749. Accessed 7 June 2016.

Hampton, Christopher. 2007. *Atonement: The Shooting Script*. Based on the novel by Ian McEwan. New York: Newmarket Press.

Heldt, Guido. 2013. *Music and Levels of Narration in Film: Steps Across the Border*. Bristol: Intellect.

Kalinak, Kathryn. 1992. *Settling the Score: Music and the Classical Hollywood Film*. Madison, WI: University of Wisconsin Press.

Kaplan, Jon, Al Kaplan, and Tim Curran. 2008. Nothing to Atone For: Dario Marianelli's Atonement Score, Boldly Front and Center. *Film Score Monthly Online*, Vol. 13, No. 1 (January), http://www.filmscoremonthly.com/fsmonline/story.cfm?maid=1193

Karlin, Fred. 1994. *Listening to Movies: The Film Lover's Guide to Film Music*. New York: Schirmer.

Klein, Michael L. 2005. *Intertextuality in Western Art Music*. Bloomington, IL: Indiana University Press.

Koppl, Rudy. n.d. Atonement: A Twist of Mind. http://www.musicfromthemovies.com/index5.php?option=com_content&view=article&id='. (2743). Accessed 1 June 2015.

Laing, Heather. 2004. *Gabriel Yared's the English Patient: A Film Score Guide*. Lanham, MD: Scarecrow Press.

Levinson, Jerrold. 1996. Film Music and Narrative Agency. In *Post-Theory: Reconstructing Film Studies*, ed. David Bordwell and Noël Carroll, 248–282. Madison: University of Wisconsin Press.

Macauly, Scott. 2007. Dario Marianelli. Playing to Type: Scoring Atonement, 30 November. www.focusfeatures.com/article/dario_marianelli. Accessed 8 June 2015.

Macdonald, Hugh. 2002. *Berlioz' Orchestration Treatise: A Translation and Commentary*. Cambridge: Cambridge University Press.

Marianelli, Dario. 2005. Note from the Composer, Dario Marianelli. Liner notes to *Music from the Motion Picture 'Pride & Prejudice'*. Decca B000AD1NXK.

Moggach, Deborah. n.d. *Pride and Prejudice*. The Internet Movie Script Database (IMSDb). http://www.imsdb.com/scripts/Pride-and-Prejudice.html. Accessed 21 May 2016.

Reesman, Bryan. 2006. Dario Marianelli. *Mixonline*, 1 June. http://www.mixonline.com/news/films-tv/dario-marianelli/369137. Accessed 24 May 2016.

Spunberg, Adam. 2011. Scripting Pride & Prejudice with Deborah Moggach Pt. II. *ScreenPicks*, 5 April, http://screenpicks.com/2011/04/scripting-pride-prejudice-with-deborah-moggach-pt-ii/. Accessed 12 June 2016.

Wagner, Annie. 2005. Weeping into a Pint of Lager: Joe Wright on the Making of 'Pride & Prejudice. *The Stranger*, 10 November. http://www.thestranger.com/seattle/Content?oid=25183. Accessed 5 June 2016.

Wilson, Alexandra. 2015. Unreliable Authors, Unreliable History: Opera in Joe Wright's Adaptation of *Atonement*. *Cambridge Opera Journal* 27(2): 155–174.

Wright, Joe. 2010a. Commentary. *Pride & Prejudice*, Blu-ray Disc. Directed by Joe Wright. Universal Studios.

———. 2010b. Feature Commentary. *Atonement*, Blu-ray Disc. Directed by Joe Wright. Universal Studios.

CHAPTER 12

Mychael Danna Interview

Lindsay Coleman

A versatile Canadian composer, Mychael Danna often co-composes with his brother Jeff. He first came to prominence with his evocative score for Atom Egoyan's *Exotica* in 1994, and has continued to produce spine-tingling music to accompany Egoyan's images in films such as *The Sweet Hereafter* (1997) and *Devil's Knot* (2013). Concurrent to his work with Egoyan has been an equally celebrated collaboration with Ang Lee, resulting in an Academy Award for Best Score for the film *Life of Pi* (2012).

Mychael Danna was interviewed, via Skype, in early 2013, by Lindsay Coleman.

Q: The *Little Miss Sunshine* (Jonathan Dayton and Valerie Faris, 2006) score has been used to advertise a very wide variety of products. How do you feel about that?
A: Whenever people enjoy the music I always feel complimented, however it gets used. Once you've written a piece of music, it's like your child. You pat it on the head, and out it goes into the world. At that point your ownership ends, people make of it what they like.
Q: Do you feel the same way about the score for *Life of Pi*?

L. Coleman (✉)
Nunawading, Australia

© The Author(s) 2017
L. Coleman, J. Tillman (eds.), *Contemporary Film Music*,
DOI 10.1057/978-1-137-57375-9_12

A: All my scores are personal, but *Life of Pi* was particularly personal, because there were so many connections with my own life. Everything I do I make personal. I always put myself into it. I think when you write film music you are writing it in the context of the film. There is a unity between the two. If you take it out it becomes a different thing. It's not what it was designed for. Even the CD for *Little Miss Sunshine* or *Life of Pi*, that is not how the score was designed. It was designed to fit with the 3D images created for the film. After a project finishes, though, I compare it to what an architect goes through. You design a building and then, 100 years later, someone completely different is living in it. It is really beyond your jurisdiction, in a way. All I can control is writing the music for the images, in collaboration with my director.

Q: You have noted that you always wanted to be able to make a living as a composer. Would you say that what you just described is one of the necessary approaches to being a commercially viable composer?

A: When I discussed being 'commercial' it wasn't really meant in the context of 'making a lot of money'. It was more 'commercial' as in people are actually consuming the music, it is reaching an audience. In twenty-first century terms we would refer to it as 'consuming', in nineteenth-century terms as 'listening' to it. I went to college and studied composition. I didn't want to be an ivory tower composer. I didn't want to be working in a vacuum, to be writing music just for myself. I wanted it to relate to the society I was a part of. In today's terms that means commercial. It doesn't mean I will strive to make as much money as possible. It just meant I wanted to be part of the society in which we live in, and that people would use and enjoy my work.

Q: You once said worrying about how a score would translate to an audience once you have completed it was too taxing. Is that something you still operate by?

A: Yes. I wanted to operate in a world where I was interacting with the society, yet at the same time I didn't want to plan my work out in such a way that I was always striving to predict what this audience member, or that audience member, might feel. You have to make it your own. You have to be true to what is inside. The paradox is, that to connect with an audience, you have to be true to your own instincts and intuitions. Even the most naïve listener can distinguish truth from bullshit. Sincerity is just based on being true to your own feelings, and then turning it into whatever art you are working on.

If you've got a C minor chord you can't be worrying about whether you should go to F major, based on what your neighbour might think of that. You can't worry about that, or you will paralyse yourself.

Q: Many people feel that is where the creative impulse comes from.

A: Sure. Let's look at *Life of Pi*. That film had to have a big box office. We couldn't say, 'We liked it, sorry nobody else seemed to get it.' The parameters that were set up in that project, the fact that it cost well over $100 million, it had to play on a lot of screens, all over the world. That does depend on being true to oneself, and getting outside responses. We did test screenings. Nobody finds them very fun, but they are incredibly educational. You get a lot of information, a lot of feedback, from these screenings.

Q: Would you make a film on the scale of *Pi* again?

A: That's a good question. I've done films of many varied scales. They are all different. There are many different rewards and costs. On a small film you are working intimately, just you and the director. The sandbox is smaller, your choices are more limited. On *Pi* we had the best of everything, at a moment's notice. I also had ten people in a room who would very quickly hit the eject button if things were not going well. It's a much more stressful situation. The rewards are bigger, too. I'm not just speaking about awards, or box office. It means so much to me to know that the film has been seen in so many countries in the world. That it has been such a big film in China, in India, in Russia. It means a lot to know that I have taken so many musical forms from different cultures, and now I can finally give it back. To know I am part of something which people around the world can respond to. On a smaller budget that kind of thing can't really happen. I wouldn't want all my films to be of this scale. It's fun to have different problems, film to film.

Q: Elliot Goldenthal feels his work is a conversation with composers from the past, from previous centuries even. Do you feel similarly about your own work?

A: I said something similar at a dinner the other night, and I have actually never heard that quote from Elliot before this moment, so that is very interesting. I've never met him in fact. One of the reasons I became a composer is because when I was younger I loved composers, I wanted to know more about them. The closest you can get to Henry Purcell, or J. S. Bach, is to do what they do. It is like Mozart staying up all night to finish the overture to one of his operas, because he had spent too long procrastinating. I've had that experience. So

I feel I do know him better. The concept of deadlines, their having to relate to an archbishop, or emperor, or some other patron, I can align that with interacting with a director. I am quite conscious of that sense of lineage, or being close to the human beings I am most drawn to in my own life, from throughout history. I now feel, when I listen to Debussy, I can hear it from a different perspective. It is one of my favourite things about choosing this career. But, you know, I would say I'm more of a filmmaker than a composer. I tell my assistants, 'we are not composers'. We're part of the filmmaking team. Our decisions should not be based on those of a composer. They can be buried deep down in our process, yet the higher decision-making is based around story, around the director's vision. We are serving that.

Q: The track from *Pi*, 'Godstorm', has a devotional aspect to it. Your description of the track is that it depicts a pitiless God. I feel the scene evokes awe of God's power and creation. Could you elaborate?

A: 'Godstorm' is a three-way conversation going on between Pi, Richard Parker, and God. The way Ang would describe it is the idea that there is God, and the human scale, and the animal scale, all kind of relating to each other in an adversarial triangle. I agree with what you say, though, that there is a conflict between worship of the awe-inspiring universe we live in, of nature as an extraordinary force which is beautiful, and yet as one which is also pitiless, and without any of the human characteristics we would find comfort in. It's not cruel, it's not kind. It's completely neutral, and has no care for our existence in any way whatsoever. Your interpretation is the wonderful thing about art, and this film specifically. What Ang and I have been trying to say isn't necessarily how an audience will interpret our work, and I'm very happy about that. For me, the scene is about unrequited love. Pi is trying to have a conversation with God, and trying to throw himself on God's mercy. Yet, God is oblivious, without any care for his predicament. In that moment he snaps, and is angry with God. He is angry his pleas have been without a response. There's that sadness of that unrequited love. There is that pathetic nature of someone who wants another's attention, and love, and isn't getting it, and now they're angry. That is what is moving about that music for me. But everybody has their own way of looking at the universe. Yet, that's how I see the scene. I feel sorry for Pi, but also he is all of us. We all live in this world which is something we don't understand, and which doesn't respond to us in the way we would like it to. It is also beautiful, and majestic, and we love it. It is an unrequited love. My opinion is no more important than any other audience member's.

Q: Is the score in that scene from Pi's perspective, or God's perspective?

A: It's from an observer's perspective, it's from my perspective. As an observer watching, I am perceiving a mirror of my experience, of a puny human being tossed around like a rag doll, by a universe which is completely unconscious of his existence. Not in an evil way, it is just the reality of it. It is kind of heartbreaking. That's the perspective the music was written from. At the same time, that's me, that's you, that's all of us. We are all Pi on that boat.

Q: 'First Night, First Day' is essentially a musical interlude. There is no major sound in the scene. The images are more or less static. It is a longer piece of music. Did you feel that was a particular showcase for you?

A: There is no showcase in this film. Believe me, I tried to write them. Over the year I worked on this score I had to recompose, rescore scenes many times. There were early versions of the score set to scenes which were more obvious showcases, which were more obviously melodic. The scene you described, and the later scene in which Pi hallucinates, were examples of such. Ang felt, quite rightly, that the film always had to be in image, that there always had to be a balance between music and image. Not just image and music, but character and narrative, between special effects and sound, everything had to be balanced like this. Orchestras are asking me for a suite, to take music out of the score for this, but I don't think it will work. It can't be done because the music is embedded in the visuals, in the story.

Q: It wouldn't translate to a musical?

A: It could translate to an opera. It could translate to a ballet. It could be translated to another art form. But if you take the music out of this film it is not a complete thought, in and of itself. That is rightly so. That would not be how the music was designed. It was designed not to say too much, not to be the whole story, to suggest, to make the emotional environment of the story. So, it is not a showcase. It has to be in balance, like everything else.

Q: The visuals set against 'First Night, First Day' are very beautiful, but your music does suggest a threat.

A: It was more of a complete feeling of rest. The film has barely started. But, we needed to keep the feeling of the journey in the forefront. Again, this is a conversation Pi has with God. Pi says 'it's over to you, I surrender'. In one interpretation God is not listening. Pi is still in the frame of thinking that God has a human-like personality. I was attempting to say, 'Pi, things are not as you would like them to be. You are having a 24-hour test, which is now just about over. You think you will say to God 'I surrender', and a ship will pull up. That is not going to happen. That is not where we're headed. The tiger is not your friend. This is my interpretation. Mine is no more correct than anyone else's. And, it is worth mentioning that Ang's interpretation of this film is slightly different from my own. That is the magic of this film. When young Pi says he can see a soul in the tiger's eyes the father says, 'No, you are just seeing your own reflection in his eyes.' That's one of the essential questions of the film for the audience. That is not just a question about Richard Parker, but also about God. When we are looking at God, are we just seeing our own reflection? That is not an answered question, but it is a question that is asked. In the music, that is what is being suggested in 'First Day, First Night'. Pi is still thinking in a way he still claims to when he is an older person. I think it is one of the lessons of the journey, that what you are seeing is a reflection of yourself. Is the reflection of yourself God? I would say 'yes'. But that is where things get way too fuzzy in terms of what anyone could hear in the music itself. But, this is what goes through my mind while I'm writing the music.

Q: Probably, given the state in India which Pi originates from, there would likely have been more quarter tones in 'Pi's Lullaby'.

A: Certainly. This comes back to our earlier discussion that this is a $120 million movie. It can't have the approach of an art film. If this were a $3 million movie it would have had a different approach, and one which might have been recognized as more 'Indian'. You can certainly imagine the studio's response, without my spelling it out to you, to an opening song in Tamil. It certainly sounded to them non-Western, and to them it didn't really sound like a very good idea. Ang wanted to, and rightly so, plant the seeds of our understanding of Pi's world. We need to understand that, we need to feel it emotionally, so that when we take it all away from him we understand what he has lost. The Indian elements were for that. But you are right, there was a fine balance to be struck. The most important thing was that people connected emotionally. If you're born in Kansas, you still need to relate to what Pi's early life was. It's a very different environment, but it's very welcoming. The sense of family love, and a mother's love, which is given in the song, is the most important thing. When I selected a singer, I selected someone whose voice was very listenable to for a Western ear. It's not too alien, it's not too specific. Pi is also born into a place which is a cross-cultural world, Pondicherry. People speak French, they eat croissant. That in turn influences his way of looking at the world. To him, Hinduism, Judaism, Christianity are all facets of the same gem. Even without worrying about this being too 'Indian' it still would not have been more 'Indian', because Pi is a world citizen.

CHAPTER 13

Mychael Danna: Music as Metaphor

Peter Golub and Katy Jarzebowski

In an interview about *Moneyball* (Bennett Miller, 2011), Mychael Danna reveals the essence of his collaborative vision—an active role as storyteller:

> I have always aspired to look at film music in a new way, not based purely on what has gone before, but on what is best for the film at hand. To find the best solution, starting with a blank slate, and to not be afraid of doing the unexpected, with the prerequisite of knowing exactly why you are making choices, and not basing those choices on things outside of the deepest meaning of the film.[1]

As a prolific film composer, he sets his work apart by choosing nuance over convention; Danna understands our expectations and plays against them, treating each score as an opportunity to create an autonomous musical language specific to the context of its film. Because the relationship between music and moving images in the cinematic storytelling tradition has groomed our responses to Pavlovian proportions, today's collective film audience associates certain musical language with an exact genre, or emotion, or tone, or atmosphere; being conditioned in this way can

P. Golub (✉) • K. Jarzebowski
Los Angeles, CA, USA

limit the possibility for a nuanced perception of the cinematic experience. Academic jargon aside, Royal S. Brown offers a very sensible explanation:

> ... film music can contribute in an overwhelming way, via its tendency to hyper-explicate, to passivity in the viewer/listener. In other words, a given passage of music, instead of leading the viewer/listener towards an open and/or paradigmatic reading of a given situation, imposes a single reading by telling the viewer/listener exactly how to react to and/or feel that situation.[2]

Danna, contrastingly, arrives at meaning by creating a suggestive juxtaposition of musical language, persuading the passive viewer to turn active by offering the unexpected. His expanded musical language introduces a kind of tonal dissonance within the narrative, a scene, or even a single character—a choice which Brown defines as 'alternation'—engaging the viewer to resolve, or 'transcend', that dissonance by understanding its place within the meaning of the film.

During a 2014 radio interview aired on NPR's programme *All Things Considered*, Danna stated, 'a good film score ... asks more questions than [it] answers, and it helps the audience ask those questions. But it doesn't solve the problems. I think that's something that's really changed in the last generation or two of film music'.[3] Danna's approach shows a respect for the audience by encouraging a thoughtful—and deeply emotional—response to the film. This approach functions much like the literary metaphor, a device which complicates the text in order to facilitate a reader's understanding; each juxtaposition between music and image serves to complete a film's tonal context and deepen the viewer's awareness. To this end, Danna makes use of unexpected instrumentations in films such as *The Ice Storm* (Ang Lee, 1997) and *Life of Pi* (Ang Lee, 2012), in which the music weaves instruments and ensembles from non-Western cultures together with orchestral elements, enlivening the interplay between music and image. With a discussion of *Moneyball*, we will examine an approach that uses a more traditional ensemble, the orchestra, in a reimagined way.

Danna's many enduring artistic partnerships serve as testimony to the success of his approach to scoring; with such notable directors as Ang Lee, Bennett Miller, Atom Egoyan, and Mira Nair repeatedly collaborating with the composer, his music becomes an inherent extension of their creative voices. Each relies on Danna's music to pull back the layers of the narrative, suggesting an emotional depth that further deepens the story. In accomplishing this, a composer must not only possess the expected skills of a musical craftsman, but also an acute awareness of the filmic medium itself, and the way films are experienced by today's audience.

In a career that spans almost 30 years, Danna's output demonstrates continuous nuance and invention. From his early days in Toronto, where for five years he was composer-in-residence at the McLaughlin Planetarium, through his recent Oscar and Golden Globe Awards for *Life of Pi*, Danna has amassed a body of work that is varied, original, and unmistakably his own. Born in Winnipeg, Manitoba in 1958, Danna has credited his Canadian roots as beneficial to his ability as a storyteller. While discussing *Monsoon Wedding* (2001), one of his frequent collaborations with Indian director Mira Nair, the composer stated, 'I want to respect the cultures that I'm referring to and working with. And I think Canadians and maybe someone from Winnipeg or Toronto is really well-qualified for that, because Canadian culture is so new and almost nonexistent in a way that it's easy for us to see through the eyes of other nations and other cultures and other people.'[4]

At the University of Toronto, where he was awarded the inaugural Glenn Gould Composition Scholarship in 1985, Danna's first exposure both to early music and world music would leave an impactful and lasting influence on his work. There Danna scored shows for student theatre groups, experiencing first-hand the emotional immediacy that music can add to the storytelling process. It was also during this period in Toronto that the composer would begin his now 28-year artistic partnership with director Atom Egoyan on the film *Family Viewing* (1987). To date, five of the pair's collaborations, including the score for the cult classic *Exotica* (1994), have each earned Danna the Genie Award from the Academy of Canadian Film and Television.[5]

Danna continues to attribute his extensive familiarity with varied compositional languages to his background and cultural experiences, stating in a 2012 interview, 'What really excited me was this collision and collusion of all these different cultures ... this is the vanguard of where our species is headed, and artistically we are reflecting that.'[6] After all, the suggestive nature of setting a particular musical language against a moving image has become a universal signal for meaning, just as our collective consciousness of cinematic language has become as fluent as our mother tongues; for almost a century, the filmic narrative has continuously been evolving, from the earliest implementation of montage towards an established visual language. As early as the 1920s, film theory, which served to legitimize the artistic integrity of the moving image, began at once proposing, identifying, and defining the concept of montage as the basic form of filmic language; Russian filmmaker and theorist Sergei Eisenstein published his manifesto *Film Form* in 1928, evangelizing for the potential of 'montage by attraction', or as renowned film critic André Bazin put it:

> In this extreme form, montage by attraction was rarely used even by its creator but one may consider as very near to it in principle the more commonly used ellipsis, comparison, or metaphor ... There are of course a variety of possible combinations of these three processes. Whatever these may be, one can say that they share that trait in common which constitutes the very definition of montage, namely, the creation of a sense or meaning not objectively contained in the images themselves but derived exclusively from their juxtaposition.[7]

This concept of 'juxtaposition' within the context of filmic language echoes Brown's notion of 'alternation' in film scoring—or the suggestion of deeper meaning through playing against audience expectations—which, in turn, echoes Danna's approach as a film composer. Similar to the developmental and technical progression of most visual media, film has endeavoured from its conception to accomplish objective realism. While cinema has continuously assimilated new devices into its language—from sound to music, colour to special effects, and now virtual reality—its origins rest simply in the animation of the photographic image, itself a manifestation of the plastic arts' quest for the ultimate expression of reality. The years following World War II marked a period of fervent advancement in film technology, but Bazin lamented that by bowing to literal depiction—specifically alluding to a reliance on sound devices—cinema 'turned its back on metaphor and symbol in exchange for the illusion of objective presentation'.[8] Nonetheless, since Bazin's observation, cinema has steadily shown it can go beyond literal depiction and, sometimes, create powerful and beautiful works in the process.[9]

Filmmakers during the Golden Age of Hollywood were so adept at creating a foundational cinematic language that audiences fluently follow such devices as panning, jump cuts, time cuts, montage. Likewise, the use of music has for many years produced specific conditioned responses. Before filming the final scene of *Dark Victory* (1939), in which a blind Bette Davis walks up a flight of stairs to meet her death, the actress famously asked director Edmund Goulding, ('is [composer] Max Steiner going to get to the top of the stairs before I do?') Here we see that just as the language of film, in general, has imprinted itself on audience response, so too has that of music. Yet, when music is freed of this role of obvious literal depiction and manipulation, new possibilities emerge. Brown, the aforementioned film music scholar explains: 'the image becomes superior to its referent ... music can take on a very privileged status as the ideal image, precisely because of its apparent non-referentiality.'[10] This points us to Danna's compositional approach as 'transcendent' in nature: the specific choice of one musical language over another has the power to recontextualize an entire film.

THE ICE STORM

The Ice Storm, based on Rick Moody's novel, is a study in alienation. About the best you can claim for the characters is that, in the end, they are resigned to the awfulness of it all. Set on Thanksgiving weekend in suburban Connecticut, it is a period piece set in 1973, replete with bell-bottoms and sideburns, Nixon and Watergate never far away. The deeply alienated adults are having affairs; their kids—on the brink of adolescent sexuality, which is inherently awkward—are *really* messed up. There isn't a lot of communicating going on. This movie about messed-up suburbanites, and their messed-up kids, treats the community 'anthropologically', as if the filmmakers are viewing things from a completely different time and place. Fittingly, the film's director, Ang Lee, is Taiwanese-born, American-educated, and heavily influenced by Chinese culture and cinema; his personal experience offers an outsider's perspective on the American dystopia.

Whereas film music is often charged to impart 'time and place', this practice is consciously avoided here. Danna has said, 'Music doesn't really need to repeat ... "where" we are and "when" we are. Music has powers beyond that. It has the power to touch us and to relate to the characters.'[11] Here, he chooses a musical language which suggests a structural dissonance to the film's setting, a juxtaposition that recontextualizes the narrative. The music employs gamelan, North American wooden flute, and strings and woodwinds in a Western orchestral style.

Throughout the film, these three musical elements (never calling attention to themselves, but never afraid to be heard) are utilized and combined in different ways as the story develops, with music placed as judiciously as the sound design and source music; silence is equally well chosen and eloquent.

Because the sound design and source cues give us a penetrating sense of time and place (see below for a discussion of sound and Muzak in the pharmacy scene), music can stand somewhat apart, functioning as metaphor. Film editor, sound designer, cinematic innovator, and thinker Walter Murch has written:

> Every successful reassociation is a kind of metaphor—what Aristotle called 'naming a thing with that which is not its name'—and every metaphor is seen momentarily as a mistake, but then suddenly as a deeper truth about the thing named and our relationship to it. The greater the stretch between the 'thing' and the 'name', the deeper the potential truth.[12]

At the instant when 'reassociation'—the 'mistake'—occurs, there is a grasping of metaphor. What Ang Lee and Danna have achieved through their musical choices is to position the audience as a kind of anthropologist studying the odd habits—mating and otherwise—of the strange tribe of people who live in suburban Connecticut in the 1970s, as if from very far away. They had, as Danna told Peter Golub, originally experimented with music that was more on-the-nose and of the period—but it didn't work. By weaving a score that includes Native American flute, a gamelan ensemble, and Western orchestral music, we experience the characters with detachment, as if we were anthropologists, removed from the specific locale with a licence for clinical observation.[13]

The opening credits of the film are accompanied by the solo Native American flute playing a lonely, freely floating, and somewhat icy pentatonic melody. This flute melody, combined with cold outdoor sounds, is the first thing we hear as we see images of icicles and a suburban train stuck in a winter storm. We see stills from comic books, and then teenager Paul. When the music stops, the sounds of the train coming to a halt, and the various electric effects create an almost violent mini-overture, foreshadowing the final scene in which young Sandy is electrocuted in the storm. As this brief *musique concrète* montage ends, we hear our first dialogue—the conductor's announcement that the train is back in service.

Paul's voice-over narration begins, relating the plot of the *Fantastic Four* comic he is reading, accompanied by a minor third tremolo (between B and D) played on two vibraphones, and doubled an octave lower by cellos performed *sul tasto* (a technique positioning the bow over the fingerboard to reduce the higher overtones and effect a thin but dark tone). This effect gives the scene of Paul's family greeting him at the train station a quality that is at the same time muted, tragic, and yet detached. The flute floats over this quasi-tragic sound-world, joined by mournful oboe and clarinet. A return to the solo wooden flute brings this opening section to a close. The contrast of the film's source cues and sound design, against Danna's musical language, recontextualizes the story by suggesting a kind of narrative dissonance.

Fifteen minutes into the film, we come to the end of the first chapter. Following the powerful use of score and sound in the opening segment, the film now begins to integrate source cues—or diegetic music which lives within the world of the film, and is simultaneously experienced by its characters. Ang Lee has established awkward family relationships beneath a veil of forced normalcy among Paul and his parents, Ben and Elena. Through artfully subtle direction, Lee has painted a deep impression of their dystopia: Elena's indifferently scolding dismissal of Ben's affection in bed, or Paul at boarding school, struggling through a phone call from his father. Despite keeping up deceptive appearances for their friends, something is broken in the family. Music inaugurated us into this world at the top—with the credits folding into the stalled train—and now we segue elegantly into the next section with another train and a fresh musical piece of score.

With Elena's rejection of the night before still in his consciousness, Ben boards a commuter train to Manhattan. The shot of the platform offers an iconic sight: the men dressed uniformly, their suits and briefcases prepared just as we expect for the workday. The music here is a jaunty, minimalistic, eighth-note texture alternating between 4/4, 7/8 and 9/8, with syncopated accents both on the beat and staggered, keeping you in a groove but off-balance. The tonal colour is distinctly that of an Indonesian gamelan orchestra (panerus, bonang, gambang, jenglong, kendang and various gongs) that doubles the strings in the perpetual motion part of the texture. It is interesting to note that the tuning of the gamelan instruments does not perfectly match that of the strings, and the effect suggests a wonderfully unexpected 'off-ness' against the conformity of the commuters. After a little while, a sustained and slightly melancholy oboe/clarinet melody floats over the rhythmic motor as Ben looks up distractedly from his *Wall Street Journal* while the other commuters continue reading. Jabs from the contrabasses, doubled with jenglong, provide a counterline that adds intensity and drive.

This music gives us a sense of these men, and so many like them, going off to work in mechanized fashion, their organization akin to that of worker bees. Murch's concept of reassociation, mentioned above, comes through magnificently here. It's as if the music has a different DNA than these people and their situation but, at the same time, the repetitive aspect of the minimalist figures works to universalize these commuters; yet, while there's something downright tedious and mechanized about the situation, there is also a distinct energy communicated that makes the whole thing bearable, even ironic, almost funny.[14]

What is truly instructive about this scene is the functionality of the sound-world as a whole, specifically the way music and dialogue are manipulated by Ang Lee and his team. After Ben looks up from his newspaper, the camera pans to a conference room in his Manhattan office. Here, the cue becomes overpoweringly loud, rendering the dialogue almost inaudible. The point is very clear that Ben is literally unable to hear the dialogue over the noise in his head. We experience his sense of personal submersion—his alienation from his world—as he carries the bedroom scene from the night before with him into his workday. The sheer monotony of the perpetual motion figure, though geographically from somewhere else, is the perfect counterweight to Ben's experience. It's the music and sound that make this vivid.

From the conference room, the music leads us back to Connecticut, where a yard sale is taking place in front of a Protestant church. The imagery is rich in visual minutiae of the time and place; we see a table of secondhand books on sale—*Siddhartha*, Doris Lessing, *Being and Nothingness*, Joseph Cornell, Camus—that tells us everything about the world of these characters, and their preoccupation with alienation and sexuality. As the music ends, it hands off to a tall, good-looking young man with very long hair who introduces himself to Elena: 'Reverend Edwards—Philip Edwards—you came by and checked out the congregation a couple of times last year.' His shoulder-length hair and colloquial language, plus the array of books about alienation and sexual liberation—all of this goes a long way to create a vivid sense of time and place, allowing the music to inhabit a more internal and psychological space.

After the awkward semi-flirtation/provocation in the Reverend Edwards-Elena exchange, there is an even more awkward school-yard conversation among Wendy, Paul's sister, and her friends involving the grossness of 'licking Dave Brewster's weenie in the third floor bathroom', which leads into a short and memorable moment. The boy with whom Wendy has an ongoing flirtation, Mikey, is playing football; he goes out for a pass, and as the ball is momentarily suspended in the air, the natural sound design drops out, leaving only a low rumble, as if the earth is moving. Mikey loses focus and misses the pass to the consternation of the quarterback, who makes a gesture that says, 'what are you, stoned?' Motivated by sound, this artfully revealing moment introduces us to Mikey and his adolescent vulnerability, suggesting that there are deep-seated anxieties and troubles just below the surface.

Back at the church sale, Elena notices her daughter, Wendy, riding a bike down the street and wistfully comments to Reverend Edwards that she, herself, hasn't been on a bike for years. We then follow Wendy into a pharmacy, where she shoplifts a Devil Dog (paging Dr Freud), only to be caught red-handed by a spooky, older fellow-shopper. The pharmacy's Muzak eloquently underscores the surreal quality of the situation—a wealthy girl perversely, and for no reason, stealing a Devil Dog.

Back on her bike, Wendy has another awkward exchange with Sandy, Mikey's little brother; after they greet each other, he proceeds to perform a mock execution on her with the little G. I. Joe figure he's carrying. Wendy trails onward alone, riding out of town and into a more rural area, where we hear the haunting wooden flute theme from the start of the film. The flute revives the demons from the opening storm as she approaches Mikey in a fabulously lonely and empty leaf-strewn swimming pool. After a preliminary adolescent back-and-forth involving chewing gum and Devil Dogs, and alluding to the fact that these two have had sex, the young lovers engage in a heavy, awkward French kiss.

Their kiss segues into the next scene in which Ben and his neighbour Janey, Mikey and Sandy's mother, are having sex. It is instructive to examine how Ang Lee and Mychael Danna negotiate this significant transition, ending the scene of the two kids making out and taking us into grown-up adultery. As the kids begin their heavy and awkward kiss, we hear lush strings bordering on the romantic; on top of this enters a slow variation of the eighth-note gamelan figure last heard in the commuter train cue; and on top of that wafts the solo wooden flute melody. At this structurally important moment in the story all the musical elements are combined to create a sense of the oneness—the intertwining—of the various story elements: the children's awkward sexual exploration, the parents' awkward affair, the utter lack of joy and connection in the entire community. The music provides a poignancy—a human-ness—amidst this sea of alienation.

To reinforce the absurdity of it all, Ben now lies in bed after having had sex with Janey, and talks quite animatedly about golf. She cuts him off: 'Ben, you're boring me. I have a husband. I don't particularly feel the need for another.' He agrees with her ('You have a point there. Right. We're having an affair, an explicitly sexual affair'), and the scene comes to an end. A shot of Ben slipping away from the wooded house (he actually slips on a rock) cues the perpetual-motion gamelan music. He's on his way—a mechanized figure just as he was on the commuter train. The strings and winds join in their sorrowful melody as he makes his way home through the woods, and we cut to Elena at home, preparing a pot of rice. There's a primitive quality to the imagery, as if alluding to Elena playing the part of a tribal woman in some primeval cave. The inherent sadness of the theme in the strings and winds joins Ben's adulterous actions to Elena's faithful dinner preparations, the music providing a melancholy connection between the two worlds.

The rest of the movie will not be discussed in scene-by-scene detail.[15] There are, however, a couple of key moments. There is a marvellous scene in which Elena, accompanied by the gamelan theme, is riding her bicycle to the same pharmacy where her daughter had stolen the Devil Dog. As the cue almost winds down, she picks up a lipstick and slips it into her pocket; the music revs up again. Whereas the daughter was accompanied only by Muzak and the sound effects of the store, the mother is fully scored. Perhaps the daughter is less fully formed, more unconscious—she's newer to this—and so, hasn't earned a score but has the source music, the actual diegetic music of the scene, following her moment to moment. The mother, on the other hand, has probably done this habitually, and the use of score makes her action seem ingrained and, ultimately, sadder.

In a later scene, we hear a surprising and telling use of the solo flute theme. As Ben and Janey are having another go at it, she leaves him alone in her room. She says she is going to get birth control, but he looks out of the window to see her drive away. Ben sits in his underwear on her waterbed, armed with a bottle of vodka, and the solo flute theme enters again, giving us a feeling somewhere between lonely hollowness and absurdity.

Skipping ahead to the last section of the movie, there are several musical moments that bring together the elements of the score in dramatically suggestive ways. At the end of the bizarre swingers party—in which the guests pick a key out of a bowl and go home to sleep with the owner of that key—Elena and Janey's husband leave together and have a kind of sexual exchange in the car. She returns home deeply alienated. Here, the musical language is particularly effective. The gamelan theme first heard at the train station is reiterated in a slower and icier variation (augmentation), with the woodwind theme above dark chords in the strings. The three elements combine as Elena finds her husband, Ben, sitting drunkenly on the bathroom floor—a moment made particularly dark by the union and slowing down (again, augmentation) of themes, anchored by full-bodied strings. By elaborating the woodwind theme, and thickening the strings, a feeling of tragedy falls over the scene. As we see the car driving in the icy night, the music trails out, leaving the natural sound as expressive accompaniment. The filmmakers have waited for this moment to unleash the full emotional potential of these messed-up characters.

As Janey walks into her house, we hear a cue with harp, piano and eventually winds that sums up all the sadness and missed connections of an emotionally chilly evening. The piece ends as we go outside and see Mikey playing in the ice storm to the natural sounds of the night. The climactic scene that follows, in which Mikey is electrocuted, and his dead body slides down the street, has no music; it doesn't need it, as the filmmakers determine that the eloquence of the scene needs no additional comment. This marks the end of the story. An epilogue, with a voice-over by Paul, begins with a kind of stuck version of the gamelan theme; circling around the opening bars, this time the familiar theme can't get itself off the ground. As Ben finds Mikey's body on the street, the gamelan sounds take a lower and darker shape, along with a new statement of the flute theme.

Here, at the end of the film, the musical elements continue coming together, overlapping and stretching. We end where we started, with Paul on the train, which has started up again after the ice storm. As Ben brings the dead Mikey home, the woodwinds offer an elegiac release for the audience. It's not ironic or alienated this time, it's a true expression of grief, a moment of profound tragedy breaking through delusion. The score's direct expression of sadness makes this more poignant for having been withheld from us throughout the film until now. Ben and Elena and Wendy drive Paul back to the train station; Paul looks at his family and breaks down sobbing. It isn't exactly hopeful, but at least it's real. Death has forced them to examine the hollowness of their lives.

Moneyball

Moneyball is a sports movie unlike any other. It's not the usual story of a rag-tag team that overcomes impossible odds to pull out a victory through sheer spirit and will, nor is it a sports tragedy à la *Jim Thorpe, All-American* (Michael Curtiz, 1951), nor still a quirky tale of pluck and determination like *Rudy* (David Anspaugh, 1993). Instead, *Moneyball* shows how the mundane application of statistical probability can lead to winning. It isn't individual heroism, or personal breakthrough, or even dogged determination that leads to victory, but adherence to mathematics. With the main character's backstory of personal loss in his own career permeating the movie, one comes away with an odd sense of things not quite working out, even though the team and the method are winners. Is this all we are, mathematics? Where does individual human heroism come in? Even though the film is hugely entertaining and interesting, it has a fundamental sadness. Mychael Danna, with his ability to tap into the dark side, provides the perfect score.

Throughout the film, director Bennet Miller utilizes numerous montage sequences, offering the viewer a specific interpretation of past or present events. Often, a series of selected shots is quickly intercut, building a slideshow of moving images. Dialogue overlaps from one shot to the next, connecting the montage in both meaning and tone as voice-overs become diegetic sound. Most notably, Miller employs this narrative device during the losing-stretch-turned-winning-streak of the Oakland A's, as well as Billy Beane's flashbacks to his failed career as a baseball player. The latter occasions are specifically presented as Billy's personal memories, offering, in hindsight, a direct connection between the protagonist's past regrets, and the reasoning behind his current attraction to the method of deductive player selection introduced to him by Paul DePodesta; indeed, Paul himself admits to a tipsy Beane that in lieu of the favourable first-round projections, he would have pegged him a ninth-round draft pick.

Montage sequences tend, momentarily, to alter the narrative pace of a film; the story can come at the audience in a non-linear way. Miller strategically bookends Beane's initial flashback with an uninspired pow-wow with his own aging pool of Oakland A's scouts and his first introduction to Paul DePodesta. Beneath the seductively optimistic projections of an elderly scout, glimpses of a much younger, and yet unbroken, Billy Beane, circa 1979, are juxtaposed against Danna's cue, pregnant with anticipation.

Danna's score suggests meaning through tonal colour, while simultaneously grounding the audience's experience during a fleeting moment. Effectively, this cue works in juxtaposition to the narrative function of the sequence; as Miller peels away the layers of Billy's history, Danna's music poses a question, 'What happened to Billy Beane?' At roughly 13 minutes into the film, young Beane's decision, and its outcome, are as yet unknown to the audience; and by itself, Danna's music gives no definitive answer. Played against images and text that would otherwise build excitement, however, the cue—trapped in a state of unresolved anticipation—suggests a sense of foreboding.

Beginning with six quivering violins, playing a single mid-range pitch at tremolo (D4) against the image of a captivated elderly scout whose watchful stare exudes fascination with the display of youthful talent before him, Danna introduces a sparse piano theme which will hereafter become associated with the younger Billy. Comprising consecutively repeated two-note phrases, paired in sets of two, and moving in stepwise motion (first rising, then falling) at a steady 60 beats per minute, the piano leads the theme melodically while the strings slowly build a delicate, trembling tone cluster below. Mimicking the dissonant quality of the violins, Danna soon introduces clusters in the piano as well, and the stepwise rise and fall of the theme builds more and more complex unresolved suspensions.

Digging further past the musical elements that comprise the essential nature of the cue reveals a thoughtfully structured dance between music and sound design. As the first baseball cracks against Billy's bat off-screen, Danna immediately introduces the initial iteration of the cue's thematic motif, and he repeats this pattern (crack-piano) three times more, each instance floating forwards in the mix until finally landing on the reveal: a close-up disclosing that the young player, who the scout predicts will be 'going in the first round', is Beane himself. Establishing a close marriage between score and sound allows Danna to control imperceptibly the pace of the sequence, which may otherwise seem fleeting or even abrupt; he anchors the montage to an invisible musicality.

The cue builds and shifts, and so, too, does the viewer's awareness. As discussed earlier, today's typical audience is a veritable Pavlov's dog—image set to music triggers our emotions. Traditionally, film scores support the narrative emotional journey by *reflecting* the sentiments on-screen. In her writings on 'narrative film music', fittingly entitled *Unheard Melodies*, Claudia Gorbman infers that the establishment of musical codes and conventions during the Classical Hollywood era 'expresses moods and connotations which, in conjunction with the images and other sounds, aid in interpreting narrative events, and indicating moral/class/ethnic values of characters ... music reinforces what is already signified by dialogue, gestures, lighting, color, tempo ... editing, and so forth'.[16] Indeed, Gorbman's observations shed light on the dominant tendencies of film scores since the advent of sound films in the 1920s. Most top-grossing Hollywood movies today continue to employ music primarily to enforce tonal shifts, narrative pacing, and emotional direction.

Danna, however, remains faithful to a more progressive and, we would argue, more metaphorical mentality in his work, as explained in his aforementioned observation that the score's responsibility is to 'ask more questions than [it] answers'.[17] This attitude offers a fresh approach, both to the relationship between sound and image, and the collaborative process between directors and composers. His approach offers new possibilities to today's filmmakers, as audiences' familiarity with film language becomes second nature and the dependence on music as an explicitly narrative device decreases. To repeat the quote from Murch: 'Every successful reassociation is a kind of metaphor ... and every metaphor is seen momentarily as a mistake, but then suddenly as a deeper truth about the thing named ...'[18]

Beane's first flashback never musically satisfies the curiosity this cue so potently suggests. Instead, the young Billy's theme, in this initial rendering, demonstrates a steady emotional diplomacy; maintaining a suspended anticipatory quality, the cue avoids both harmonic and melodic resolution, and if heard autonomously, could easily signify either suspense and foreboding or excitement.

Without explicitly answering the questions posed by this first peek into Beane's past, Danna nonetheless subtly supports Miller's visual hints by adding meaning through contrast. During the scouts' fantastically auspicious, and laughably useless, observations (at one point the voice-over cites Beane's 'good face' as a promising quality for a baseball player), Danna gently overwhelms the melodic anchor by shifting dominance in the mix from the piano to the strings with a subdued wave of harmonic dissonance, seething with uncertainty. This tonal shift occurs amidst a telling shot set in Billy's childhood home: as his son shakes hands with a scout in the frame's foreground, Billy's father comes into focus in the background, his countenance troubled and perhaps even disappointed. While this musical choice might seem to follow the path of a traditional film score, insomuch as it supports the narrative shift expressed on-screen, Danna actually diverges from expectation. In lieu of creating direct parallels between image and score, he instead favours contrast.

Upon exiting this montage sequence, Miller relocates the audience with the present-day Billy Beane, who awaits a meeting with Paul. While Billy contemplatively stares at a framed black-and-white photo of a Cleveland Indians player sliding into home base, his thoughts remain on his past choices as the voice-over and score persist, tapering off slowly. The frame subtly pans in closer on his face, mouth agape and mind decades in the past. By extending the cue into the next scene, Danna suggests that Billy's choices, whatever they may have been, continue to haunt him, and the young Billy's theme takes on further meaning: regret.

Having created an audio-visual dissonance, Danna establishes the metaphorical meaning which Murch labels a 'successful reassociation'.[19] With each reinforcement of this contrast, the theme further builds a connotative function for the audience. Danna next employs this theme in a similar fashion ten minutes later when Miller reveals the devastating repercussions of Billy's decision to play baseball over accepting a full scholarship to Stanford. Perhaps the most satisfying use of the theme, however, occurs during the Oakland A's first failed application of the Billy James method. Danna directly quotes the theme amidst an entirely separate melody; hearkening back to Billy's regrets, the musical quotation, paired with inserts of a struggling young Beane on the field, can now act as an autonomous musical signifier for the audience, entirely specific to the film.

LIFE OF PI

Fifteen years after *The Ice Storm*, Mychael Danna teamed up again with Ang Lee on their fourth collaboration, *Life of Pi*. The film was an undeniable success, both critically and with audiences, winning four Academy Awards—including best director and best original score—and earning over 600 million dollars worldwide. In his 2012 Academy Awards speech, Danna celebrated the partnership with Lee, stating, 'I share this award with our visionary captain who guided a global cast and crew in the telling of this truly wondrous, beautiful story that transcends culture and race and religion.'

The film follows Pi, a teenage Indian boy who loses his family after a shipwreck, and is stranded on a lifeboat in the company of a Bengal tiger named Richard Parker for 227 days in the Pacific Ocean. Narrating the film as an adult living in Canada, Pi's story is told entirely through his own recollection upon the request of a curious journalist. In fact, Richard Parker is Pi's alter-ego, and the tragic reality of Pi's experience on the lifeboat involves witnessing the murder of his mother by a brutish cook and the subsequent murder of the cook by Pi himself. The story of the film becomes a metaphor that recounts Pi's survival and test of faith, and Danna's music adds another layer of metaphor.

Incorporating a wide palette of musical styles and instrumentations, the score itself is a big part of the all-embracing reach of the film. Pi's journey takes him from youth to adulthood, India to France, zoo to dance studio, and eventually from the arms of a loving family to orphaned solitude. Equally epic in scope, Danna's score weaves traditional Western orchestrations with gamelan ensemble, transitioning into French *chanson* and Indian-inspired vocalizations to support cultural references and settings; the orchestra was Los Angeles-based, while non-Western instruments like the *bansuri*, an Indian bamboo flute, and the *santur*, a Persian hammered dulcimer, were recorded in Toronto and Mumbai, respectively.[20]

More important, however, is the shift in tone as Pi describes his struggles and triumphs with Richard Parker, or rather, with his own existence and faith. Danna has asserted that his cues are written so specifically to the film that, taken out of that context, they would not work as autonomous concert music. Doubtful that the score can be reworked as a suite, he feels, 'It can't be done because the music is embedded in the visuals, the story.... But if you take the music out of this film it is not a complete thought, in and of itself.... It [the score] was designed not to say too much, not to be the whole story, to suggest, to make the emotional environment of the story.'[21] He proposes a universality similar to that of the film—the struggle of its protagonist to know himself and his place in the universe. 'We are all Pi on that boat.'[22]

Early in the film, during Pi's youthful curiosity about different gods and religions, his mother narrates the story of the Hindu deity Krishna, who carries the universe in his mouth. As she speaks, the theme 'Pi's Lullaby' floats through the scene as a solo female vocalization, melismatic and Indian in nature. Danna states that he wanted to include an Indian-inspired theme to share a piece of Pi's world with the viewer because 'we need to feel it emotionally, so that when we take it all away from him, we understand what he has lost'. The composer specifically chose an Indian singer, Bombay Jayashri, whose voice was 'listenable to for a Western ear'.[23]

Throughout the film, the immensity of the ocean's underwater world becomes a metaphor for the inescapable vastness of the human experience—the universe that Krishna shelters in his mouth. To support this figurative imagery, Danna uses a foundation of gentle gamelan ostinato with alternating rhythmic patterns to suggest the otherworldly. During a cue titled 'The Whale', Pi peers over the edge of his raft at night, staring at bioluminescent jellyfish. Their glow is alien in the darkness, and he is captivated. The percussive gamelan churns out a moderate four-beat pattern spelling out a tonic-to-submediant (i 6/4 to VI) looping harmonic pattern, allowing a stepwise chromatic shift in the bass. The instrument's timbre is ambient and mysterious; paired with the chromatic bass pattern, it suggests the macabre. Deep below, Pi notices an approaching light—a massive whale, the mystery and vastness of the universe revealed.

Ninety minutes into the film, in an emotionally charged existential climax, Pi faces off against a violent storm which he believes to be God communicating directly with him. In a cue called 'God Storm', the composer expresses the protagonist's struggle through the loosely structured use of traditional Western sonata form. Danna first establishes a primary theme and, later, a contrasting secondary theme. Here, each theme is treated as a motivic 'cell'—a thematic phrase which can be reiterated as variations to further develop a piece of music.[24] Other aspects of traditional sonata form are also featured, such as development and recapitulation. Danna's departure from the expected order of sonata form suggests an underlying chaos—the quick shifts and sudden transitions, along with a musical language of opposing forces, magnify Pi's internal crisis over the violence of the storm.

Yelling a soliloquy to God over nature's forceful roar, Pi implores Him to appear, celebrates Him, and finally curses His fearful wrath. The scene opens on a wide-shot with Pi in the foreground preparing the lifeboat for the storm clouds looming in the distance. A large wave knocks Pi out of balance and he loses his precious journal to the rising winds. Sound design suspends the anticipation alone for a few moments as Pi stumbles into the ocean; splashes, whistling winds, and waves provide white noise, subtly invoking a sense of cleansing before Pi's POV point of view instead. On this shot music enters with a weighted immediacy in what can be considered the sonata's exposition, where the primary theme is established with gentle clarity and strength. A boy's voice sings out a haunting and mysterious four-note rising motive (C–D-flat—E-flat—E-natural), repeating it with an alternate figure (C–D-flat—F–E-natural), over growing sustained tonal clusters in the choir, horns, and strings. Beneath both phrases, the altos sing an E-flat that resolves up to E-natural, suggesting a minor-major resolution. The effect is majestic and spiritual, while simultaneously implying mystery and danger.

Against the haunting vocals and shifting harmonic columns in the orchestra, the heavens part and Pi sees a massive sunbeam shining down on the ocean. He beckons God to appear and the camera jumps high above, looking down as a bolt of lightning strikes beside the lifeboat; he cheers, 'Thanks be to God! Come on, Richard Parker—you have to see this, it's beautiful! He's come to us, it's a miracle!' Just then, a massive wave pummels the boat and Pi hits the water. The music collapses momentarily, leaving only the strong hum of a men's choir singing in unison on *ah*; the Gregorian-style chant suggests the timeless primitivism of man's eternal struggle—not only as *man vs God*, but also *man vs himself*. Seeing Richard Parker cowering in the boat, Pi turns on God in rage, 'Why are you scaring him! ... I lost everything! I surrender, what more do you want!' Once a fearful opponent, Pi now defends the tiger—and his own darkness—against the judgement of God.

Following the rebellious display, an opposing force in the music, the *overdub* cue, creeps towards the action, facing off more prominently against the churning rise and fall of the foreground strings, which now begin to treat the stepwise minor-major motion in the primary theme as a motivic cell, making liberal use of the e-natural to e-flat gesture. In the traditional structure of sonata form, this section would be labelled the *development*, where the established theme, or motivic cell, is treated in variations. Meanwhile, the overdub is piercing and threatening in character—it stabs violently into the shifting harmonic columns that navigate the cue. The compositional devices which Danna employs for this overdub might be considered as musically codified and signifying certain Gorbman-esque 'moods and connotations' through long-established film scoring conventions, but this interpretation would only be citing a single gear in the machinery of this cue. Certainly, the overdub includes a grab-bag of suggestively threatening orchestral elements. The percussion section involves a wide spectrum of textures—long rolls on timpani and tam-tam, big hits and barking flams on the bass drum. Danna adds percussive colour with both gong and sizzle cymbal, the former emitting a more immersive reverberation with intense overtones while the latter offers a grating quality, like a metallic rattlesnake.

The most effective element in the overdub, however, is a repeated *cadenza* gesture—stepwise runs in the string and woodwind sections, briskly rising then falling, quickening and bending time (quadruplets become sextuplets become septuplets, and back again, contracting and stretching). In music, the cadenza allows for a solo to be played in an expressive and virtuosic fashion with a feel that is *rubato*, or rhythmically free. Jumping from one rhythmic grouping to the next, the overdub's running gestures feel free and autonomous, chaotic and unpredictable. Danna further accelerates the pace by notating tremolos in the string runs. These gestures lean aggressively into the foreground cue, intensifying Pi's struggle against the threatening storm. Naturally, the viewer knows Pi will survive—he is our story's narrator—but the real question regards his faith.

Danna shares that Ang Lee considered the scene as an 'adversarial triangle' among Pi, Richard Parker, and God, but the composer admits that he interpreted the scene differently—as '... unrequited love. Pi is trying to have a conversation with God, and trying to throw himself on God's mercy. Yet, God is oblivious'.[25] Nevertheless, from any viewpoint, the scene is about existential crisis. In his harrowing circumstance, Pi is witness to the universe's indifference towards him. The clash between the 'God Storm' cue and its overdub works to support the crisis he bares so openly—first celebrating God, then cursing Him.

Finally, the crisis turns inward. Pi sees the real Richard Parker, looking just as pitiful and helpless as he finds himself; they are both literally and figuratively in the same boat, as it were—two parts of the same soul being tested and surviving—together. A quick breath of an eighth-note rest separates the churning foreground cue from the following section. The choir enters with the secondary theme, slowly building from the top down with each phrase, both angelic and majestic. The four-note pattern is stated (F down to E-flat, F up to G-flat) and then repeated in several iterations as variations—elongated over the high strings, deconstructed in the lower strings, played backwards then forwards again. Beginning on a b-flat minor tonic, the harmonic anchor is simultaneously weakened by the strong presence of the dominant (F) and an unresolved cadential pattern, suggesting wonder and mystery.

That first iteration, however, imparts an immediate emotional effect upon us because, in fact, Danna has preceded it with variations as well—haunting meanderings throughout the previous section of the four-note pattern are woven into the churning columns, subconsciously preparing us for its full iteration. As such, its clear entrance after the brief, silent breath suggests a moment of clarity—Pi's vision comes into focus and reaches an epiphany marked by the return of the cue's primary theme, now transposed down to the key of B-flat minor (previously C minor), now with the D-flat resolving up to D-natural to emphasize the characteristic minor-major tonal shift.

In a cue laden with opposing elements (major vs minor; primary cue vs overdub), Danna now brings the music into focus. The chaos subsides and then settles; the secondary theme sings out in high, sustained strings while the primary theme returns in the low range, strong and supportive. A return of the primary theme—while not in its original key—marks the sonata's brief recapitulation, and the complementary harmony into which the two themes play perfectly against each other reflects Pi's moment of truth and epiphany. The harp rises and falls over a billowing B-flat major triadic arpeggiation leading to an ambiguous dominant cadence; as the major tonic rings out, the D-natural shifts down to D-flat, modulating the tonic to B-flat minor. Pi has found peace, however restive.

Danna's deconstruction of sonata form in 'God Storm' plays with the viewer's expectations. And while his use of a large orchestra emphasizes the chaos of the storm, Danna's shaping of the music—its structural shifts, sudden drops, choir entrances, and the employment of an agressive overdub—follows Pi's internal journey. The cue is all-immersive from any angle.

By carefully placing his musical entrances, Danna further focuses the viewer's experience. The composer has cited that a balance between sound and music in *Life of Pi* was specific to Ang Lee's vision for the film.[26] As in the approach seen in *Ice Storm*, numerous wrought moments of Pi's survival are often left unscored and supported solely through image and sound design, only to be joined by a decisive musical entrance upon the scene's resolution. The strength of this expressive effect is perhaps felt most during the awesomely chaotic shipwreck scene when, during six harrowing minutes on-screen, Pi realizes the ship is sinking in the middle of night, tries to warn his family but fails to reach them through the watery annals of the ship, and miraculously stumbles into a lifeboat that sweeps him onto the open sea. In the process, a maelstrom of sharply pounding sonic attacks hurdles the viewer into Pi's very dangerous reality; ship horns blare over an onslaught of crashing waves and intense winds, zebras neigh beneath the water and emergency whistles pierce the air, men yell hectic commands at Pi over the deafening storm. Watching the ship going under, groaning painfully as it capitulates to the relentless ocean, Pi is distracted momentarily from the spectacle by Richard Parker's unwelcome approach. Fleeing from the tiger, Pi dives into the water.

Beneath the waves, the sonic barrage is suddenly muffled; the viewer—awareness still heightened and emotions taut—is left vulnerable. As the camera slowly pans around Pi, the viola enters against stark quiet with a sustained F-sharp below middle C; the low strings meander around a natural minor line descending an octave from tonic to tonic. The hollow quality of the bellowing three-octave column on the tonic in violas, celli, and basses, against a precipitous quiet, prepares the viewer for defeat. Illuminating the depths of the ocean, the massive cargo ship drifts into the watery abyss. As the ship's eerie glow fills the frame, with Pi's silhouette floating in the foreground, the strings yield to the ship's wailing and a grieving choir that, together, seemingly trap both Pi and the viewer in absolute stillness. Without any precedent, the score instantly establishes itself as a first-person voice for Pi's very singular existential journey. The cue, 'Ship Sinks', is a ghostly example of how effective a thoughtful calibration of music and sound design can be.

Danna similarly delays cue entrances in several other pivotal moments until a scene's denouement—moments of self-discovery and spiritual enlightenment. Later, when thousands of flying fish surround the boat, their scaly wings piercing through the air and smacking into Pi and Richard Parker, slapping against their weakened bodies, the absence of music urges the viewer to experience more directly the event in all its absurdity; the fish are harmless and even welcome as a nutritious blessing, but somewhere in the chaos, Pi finds the courage to fight and subjugate the tiger, seizing a massive tuna that has landed in the boat. As he stands tall and triumphant over his opponent, makeshift weapon in hand, a direct frontal shot-reverse-shot between man and beast gives way to a wide-shot: Pi guarding his prize atop the boat. A variation on the 'Pi's Lullaby' theme enters, as the scene transitions from day to night when Pi humbly partakes of his tuna back on the raft. Alone again, and distancing himself from Richard Parker, the delayed entrance of the cue suggests a humility in Pi's solitude—a deep gratitude and relief.

By juxtaposing varied and distinct musical languages (gamelan ostinato as alien and macabre, 'Pi's Lullaby' as nostalgic and warm), Danna allows the viewer to reassociate and derive new meaning from a given scene. During an intimate moment in which Richard Parker looks into his own watery reflection, Pi asks 'What do you see?' The camera goes underwater and reveals a beautiful and eerie montage—battling underwater monsters morph into drowning zoo animals, floating about the screen, until finally, the camera lands on a cargo ship, resting on the ocean floor like a glowing coffin. The frame pulls out above the water to see Pi, now staring at his own reflection. With the colliding images of this montage Lee suggests the vastness of human experience. Danna opens the cue with the gamelan ostinato, mysterious and haunting, but as the images shift to nostalgia (zoo animals), the 'Pi's Lullaby' theme returns on a wooden flute, and the tone becomes warm. Finally, the lamenting *Requiem* choir returns upon the stark reminder that his family is gone, and he is alone.

Danna's music at the end of the film is extraordinary. Pi is on the shore, finally having reached land. As the tiger disappears into the woods beyond, the adult Pi/narrator tells us, 'Richard Parker broke my heart.' The music does something here that music uniquely does: it manages to capture conflicting emotions. What's happening on the screen is terribly poignant and complicated: the sadness of Richard Parker leaving him, the greater sadness of losing his family and being alone in the world, the kind of postpartum depression that comes from the end of his struggle to stay alive, his sheer joy at having survived his ordeal and being rescued. The music here combines all these elements, and it does so in an understated way that gives added impact.

Epilogue

The most influential antecedent of traditional film scoring—and possibly of narrative film language in general—may be the programme music of the nineteenth century. Berlioz's *Symphonie fantastique*, perhaps the mother of all programme music, sets the bar incredibly high as an example of music that depicts and projects the drama. The programme was basically a scenario, a movie of the mind. In his printed programme (which he disseminated at performances of the piece), Berlioz spells out what's going on in Part 2: 'The artist finds himself in the most varied situations—in the midst of the *tumult of a party*, in the peaceful contemplation of the beauties of nature; but everywhere, in town, in the country, the beloved image appears before him and disturbs his peace of mind.' All of this—the tumult, the party, nature, the town, the beloved image (we certainly have no trouble identifying what Berlioz calls the *idée fixe*)—can be found in the music with exacting specificity.

It is this one-to-one relationship between music and image that Berlioz and, of course, Wagner championed. Depiction in music is at the heart of nineteenth-century tone poems, and as such is the forerunner to the traditional approach to film scoring. Richard Strauss once said he could describe in music a complete dinner, down to the table setting. Early film composers such as Wolfgang Korngold, Alfred Newman, and Max Steiner were uncannily adept at this kind of thing. But their type of 'on-the-nose' scoring, where the music follows the tone and rhythm of a scene in parallel strokes, is perhaps less of a default setting today. Though many mainstream contemporary movies (e.g. horror, thriller, action, and comedy) may still employ this literal approach, the films we have been discussing have aesthetic goals that are more ambiguous, more complicated. For movies such as these, a more personal and nuanced approach to music is more appropriate. Playing against expectations, music can become metaphor, causing the momentary 'reassociation' discussed by Walter Murch.[27]

Mychael Danna is neither the first nor the only composer to take the more metaphorical approach. (James Newton Howard's score to the 2014 film *Nightcrawler* (Dan Gilroy, 2014) is a virtual case study in misdirection, bringing out the creepy essence of the main character through music that is heroic and noble.) But, Danna is singularly well-suited to these subtleties. His fluency in 'world music' and his ability to combine non-Western and Western instruments and sonorities offer him a powerful musical arsenal. Like many composers of his generation, Danna rejected musical orthodoxy and found musical nourishment beyond the Western canon—in world music, minimalism, early music. Perhaps, as he speculates, being Canadian has allowed him to be particularly open to the outside influences that have been such an important part of his language.

Most importantly, Mychael Danna has a singular ability to think deeply about the stories and characters in his films—beyond the surface particularities of time and place, beyond the specific situations of characters—as if he's pulling back the layers of an onion. By creating music that functions as metaphor, he can fulfil his stated goal that music 'asks more questions than [it] answers'.[28]

Notes

1. Jeffrey DiLucca, 'In the Dugout with Danna', *Film Score Monthly Online*, Vol. 16, No. 10 (October 2011).
2. Royal S. Brown, *Overtones and Undertones: Reading Film Music* (Berkeley: University of California Press, 1994), 10.
3. Robert Siegel, 'Scoring the Screen: A Week with Musical Storytellers of the Silver Screen'. Interview with Mychael Danna on *All Things Considered*, NPR Music, 26 August 2014. Transcript available at http://www.npr.org/templates/transcript/transcript.php?storyId=372511466, accessed 19 July 2016.
4. Siegel, 'Scoring the Screen'.
5. For a more comprehensive account of Danna's musical background and film scoring style, see Chapters 1 and 2 in Miguel Mera, *Mychael Danna's* The Ice Storm: *A Film Score Guide* (Lanham: Scarecrow Press, 2007), 1–44.
6. Anon. (2013). 'Exclusive Interview with Academy Award-Winning Composer Mychael Danna', *Examiner.com*, 24 February 2013,

http://www.examiner.com/article/exclusive-interview-with-academy-award-nominated-composer-mychael-danna, accessed 4 April 2016 (as of July 2016, this page is no longer extant).
7. André Bazin, *What is Cinema?*, Vol. 1, essays selected and translated by Hugh Gray (Berkeley: University of California Press, 1967), 25.
8. Bazin, *What is Cinema?*, 39.
9. While efforts in 3D technology and virtual reality continue to evolve towards a more actual reproduction of reality, this article frames the definition of cinema around narrative and documentary film.
10. Brown, *Undertones and Overtones*, 236.
11. Danna, Mychael (2009). Interview by Christopher Coleman. *Trackworks: The Soundtrack Experience*. Web, http://www.tracksounds.com/specialfeatures/Interviews/interview_mychael_danna_2007.htm.
12. Walter Murch, 'Sound Design: The Dancing Shadow', in *Projections 4: Film-makers on Film-making*, eds John Boorman, Tom Luddy, David Thomson and Walter Donohue (London: Faber and Faber, 1995), 247–8.
13. For a more detailed discussion of the evolution of the score, see Mera, *Mychael Danna's* The Ice Storm, 81–103.
14. Mera comes to a similar conclusion in his analysis of this cue (Mera, *Mychael Danna's* The Ice Storm, 144–5).
15. For an excellent analysis of the whole score (and the diegetic use of pre-existing songs), see Chapter 5 in Mera, *Mychael Danna's* The Ice Storm, 117–71.
16. Claudia Gorbman, *Unheard Melodies: Narrative Film Music* (Bloomington: Indiana University Press, 1987), 84.
17. Siegel, 'Scoring the Screen'.
18. Murch, 'Sound Design', 247–8.
19. Murch, 'Sound Design', 247–8.
20. Siegel, 'Scoring the Screen'.
21. Lindsay Coleman, Mychael Danna Interview, this book, Chapter 12, 191.
22. Coleman, Mychael Danna Interview, 191.
23. Coleman, Mychael Danna Interview, 193.
24. Most notably cited in the Classical era, it was Beethoven—a composer who bridged the gap into the Romantic era—who left us perhaps the most recognizable motivic 'cell' in his Fifth Symphony.

25. Coleman, Mychael Danna Interview, 190.
26. Coleman, Mychael Danna Interview, 191.
27. Murch, 'Sound Design', 247–8.
28. Siegel, 'Scoring the Screen'.

Bibliography

Anon. 2013. Exclusive Interview with Academy Award-Winning Composer Mychael Danna. *Examiner.com*, 24 February. http://www.examiner.com/article/exclusive-interview-with-academy-award-nominated-composer-mychael-danna. Accessed 4 April 2016 (as of July 2016, this page is no longer extant).

Bazin, André. 1967. *What Is Cinema?* Vol. 1. Essays selected and translated by Hugh Gray. Berkeley: University of California Press.

Brown, Royal S. 1994. *Overtones and Undertones: Reading Film Music*. Berkeley: University of California Press.

Coleman, Christopher. 2007. Composer Mychael Danna: The Music Born of a Story. *Tracksounds: The Soundtrack Experience*. http://www.tracksounds.com/specialfeatures/Interviews/interview_mychael_danna_2007.htm. Accessed 3 April 2016.

DiLucca, Jeffrey. 2011. In the Dugout with Danna. *Film Score Monthly Online*, Vol. 16, No. 10. October.

Gorbman, Claudia. 1987. *Unheard Melodies: Narrative Film Music*. Bloomington: Indiana Univ. Press.

Miguel, Mera. 2007. *Mychael Danna's the Ice Storm: A Film Score Guide*. Lanham: Scarecrow Press.

Murch, Walter. 1995. Sound Design: The Dancing Shadow. In *Projections 4: Filmmakers on Film-making*, ed. John Boorman, Tom Luddy, David Thomson, and Walter Donohue. London: Faber and Faber.

Siegel, Robert. 2014. Scoring the Screen: A Week with Musical Storytellers of the Silver Screen. Interview with Mychael Danna on *All Things Considered*, NPR Music, 26 August. http://www.npr.org/templates/transcript/transcript.php?storyId=372511466. Accessed 19 July 2016.

CHAPTER 14

John Williams and Contemporary Film Music

Emilio Audissino

A chapter on John Williams in a study of contemporary film music might sound odd. In his eighties—he was born in 1932—Williams is the last survivor of his generation, and his pre-eminent works—*Star Wars* (George Lucas, 1977), *Superman* (Richard Donner, 1978), *Raiders of the Lost Ark* (Steven Spielberg, 1981), *E.T. The Extraterrestrial* (Steven Spielberg, 1982) …—are characterized by what I have called a 'neoclassical' style, which is an updated restoration of the 'classical' style of the Hollywood music of the 1930s and 1940s.[1] Williams has continued to be an active protagonist of film scoring in the last 15 years—a period of great stylistic and industrial change—and he still is, being a permanent reference point for film music that strives for higher standards. This chapter argues that the main reason for Williams's prolonged success is a well-balanced mix of versatility and strong musical personality, the latter element being most notably reflected in his memorable musical themes. As a film historian, I shall survey Williams's versatility as the key element that has allowed him to have such long a career. In the next chapter, the musicologist Konstantinos Zacharopoulos will investigate Williams's style in terms of the strategies used to structure his famous film themes.

E. Audissino (✉)
University of Southampton, UK

A Background of Contemporary Hollywood Music

I have provided elsewhere a three-period topography of the history of Hollywood music: the classical period (1933–58); the modern period (1958–78); and, after James Wierzbicki,[2] the eclectic period (1978 to the present day).[3] In the eclectic period different stylistic traits have coexisted—disco music, new-age impressionism, world music, minimalism, electronic music, jazz, rock, pop songs—including a revival of the classical-styled symphonic film music launched by John Williams with his score to *Star Wars*. I shall further narrow the topography and sketch a background in broad lines of the most recent years of this eclectic period, in order to stress by contrast how Williams's figure is somehow anachronistic in today's film music. The first general trait is a weakening of symphonic-style film music in favour of a simplified orchestral sound resembling more rock/techno/pop music arranged for orchestra rather than symphonic music.[4] The other major trait is the massive use of computers and digital technologies, which film composers have to cope with in their work.[5] Increasingly significant and widespread signs of this technological and stylistic change can be detected around the year 2000.[6] If, in 1996, *Independence Day* (Roland Emmerich)—a sci-fi film designed to be a box-office hit—still showcased a Williamsesque symphonic score by David Arnold, the sci-fi film *Armageddon* (Michael Bay, 1998) highlighted a compilation score featuring songs by Aerosmith, Jon Bon Jovi, Patty Smith et al.—with Trevor Rabin's incidental music as a subsidiary binding element. Similarly, if the 1995 pirate film *Cutthroat Island* (Renny Harlin) had a John Debney symphonic score whose models were the old Hollywood swashbucklers, the pirate film *Pirates of the Caribbean: The Curse of the Black Pearl* (Gore Verbinski, 2003) had an orchestral score that sounds like rock music played by a big orchestra. The 1999 film *American Beauty* (Sam Mendes) had a Thomas Newman score that popularized his trademark non-symphonic minimalism—a blend of acoustic instruments, light, high-pitched percussions, and electronics in a sparse and terse orchestral texture. For the period film *Gladiator* (Ridley Scott, 2000)—set in the ancient Rome—Hans Zimmer and Lisa Gerrard took contemporary World Music and pop New Age as models, instead of Miklós Rózsa's symphonic Roman epics. And *Gladiator*'s Hans Zimmer can be considered the key figure in today's Hollywood music. His work has influenced most of the younger-generation Hollywood composers, many of them having even taken their first steps under his guidance. The two most defining characteristics of Zimmer's modus operandi are probably team-work and computer technology.

The composer for the aforementioned *Pirates of the Caribbean*, Klaus Badelt, manufactured his music within Hans Zimmer's own music studio Media Ventures[7]—now Remote Control Productions[8]—and he was only the principal of a team of composers—eight credited and two uncredited, according to IMDb. Actually, team-work and music departments are nothing new in Hollywood. There has always been a principal composer assisted by orchestrators and sometimes arrangers and ghostwriters—with diatribes about whether the merit of the music was down to the composer or his assistants—because Hollywood's deadlines are always very tight ones.[9] Yet, today's is a different phenomenon: Zimmer's Remote Control Productions is a 'music factory' capable of providing whatever music one film needs in the shortest time possible. Diatribes about authorship or *the* composer as the individual creator are pointless: Zimmer's approach is patently collectivist, his policy being to have a pool of talents that is coordinated by himself, acting more as a music producer, talent scout, and sound designer than as a composer *stricto sensu*. In *Pirates of the Caribbean* Zimmer is credited as music editor, 'music *programmer*', and score producer, and Mel Wesson as 'music *designer*' [emphasis mine]. And these 'music designer' and 'music programmer' are keywords for this post-2000 phase. Film music is now more about *designing* soundscapes rather than *composing* music in the traditional meaning of the term. Much of today's film music is not even notated in the traditional sense but directly rendered through computer technology. For example, when *Gladiator* was selected as one of the films to be presented with live musical accompaniment in the 'Cineconcerts' series,[10] its music had to be substantially adapted for the live symphony orchestra: '[the arranger] spent weeks transcribing the multiple layers of percussion because so little of it had actually been written down'.[11]

Why is musical design preferred to traditional musical composition? Because today the typical mainstream film is what Laurent Jullier calls 'film concert'.[12] In Jullier's definition a 'film concert' is one in which the sound elements are being foregrounded to such an extent that the enveloping and saturated aural experience—called 'super-field' by Michel Chion[13]—is one of the biggest attractions of current filmgoing. Despite the name, music is far from being the protagonist of the film concerts: sound effects are. This is not an absolute novelty: film composers have always had to take into account the other components of the soundtrack—dialogue and sound effects. For example, Erich W. Korngold was particularly attentive to chiselling his music around the dialogue, and sound effects in battle scenes have long posed audibility problems for music. Yet, in recent times, sound effects have decidedly been rising in importance. Digital technologies have made it possible to mix hundreds of effect tracks[14]—with sound engineers producing sound mixes of great architectural complexity.[15] Soundtracks are then rendered in the minutest detail by state-of-the-art audio equipment in the theatres—Dolby Digital, THX, DTS, and multi-point surround systems. Music now has to cope with a thicker and louder texture of sound effects.

Film composers have also to be 'music programmers'; they must be proficient with computer technologies if they want to stay in the business.[16] Today, music composition is computer-assisted, which has enormously quickened the process. And producers and executives have taken notice, shortening the minimum time they grant composers to deliver the music. If in the old days of handwritten music composers had eight to ten weeks to compose a film score,[17] now lengthy scores are to be delivered in three to four weeks.[18] Composers are also required to prepare a preliminary MIDI (Musical Instrument Digital Interface) 'mock-up' of the score, a computer-generated demo. Mock-ups allow directors and producers to get a very precise idea of what the music will sound like before the (extremely expensive) stage of recording the music with a real orchestra; this means a considerable saving of time and hence of money. But computer technology has changed film editing, too. With the use of editing software, a film can be assembled in a much swifter and more flexible way: the footage is entirely digitalized and stored in the computer station. Trimming the film is quite inexpensive, since replacing a scene with another, or moving one sequence to a different place, takes a matter of a few minutes and much less labour, and no additional (and costly) film stock has to be used. A film is never really locked until distribution copies are prepared. The consequence is that the composer is never sure that what s/he has been working on is the final cut. The composer may spot one film and tailor her/his music to the footage s/he has carefully measured; then, once the score is ready, s/he may be faced with a different film which the music does not fit as it was supposed to. The best way to survive is to adapt, in a Darwinian way, to the new environment: music that is modular and easily modifiable is the safest choice.

Given the saturated sound mix, the film's potentially ever-changing editing, and the tighter deadlines—and hence the more formulaic approach—promoted by computer-based composition, it is no surprise that elaborate formal writing and old-fashioned symphonic style have little place in today's film music.[19] Large orchestras are still used because they are able to produce a loud and massive sound that, electronically enhanced, can keep up with the level of the sound effects volume and contribute to creating the characteristic aural saturation of the contemporary 'film concert.' But large orchestras are quite rarely employed to deliver symphonic film music.

JOHN WILLIAMS AND CONTEMPORARY HOLLYWOOD

John Williams does not use a computer. His tools are 'antediluvian'[20]: pencils, paper, and a piano. He does not work in a team but he is *the* composer, as in the old days. He writes down his own orchestration in a condensed form on 8–16 staves, which are then *expanded*—not *arranged*—to a full 30–35 stave conductor's score by orchestrators acting as 'intelligent copyists'.[21] In recent cases like *Lincoln* (Steven Spielberg, 2012), *The Book Thief* (Brian Percival, 2013) and *Star Wars—Episode VII*, Williams even orchestrated all the music himself.[22] This work routine takes time and Williams typically needs no less than eight weeks to create a score—often more. He does not prepare mock-ups, but gives the director a foretaste of his in-progress music by playing it himself on a piano. His style is symphonic, his writing is technically complex, harmonically refined, and timbrically nuanced, with substantial use of counterpoint and inner voices, based on clear-cut leitmotivs and their variations and reprise, with precise split-second music/visuals coordination.[23] How come he has not only survived but stayed in the higher ranks in today's apparently incompatible environment? Alongside his innate sense of drama and knack for penning melodies that are instantly recognizable and uncannily fitting for the characters and situations they depict, it is versatility and his talent for absorbing different musical idioms that allowed Williams's career to successfully span over 60 decades of Hollywood history. Williams can write full-orchestra romantic symphonic music, atonal avant-garde, ear-catching songs, hummable marches, jazz from different ages, and even tackle the pop idioms of the day. Regardless of the period, Williams has proven a musical chameleon.

Williams entered the film-music business as a pianist in the Columbia Pictures orchestra, with an already eclectic background mixing band leading, classical music and jazz. Working as an instrumentalist and later as an orchestrator, he had the chance to do his apprenticeship during the last years of the classical period, learning the tricks of the trade from some of the fathers of Hollywood music—Franz Waxman, Alfred Newman, Dimitri Tiomkin, Bernard Herrmann ... His first jobs as a film composer were in television, where he had to learn to write fast, developing a quick instinct for what a film really needed and enough versatility to jump from one film genre to another—one week a Western, the next a thriller, then a comedy ...[24] In the 1960s, as Johnny Williams, he was promoted to the big screen and specialized in comedies, and wrote theme songs too—as required at the time. In 1969 he provided the period film *The Reivers* (Mark Rydell) with the perfect musical background in an Americana Coplandesque idiom, which would be reprised in the classically scored (à la Jerome Morross) Western *The Cowboys* (Mark Rydell, 1972). Yet, in the following year he composed a completely different pop/folk score for the Western *The Man Who Loved Cat Dancing* (Richard C. Sarafian), and would return to the genre again in 1976 with *The Missouri Breaks* (Arthur Penn), featuring a guitar-led restrained score for small ensemble in line with the post-classical Westerns like *The Wild Bunch* (Sam Peckinpah, 1969, music by Jerry Fielding). In the 1970s, Williams was generally typecast as a disaster-movie composer, with a string of films in which he rendered in orchestral settings the pop idioms of the decade—*The Poseidon Adventure* (Ronald Neame, 1972), *Earthquake* (Mark Robson, 1974) and *The Towering Inferno* (John Guillermin, 1974). He also penned one of the most avant-garde American scores ever written for a film—featuring *bruitisme* and aleatoric music—for Robert Altman's *Images* (1972)[25]; a British-sounding pastoral score for *Jane Eyre* (Delbert Mann, 1970) reminiscent of the music of Vaughan Williams; a monothematic score for *The Long Goodbye* (Robert Altman, 1973)—all based on variations on the theme song—while for *Jaws* (Steven Spielberg, 1975) he revived the swashbuckling Korngoldian fanfares for the maritime chase sequences and Herrmann's violent *Psycho* string writings for the shark attacks. With *Star Wars* he became mostly associated with sci-fi/adventure blockbusters scored with 'neoclassical Hollywood music.' While continuing to contribute the 'major' neoclassical scores that have consolidated his reputation—think of *Superman*, the *Star Wars* and *Indiana Jones* sagas, and the first three *Harry Potter* films—he also continued to demonstrate his versatility in a stream of 'minor' scores. In the 1980s he employed synthesizers—in *Heartbeeps* (Allan Arkush, 1981) and *SpaceCamp* (Harry

Winer, 1986) and later in *Presumed Innocent* (Alan Pakula, 1990)—and contemporary pop idioms—*The River* (Mark Rydell, 1984). Depending on the projects, he would put aside his trademark large orchestra and opt for small ensembles and solo instruments, for example the piano in *Accidental Tourist* (Lawrence Kasdan, 1988) and *Stanley and Iris* (Martin Ritt, 1990). Says Sergio Miceli, 'On the opposite side of the spectrum, far from his opulent and seducing scores, Williams is equally effective when he places limits to his music expression, and it is this gift [...] that makes him one of Hollywood music's principal practitioners.'[26] For the remake of *Sabrina* (Sidney Pollack, 1995) he dusted off his song-writing skills by supplementing the piano-led score with two theme songs—'How Can I Remember' and 'Moonlight'—while for *Rosewood* (John Singleton, 1997) he added three *a cappella* spirituals to the Americana folk score. Williams has no problems in absorbing idioms from other musical cultures if the film demands it: for *Seven Years in Tibet* (Jean-Jacques Annaud, 1997) he added Tibetan choirs to the cello and orchestra score; for *Amistad* (Steven Spielberg, 1997) he researched African poetry and selected Bernard Dadié's *Dry Your Tears, Afrika* as the basis for a choral piece with Mende lyrics (the dialect of Sierra Leone) and ethnic percussion patterns; for *The Terminal* (Steven Spielberg, 2004) he composed the main theme, associated with the Eastern European character, in Klezmer idiom; for *Memoirs of a Geisha* (Rob Marshall, 2005) he incorporated the pentatonic scales and traditional instruments of Japanese music, such as the Koto, into the orchestral texture; for *Munich* (Steven Spielberg, 2005) he adopted the idiom of the Middle East, featuring micro-tonal vocalises and the sound of the duduk. Two recent years are particularly emblematic of Williams's versatility: 2002 and 2005. In 2002 he worked on three scores very different from each other: *Star Wars—Episode II: Attack of the Clones* (George Lucas)—in his trademark old-fashioned style; *Harry Potter and the Chamber of Secrets* (Chris Columbus)—showcasing a lively symphonic colourism reminiscent of Russian Impressionism; *Catch Me if You Can* (Steven Spielberg)—in the idiom of 1960s cool jazz. In 2005 he worked on another *Star Wars* episode—*Revenge of the Sith* (George Lucas)—while also working on the Japanese-flavoured *Memoirs of a Geisha*, the Middle Eastern-flavoured *Munich* and *War of the Worlds* (Steven Spielberg, 2005)—a stark, mostly atonal score.

Despite not having retooled to the new computer technology, Williams is knowledgeable enough about the medium's current needs to adapt to the new industrial process. The music in the second *Star Wars* trilogy is stylistically different from the previous one. Prominently, the scores feature fewer memorable melodies—particularly in *Episodes II* and *III*—because a melody requires aural room to be heard in its entirety and then recognized, and contemporary sound mix is too thick to allow space for the same melodic flow and leitmotivic network as in the first trilogy.[27] The orchestration is also less thick and massive—in the first trilogy the middle register was particularly saturated—with more isolated instrumental groupings and timbral effects. If music wishes to find its place in today's highly saturated sound mixes, it has to emerge more timbrally than melodically. If we compare the Korngoldian pirate music for *Hook* (Steven Spielberg, 1991) to that for *The Adventures of Tintin* (Steven Spielberg, 2011) the orchestration of the latter is similarly sparser with fewer inner voices—not exactly Zimmeresque but somewhat closer to *Pirates of the Caribbean* than to the classical Korngold swashbucklers. Williams has always had an acute understanding of the issues of sound design and mix. Commenting on the music accompanying the noisy rolling boulder in the opening sequence of *Raiders of the Lost Ark*, he explained: 'The rumble of the rock in-between wiped out most of the music. [...] My solution was to get up high in the orchestra and use trumpets—I probably had three or four in the London Symphony when we recorded that—and do high repeating notes over and over and over as this rock would go [...] to penetrate the sound effect track as much as I could and to grab the ear of the listener.'[28]

I have previously discussed how contemporary film music has to be modular in order to be easily adapted to last-minute changes in the film editing. In the past, Williams would score action sequences like ballet numbers—think of 'Asteroid Field' from *The Empire Strikes Back* (Irvin Kershner, 1980)—or build a leitmotivic network that created a musical narrative on its own—think of 'The Battle of Yavin' from *Star Wars—Episode IV*. In the new trilogy, battles and action sequences are scored more rhythmically and colouristically than melodically—with the notable use of high- and low-register percussion and high-pitched woodwinds and piccolo lines, capable of piercing the sound-effect wall. Musical pieces with a looser form act more as a background for the clashes of the battle and less as musical compositions on their own: for instance, the opening battle of *Star Wars—Episode III: Revenge of the Sith*. I think the stylistic difference between *Episode I*—melodically richer and more similar to the old trilogy—and the subsequent episodes of the new trilogy has also to do with Williams making his scoring approach more modular to adjust it to the potentially unstable form of the computer-edited films. Probably Williams realized he should opt for a less thematic approach after the *Star Wars—Episode I* misadventure. Lucas decided to change the editing of the final battle after Williams had already spotted and written the music for it, with the result that the composer had to reconfigure the music on the recording stage: 'If I hit the ground running, I can write two minutes of music a day. If I were to have started all over again on the last reel, I would be ready to record in July—with the picture already in the theaters! So I've been making the music fit as we go along. That's why I'm constantly telling the players to drop measures 7 to 14.'[29] With the new *Episode VII*—released in December 2015—Williams has also adapted his working routine to the contemporary practice. Editing and sound/visual effect processing were made in parallel on one chunk of film at a time, not in separate and subsequent steps on the whole film as it used to be: since computers are now the shared platform of all post-production departments, the trend seems to be that of working on all the aspects of the film at the same moment. Reportedly, Williams did not see the whole film in a more-or-less stable rough cut but was given the film piecemeal and composed the music reel by reel, as the other departments passed him the piece they had just completed.[30] Unprecedentedly, Williams worked on the score from December 2014 to November 2015. In the process, he had to modify or completely rewrite almost one hour of the 175-minute long score because, in the meanwhile, the director, J. J. Abrams, would re-edit and make adjustments to the film. As a consequence, the recording phase took place partially in parallel with the composing phase, from June to November. Explains Williams, 'Originally we were going to London, and do it all in the space of two weeks' time, the way we've always done George's (Lucas) films. That would not have worked in this case, because J. J. (Abrams)'s editing process is very different.'[31]

Williams himself singles out versatility as the key factor for a long and successful career in film music: 'When I do a film [...] I'm not thinking about stylistic purity; I'm not thinking about anything but, "Okay, here's a film and my musical job is to construct something that will live within it and seem to be part of it and will sound like the picture looks." [...] If you have only one style of music and do only one thing [...] you're in trouble in the film business. If you want to have a career in films, and do a hundred films, you need to be very versatile.'[32] This is the central point with Williams: his versatility is uniquely balanced by a strong musical personality. Already in his first 1960s works, it can be noted that he had absorbed the then-standard Mancini-like style—ear-catching songs, pop idiom, closed musical numbers instead of Mickey-Mousing—but did not follow it too closely and impersonally; instead, he modified the current style with idioms and techniques from the classical Hollywood music.[33] Williams has an unmatched talent for taking inspiration from the most different sources that are suitable to create the right atmosphere for the film, which nevertheless are not simply plagiarized but assimilated and transformed into something that is clearly by Williams. Igor Stravinsky reportedly said that 'lesser artists borrow; great artists steal'.[34] Borrowing here means a superficial and opportunistic act—I don't have something and I need to borrow it from someone else. Stealing means to take possession of it; it is a more assimilative and personal act. If one appropriates someone else's music, that music becomes part of the composer and is likely to be transformed, personalized by the new owner—if I borrow something I don't have the authority to personalize it, which I have if I steal it and become the new owner. The criticism of those who blame Williams for plagiarizing other composers is based on a misunderstanding: Williams does not secretly borrow but 'patently steal'. This is something he does on purpose and admits candidly: 'A lot of these references are deliberate. They're an attempt to evoke a response in the audience where we want to elicit a certain kind of reaction. Another thing is that, whenever one is involved in writing incidental music—where you have specific backgrounds, specific periods, certain kinds of characters and so on—the work is bound to be derivative in a certain sense. The degree to which you can experiment, as you can in a concert work, is very limited. You're fulfilling more of a role of a *designer* [emphasis mine], in the same way that a set designer would do a design for a period opera.'[35] Williams's idea of the film composer as a 'designer' is a revealing one as it creates a point of convergence with the contemporary 'music design' trend. Though eschewing computer technology and sticking to his old-fashioned modus operandi, Williams has always had a versatile 'designer conception' of the film-music job, which has made him still successful in today's cinema.

Williams is a unique case because, in a career spanning six decades, he has been a bridge between Hollywood's past and present. He took his first steps during the twilight years of the classical-style period; he established his position in the modern-style period; he was a major player in the launch of the eclectic-style period; he has continued to be an active voice in the contemporary music-design style. Williams has artistically survived so long because he has managed to bridge film music's present and film music's past like no other, keeping passionate and curious enough about films to adapt to the new trends while retaining a strong authorial mark. One of the most outstanding traits of said authorial mark is Williams's talent for writing themes, which is investigated in the following chapter.

NOTES

1. Emilio Audissino, *John Williams's Film Music. 'Jaws,' 'Star Wars,' 'Raiders of the Lost Ark,' and the Return of the Classical Hollywood Music Style* (Madison, WI: University of Wisconsin Press, 2014), 121–2.
2. James Wierzbicki, *Film Music. A History* (New York-London: Routledge, 2009), 209–27.
3. Audissino, *John Williams's Film Music*, 9–85.
4. The terms 'orchestral' and 'symphonic' are not synonyms. 'Orchestral' refers to the instrumentation of a piece of music, i.e. an orchestra—more or less conforming to the traditional settings of a symphony orchestra (woodwinds, brass, percussions, strings in five groupings, etc.)—is employed to play the music. 'Symphonic' refers to the writing style of a piece of music: the instrumental sections in the orchestra (woodwinds, brass, percussions, strings) are engaged in contrapuntal, harmonic, and timbral interplay with each other and, within each section, with other instruments of the same section (e.g. a dialogue between oboes and bassoons). The two terms should not be confused, as a piece that is orchestral is not necessarily symphonic (for example, we can have swing music arranged for orchestra) and, even if much rarer, a piece can have a symphonic nature without being orchestral (e.g. some Erich Wolfgang Korngold piano music, in which symphonic dynamics and even timbres can be perceived).
5. My panorama of contemporary Hollywood music might appear too Manichean and lacking nuances, maybe even simplistic—for example, there are still composers using more traditional methods and having less mainstream personal voices. Yet, my scope here is not intended to provide a thorough treatise on contemporary Hollywood music but to bring to the forefront those dominant elements that serve as comparison terms with Williams's approach.

6. The year 2000 is also chosen as a landmark in James Buhler and David Neumeyer, *Hearing the Movies. Music and Sound in Film History*, 2nd ed. (Oxford-New York: Oxford University Press, 2015): 'Chapter 13: Music and Film Sound since 2000' and 'Chapter 14: Music and Film Form Since 2000'.
7. Anon., 'Media Ventures. Where Studios and Composers Meet All under One Roof!' *Studio Expresso*, 2002, http://www.studioexpresso.com/Spotlight%20Archive/Spotlight-Media%20Venture.htm, accessed 15 July 2015.
8. Jon Burlingame, 'Remote Control Prods.: Hans Zimmer's Music Factory as a Breeding Ground', *Variety*, 6 May 2014, http://variety.com/2014/music/news/remote-control-prods-music-factory-as-breeding-ground-1201173763/, accessed 15 July 2015.
9. For a description of music departments in classical Hollywood, see Fred Karlin, *Listening to Movies. The Film Lover's Guide to Film Music* (Belmont CA: Schirmer, 1994), 177–195.
10. http://www.cineconcerts.com, accessed 5 November 2015.
11. Jon Burlingame, 'Live Concerts a Cash Cow for Orchestras', *Variety*, 28 April 2015, http://variety.com/2015/music/features/live-movie-concerts-a-cash-cow-for-orchestras-1201483456, accessed 5 November 2015.
12. Laurent Jullier, *L'écran post-moderne. Un cinéma de l'allusion e du feu d'artifice* (Paris: L'Harmattan, 1997), Italian trans. Carla Capetta, *Il cinema postmoderno* (Torino: Kaplan, 2006), 37.
13. Michel Chion, *L'audio-vision. Son et image au cinéma* (Paris: Nathan, 1990), English trans./ed. Claudia Gorbman, *Audio-Vision* (New York: Columbia University Press, 1994), 73.
14. *Star Wars—Episode III: Revenge of the Sith* (George Lucas, 2005) had as many as 200 audio tracks. Ben Burtt in *Within a Minute. The Making of 'Episode III'*, documentary by Tippy Bushkin, Lucasfilm 2005, in *Star Wars Episode III: Revenge of the Sith*, DVD, 20th Century Fox Home Entertainment, 2005, F4-SITSSE 29309DE.
15. Two recent practice-oriented books are David Sonnenschein, *Sound Design: The Expressive Power of Music, Voice and Sound Effects in Cinema* (Studio City, CA: Michael Wiese Productions, 2001) and, more technical and detailed, Andy Farnell, *Designing Sound* (Cambridge, MA: MIT Press, 2010).

16. In his keynote speech at the 2014 Music and the Moving Image Conference in New York, composer/orchestrator Patrick Russ made it very clear that a knowledge of MIDI and computer technology is a must for film composers today: Patrick Russ, 'The Changing Face of Orchestration for the Moving Image', keynote presentation, Music and the Moving Image IX Conference, 30 May 2014, NYU Steinhardt, New York. On the contemporary film-music business see Jeremy Borum, *Guerrilla Film Scoring. Practical Advice from Hollywood Composers* (Lanham, MD: Rowman & Littlefield, 2015), ix–xix in particular.
17. Karlin, *Listening to Movies*, 200–1.
18. Jeff Bond, 'Horner Revealed', *Film Score Monthly*, February 2004, 20.
19. A very recent example that stresses how the dominant trend is orchestral but not symphonic is the third trailer for *Star Wars—Episode VII: The Force Awakens* (J. J. Abrams, 2015). It features some of Williams's canonical themes arranged into a more contemporary sound: 'Maximum volume and density at all times appears to be the desired impact, at the pronounced expense of orchestrational clarity. Far more in-line with practices of Hans Zimmer and his epigones than of the original model of Golden Age Hollywood, trailer three sounds assertively and symptomatically "contemporary." Observe the electronically overproduced textures, the crashing drums, the musicalized (mostly synthetic) sound effects. For better or worse, here, the *Star Wars* musical idiom is for once not pure symphonic throwback' (Frank Lehman, 'Trailers, Tonality, and the Force of Nostalgia', *Musicology Now*, online, 4 November 2015, http://musicologynow.ams-net.org/2015/11/trailers-tonality-and-force-of-nostalgia.html, accessed 5 November 2015). Trailers, of course, are designed to attract the largest possible audience by catering for the current tastes: if producers felt that the sound of the *Star Wars* music had to be updated for the final trailer, this is, I think, a meaningful enough sign that symphonic film music is hardly considered fashionable today.
20. John Williams calls himself 'antediluvian' in an interview by Brian Williams, 'Rock Center', NBC, 26 July 2012, http://www.nbcnews.com/video/rock-center/48347279, accessed 15 July 2015.
21. Lawrence Morton in James Wierzbicki, Nathan Platte, Colin Roust, eds, *The Routledge Film Music Sourcebook* (Oxon-New York: Routledge, 2012), 134.

22. Unlike other projects, there are no orchestrators credited for *Lincoln* and *The Book Thief*, and Conrad Pope—who orchestrated the second trilogy—confirmed that Williams was personally orchestrating *Star Wars—Episode VII*: Conrad Pope, Facebook post, 6 June 2015, https://www.facebook.com/conrad.pope, accessed 5 November 2015.
23. John Williams's style and modus operandi is examined in Audissino, *John Williams's Film Music*, 122–33.
24. Ibid., 87–9.
25. See Royal S. Brown, *Overtones and Undertones. Reading Film Music* (Berkeley, CA: University of California Press, 1994), 178–9.
26. Sergio Miceli, *Musica per film. Storia, Estetica, Analisi, Tipologie* (Lucca-Milan: LIM-Ricordi, 2009), 250, translated from Italian.
27. Williams adapted 30-minute concert suites from each film of the classic trilogy and a 15-minute concert suite from *Star Wars—Episode I* but no concert suite at all from either *Episode II* or *Episode III*, which is a sign of the less-melodic nature of the latter two.
28. John Williams interviewed by Gene Shalit in *Evening at Pops*, WGBH/Boston Symphony Orchestra, episode # 2105, 1997 (WGBH Archives, Boston, MA, USA).
29. Richard Dyer, 'Making *Star Wars* Sing again', *The Boston Globe*, 28 March 1999, reprinted in *Film Score Monthly*, June 1999, 18–19.
30. Anon., 'Back to a Galaxy Far, Far Away', *International Musician Magazine*, June 2015, 16–17.
31. Jon Burlingame, 'Film Score Icons Williams, Morricone and Horner Loom Large in Oscar Race', *Variety*, 9 December 2015, online, http://variety.com/2015/music/awards/oscar-icons-williams-morricone-and-horner-loom-large-in-score-race-1201657637, accessed 10 December 2015.
32. David Vernier, 'Magnificent Modern Maestro', *Digital Audio*, March 1988.
33. Audissino, *John Williams's Film Music*, 91–103.
34. The attribution of this quote to Stravinsky is shaky as it is equally attributed to Picasso and T. S. Eliot.
35. Kenneth Terry, 'John Williams Encounters the Pops', *Downbeat*, March 1981, 21.

Bibliography

Anon. 1997. *Evening at Pops*, WGBH/Boston Symphony Orchestra, TV show, episode # 2105. WGBH Archives, Boston MA, U.S.A.

———. 2002. Media Ventures. Where Studios and Composers Meet All under One Roof! *Studio Expresso*, online, http://www.studioexpresso.com/Spotlight%20Archive/Spotlight-Media%20Venture.htm. Accessed 15 July 2015.

———. 2015. Back to a Galaxy Far, Far Away. *International Musician Magazine*, June, online. Accessed 5 December 2015.

Audissino, Emilio. 2014. *John Williams's Film Music. 'Jaws,' 'Star Wars,' 'Raiders of the Lost Ark,' and the Return of the Classical Hollywood Music Style*. Madison, WI: University of Wisconsin Press.

Borum, Jeremy. 2015. *Guerrilla Film Scoring. Practical Advice from Hollywood Composers*. Lanham, MD: Rowman & Littlefield.

Brown, Royal S. 1994. *Overtones and Undertones. Reading Film Music*. Berkeley, CA: University of California Press.

Buhler, James, and David Neumeyer. 2015. *Hearing the Movies. Music and Sound in Film History*. 2nd ed. Oxford and New York: Oxford University Press.

Burlingame, Jon. 2014. Remote Control Prods: Hans Zimmer's Music Factory as a Breeding Ground. *Variety*, 6 May. Online. http://variety.com/2014/music/news/remote-control-prods-music-factory-as-breeding-ground-1201173763/. Accessed 15 July 2015.

———. 2015a. Film Score Icons Williams, Morricone and Horner Loom Large in Oscar Race. *Variety*, 9 December, online, http://variety.com/2015/music/awards/oscar-icons-williams-morricone-and-horner-loom-large-in-score-race-1201657637. Accessed 10 December 2015.

———. 2015b. Live Concerts a Cash Cow for Orchestras. *Variety*, 28 April. Online. http://variety.com/2015/music/features/live-movie-concerts-a-cash-cow-for-orchestras-1201483456. Accessed 5 November 2015.

Chion, Michel. 1990. *L'audio-vision. Son et image au cinéma*. Paris: Nathan. English trans. and ed. Claudia Gorbman, *Audio-Vision*. New York: Columbia University Press, 1994.

Dyer, Richard. 1999. Making *Star Wars* Sing again. *The Boston Globe*, 28 March. Reprinted in *Film Score Monthly*, June 1999, 18–19.

Farnell, Andy. 2010. *Designing Sound*. Cambridge MA: MIT Press.

Jullier, Laurent. 1997. *L'écran post-moderne. Un cinéma de l'allusion e du feu d'artifice*. Paris: L'Harmattan.

Karlin, Fred. 1994. *Listening to Movies. The Film Lover's Guide to Film Music*. Belmont, CA: Schirmer.

Lehman, Frank. 2015. Trailers, Tonality, and the Force of Nostalgia. *Musicology Now*, online, 4 November. http://musicologynow.ams-net.org/2015/11/trailers-tonality-and-force-of-nostalgia.html. Accessed 5 November 2015.

Miceli, Sergio. 2009. *Musica per Film. Storia, Estetica, Analisi, Tipologie*. Lucca-Milan: LIM-Ricordi.
Sonnenschein, David. 2001. *Sound Design: The Expressive Power of Music, Voice and Sound Effects in Cinema*. Studio City CA: Michael Wiese Productions.
Terry, Kenneth. 1981. John Williams Encounters the Pops. *Downbeat*, March 21.
Vernier, David. 1988. Magnificent Modern Maestro. *Digital Audio*, March.
Wierzbicki, James. 2009. *Film Music. A History*. New York and London: Routledge.
Wierzbicki, James, Nathan Platte, and Colin Roust, ed. 2012. *The Routledge Film Music Sourcebook*. Oxon-New York: Routledge.
Williams, Brian. 2012. Rock Center: Interview with John Williams. NBC, 26 July, TV show. Online. http://www.nbcnews.com/video/rock-center/48347279. Accessed 15 July 2015.

CHAPTER 15

Musical Syntax in John Williams's Film Music Themes

Konstantinos Zacharopoulos

In their book *Composing for the Films* Theodor Adorno and Hanns Eisler question the usability, in film music, of the forms which were developed and became part of the theoretical framework of Western-European musical tradition.[1] Although referring to higher-level forms that are beyond the scope of my analysis here, what Adorno and Eisler claimed poses some questions as regards the significance of the organization of smaller structures—particularly of the themes themselves—and the importance a composer gives to their syntax.

This chapter is an abridgement of a chapter from my forthcoming doctoral dissertation (Konstantinos Zacharopoulos, 'The Film Music of John Williams (1975–2015)', University of Athens, Ph.D. diss., forthcoming). In the dissertation, I analyse 4–10 themes of each type, thus trying to consider many possible deviations from the most characteristic stereotypes, while in this essay the discussion is limited to one or two of the most typical themes of each type. Furthermore, an effort has been made to omit most technical harmonic references for reasons of brevity, as well as to make the text more comprehensible. The text was translated from Greek into English by Athanasia Agistriotou.

K. Zacharopoulos (✉)
Department of Music Studies, National and Kapodistrian University of Athens, Athens, Greece

© The Author(s) 2017
L. Coleman, J. Tillman (eds.), *Contemporary Film Music*,
DOI 10.1057/978-1-137-57375-9_15

To paraphrase Nicholas Cook's definition of what constitutes a theme in music, in film music the term refers to a 'readily recognizable musical element' which serves a dramatic (and not formal) function,[2] which can consist of a few notes (motif) or be a fully developed melody.[3] The narrative role, as well as the descriptive function carried out by musical themes, is also recognized by Gorbman, since themes function as signals associated with a particular character, locale, situation, emotion, etc.[4] While the dramaturgical implications of themes in film music have often been discussed, the absence of a thorough musicological study of them (and particularly of their syntactic structure) is quite noticeable.[5] Adorno and Eisler suggest that 'principal themes, transitions, secondary themes, closing themes, or thematic resolutions, should be liberated from the formal pattern and made independent',[6] while elsewhere they mention that 'in short musical forms, each element must be self-sufficient or capable of rapid expansion'.[7] If we wish to identify two types of formal lower-level constructions in what Adorno and Eisler are describing, the most appropriate are the period and the sentence, two of the most important theme-types[8] of classical instrumental music.

It may seem uncommon for a film composer, in the second half of the twentieth century, to resort to these traditional types from the classical music period. However, it must be noted that such types, whether intact or varied and developed, were combined with an expanded harmonic language and already used by such composers as Bartók, Prokofiev or even Debussy, among many others, mainly in the neoclassical period.[9] Williams himself has often expressed his admiration for the masters of classicism: 'I can study the finale of (Mozart's) "Jupiter" Symphony with the greatest pleasure, a lot more pleasure than studying "What Next," the Elliott Carter opera',[10] while elsewhere he mentions that 'Haydn is "one of the all-time great musical talents" [...] Without Haydn, we probably wouldn't have Mozart or Beethoven'.[11] We are also informed that his favourite bedtime reading is a score of Beethoven sonatas that 'reads like a novel!'[12] The love he shows for the classical period undeniably reflects in the syntax of most of his themes: repetitions, symmetry and metrical clarity, as well as the boundaries and grouping of phrases are among his dominant traits. Nevertheless, it must be pointed out that this association with tradition does not constitute a sheer imitation of the microstructures of the past but their smooth integration into Williams's harmonic thinking as well as into his general style, which is accompanied by their simultaneous evolution and development into embellished mature forms, as will be indicated below.

The sentence and the period have undergone an in-depth analysis in the theoretical works of Arnold Schönberg (1874–1951),[13] his pupil Erwin Ratz (1898–1973),[14] and more recently in William Earl Caplin's (b. 1948) monograph *Classical Form*.[15] The following syntactic analysis of Williams's themes is based primarily on the simple types suggested by Caplin (in a less strict manner), while some varied and singular forms of the sentence, which are updated versions of the classical archetypes and also appear in several Williams themes, stem from those studied in more recent musicological research by such theorists as Matthew BaileyShea[16] and Mark Richards.[17]

Sentence

The sentence is regarded by Schönberg as a 'higher form of construction than the period. It not only makes a statement of an idea, but at once starts a kind of development'.[18] As BaileyShea remarks, it may be the only form in the history of Western music theory that has been associated with, and determined by, a unique *locus classicus:* the opening theme of the first movement of Beethoven's Piano Sonata in F minor, op. 2 no. 1.[19] This eight-measure theme perfectly expresses the form of the sentence, which belongs to a set of tight-knit themes, and demonstrates all the typical elements that define it: the statement of a basic idea,[20] its repetition and development through specific procedures leading to the final cadence.[21]

If Beethoven's theme constitutes a model of this lower-level form, then I think that the corresponding original model in John Williams's film themes could be the 'Main Theme'[22] from *Superman* (Richard Donner, 1978) (Fig. 15.1)[23], which follows all the standards of a typical sentence.

The theme starts vigorously with a two-measure distinctive basic idea played on the trumpets (mm. 19–20) that is repeated slightly varied in the next two measures (mm. 21–2). The four-measure phrase which is created in this way, and is supported harmonically throughout by a prolonged tonic chord,[24] constitutes the *presentation* of the sentence. Here lies the fundamental melodic-motivic content of the theme, which is established through the repetition of the basic idea within a stable harmonic environment. The *continuation* of the sentence follows shortly afterwards

Fig. 15.1 'Main Theme' from *Superman*. Adapted from 'Superman March' from *Superman* (mm. 19–26), © 1978 Warner-Tamerlane Publishing Corp, Hal Leonard Signature Edition, 04490228

through a structural fragmentation. This means that while the first part of the theme initially consists of two-measure groups, now the structure breaks down in one-measure units (mm. 23 and 24), leading, through an acceleration of harmonic rhythm, to the perfect authentic cadence at mm. 25–6. The *continuation* of the sentence constitutes the development to which Schönberg refers, since in a way it 'develops' and elaborates the material stated in the initial *presentation*.[25]

This eight-measure theme is constructed as follows: (2 + 2) + 4 measures. This means that there is a perfect balance and symmetry between its two main parts: the *presentation*, which features the statement of a basic idea and its repetition (2 + 2 mm.) and the *continuation* of the sentence (4 mm.), thus defining the above-mentioned type as an ideal expression of the sentence.

Another element worth noticing is this: the *continuation* itself is articulated as a 'mini-sentence' in a sublevel. In other words, in m. 23 there is a subordinate basic idea, which is repeated in the following measure, and then develops and ends in m. 26, forming the structure 1 + 1 + 2 (mm. 23–6). This embedded micro-sentence in the *continuation*, a phenomenon for which BaileyShea proposes a distinct type,[26] results in a more stable structure since the basic organizational features of the whole form are also reflected in a part of it (in its *continuation*).[27]

Period

Theorists seem to disagree on how frequently the period occurs in classical themes. Schönberg mentions that the period occurs only at a small percentage with romantic composers using it even more rarely,[28] whereas Caplin considers this lower-level form the 'most common tight-knit theme-type in instrumental music of the classical style'.[29] It is evident from the study of John Williams's themes that the period holds a prominent position as a type of structural organization, since the number of periods is almost three times the number of sentences.[30] The simple type period consists of two four-measure phrases (like the sentence): the first four-measure phrase, the *antecedent*, begins with a two-measure basic idea followed by a two-measure contrasting idea ending with a weak cadence; the second phrase, the *consequent*, repeats the *antecedent* with a modification of the contrasting idea (usually), or with a new thematic content, leading to a strong cadence at the end of the theme (perfect or, less frequently, imperfect).[31] Thus, a more 'closed' form is created, compared with the 'open' sentence, which has a developing nature that causes its openness.

The 'Remembrances Theme' from *Schindler's List* (Steven Spielberg, 1993) (Fig. 15.2) corresponds to a typical eight-measure period which is divided into two same-sized parts (despite the frequent shift of the meter between 3/4 and 4/4). The *antecedent* begins with a lyric two-measure basic idea, followed by a contrasting idea, and closes with a half cadence;

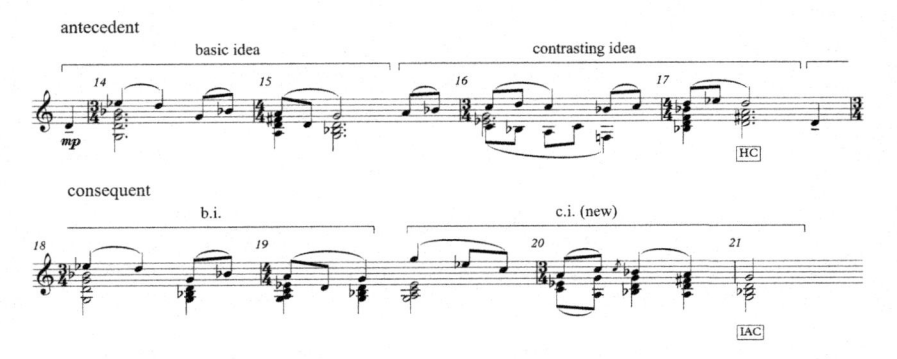

Fig. 15.2 'Remembrances Theme' from *Schindler's List*. Adapted from 'Three Pieces from *Schindler's List*, Remembrances' (mm. 14–21), © 1993 by Music Corporation of America Inc., Hal Leonard Signature Edition, 04490011

while the *consequent* repeats the initial idea and ends with a new contrasting idea with an imperfect authentic cadence.

The contrasting idea in a period is one of the vital differences that distinguish this form from the sentence. The second two-measure unit of a theme is of decisive importance because it tells us if what follows is a sentence or a period. However, the extent to which this second idea contrasts with the initial one differs in a number of themes, and can often create wrong perceptions, or anticipations about their subsequent course.

For example, in many cases, and specifically in Williams's themes, the contrasting idea bears a striking resemblance to the basic idea (usually in its opening). As a result, it may be misinterpreted as its repetition. However, the different harmony that supports it, as well as the return to the initial idea in the *consequent*, makes things clear,[32] and helps identify such themes as periods.[33] The 'Basket Game Theme' from *Raiders of the Lost Ark* (Steven Spielberg, 1981) (Fig. 15.3) is a typical instance of the aforementioned type of period: mm. 5–6 are almost a duplication of mm. 3–4,[34] giving at first the impression of a sentence in the making; nevertheless, the following mm. 7–8 correct this false impression since they constitute the actual repetition of the initial two measures. The theme ends with another two-measure unit (mm. 9–10), which seemingly restates the same basic idea, but later employs new motives of sixteenths, leading

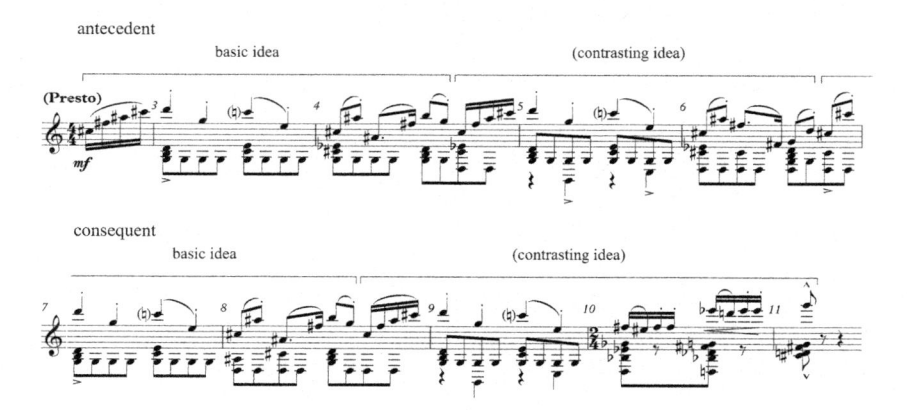

Fig. 15.3 'Basket Game Theme' from *Raiders of the Lost Ark*. Adapted from '*Raiders of the Lost Ark*, The Basket Game' (Excerpt) (mm. 3–11), © 1981 Bantha Music and Ensign Music Corporation (in the piano folio the final bar is 10, but in the handwritten score it's 11 due to the time signature change)

to a conclusion in m. 11. In this case the harmonic factor alone wouldn't be enough to clarify the confusion, because in all three ideas the chord progression remains about the same.[35]

The sentence is 'an extraordinarily malleable form; its very nature defies strict definition. Few themes are designed with the tightness of the Beethoven model, but there are countless passages that fall under the general umbrella term "sentential".'[36] The unambiguous definition given by Caplin has raised a major problem for the next theorists, about the applicability of this inflexible and narrowing type in a wider sense on themes that seem to present some of the characteristics of the sentence. Although most of Williams's themes can be interpreted, more or less, according to the lower-level forms suggested by Caplin (often differing from his view of harmony as the determinant of form),[37] there are several themes that reveal the inefficiency of the 'Caplin models'. In his dissertation, BaileyShea expands the model of the sentence in Wagner's music, with 'Wagnerian Satz' determined more by motivic factors than harmonic.[38] Eventually, in a later article, he comes to the conclusion that the sentence is best understood as a twofold form, which is divided into the *presentation phrase* (marked by the repetition of the basic idea, decisive for defining the theme as a sentence) and the *continuation phrase* (which corresponds to Caplin's definition but without any harmonic restrictions).[39] On the contrary, Richards claims that 'the defining feature of a sentence is a continuation that accelerates motivic, harmonic, or rhythmic material in relation to the basic idea'.[40] In this light, the presentation can contain one, two, three and more statements of the basic idea. Combining the views of these two theorists, I have noticed that the types suggested provide an appropriate theoretical background on which a considerable number of Williams's themes with a sentential quality are based, and facilitate the task of interpretation and grouping of the themes in question. The novelty of these types does not lie so much in new conceptual definitions (since they have already been alluded to in Caplin's work) as in that they offer an organized theoretical framework and are now recognized as self-sufficient types which can also be applied beyond the classical period.

Trifold Sentence

Although the definition of the *presentation* in a sentence involves the statement of the basic idea and its repetition, it is not uncommon to have a third statement of this idea. The 'trifold sentence', as defined by

Richards,[41] does not present anything innovative or strange, since Caplin has already noticed an additional repetition of the basic idea in some classical (mainly subordinate) themes as a means of loosening the sentence structure.[42] However, the fact that this form has evolved into an independent structure that can be found in different parts of a higher-level form, particularly when it extends up to the eight measures of the tightly knit typical sentence, constitutes a new foundation on which we can reinterpret many themes without seeing them as exceptions or 'distorted forms of the bifold type'.[43] An important element of this type, as we shall see, is that every restatement of the basic idea, particularly its last one, departs further from the original, whether harmonically or motivically.[44] In this type, the *continuation* features one or more typical characteristics, also featured in the simple sentence (namely fragmentation, harmonic acceleration, cadence, etc.).

An example of this form is the 'Main Theme' from *Presumed Innocent* (Alan J. Pakula, 1990) (Fig. 15.4), which extends to four two-measure phrases. The basic idea is stated in the opening two measures (mm. 9–10); it's a descending Dorian-type melody supported harmonically by a I[7]–III progression, which lies on a stepping bass line moving in an opposite

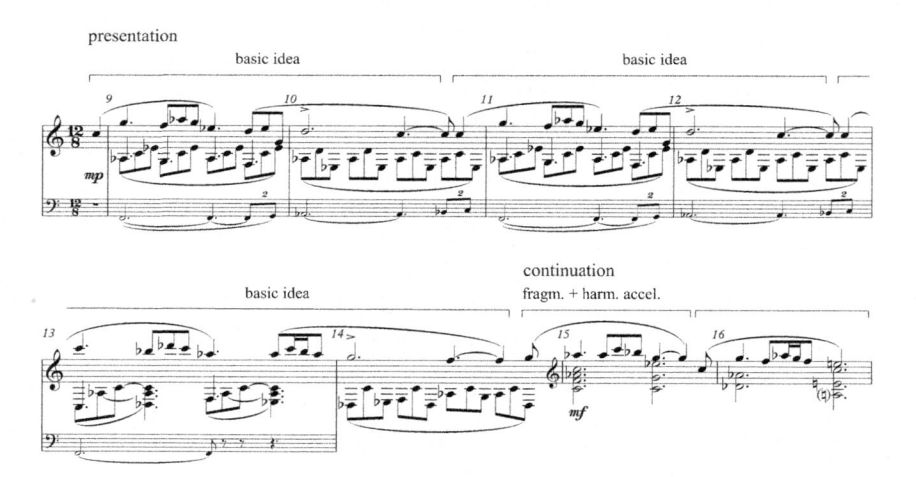

Fig. 15.4 'Main Theme' from *Presumed Innocent*. Adapted from John Williams 'Anthology, Remembering Carolyn (A Theme from "Presumed Innocent")' (mm. 9–16), © 1990 Warner-Tamerlane Publishing Corp, © 1991 Warner-Bros Publications Inc. VF1774

direction. This idea is repeated unchanged in mm. 11–2, while in the following two measures (mm. 13–4) there is a second restatement (or a third appearance), this time a fourth-interval higher with an Aeolian colour and slightly varied, ending on the submediant chord. The concluding two-measure phrase (mm. 15–6) leads to the final cadence (to an unexpected raised mediant chord [A minor]), and at the same time it shows fragmentation of the initial idea, as well as harmonic acceleration, thus constituting a typical—but compressed—*continuation* that follows an initial six-measure *presentation* (mm. 9–14).[45] This eight-measure theme, then, is built like this: (2 + 2 + 2) + 2 measures. This asymmetry, in favour of the *presentation* of the thematic content, is typical of those Williams themes that are stated as a trifold sentence. Furthermore, a greater thematic clarity emerges—due to repetitions—compared with simple sentences, since the three statements of the basic idea impress the fundamental motives more strongly in the listener's memory and, in my opinion,[46] thus create a tightly knit theme.

Sentence with a Dissolving Third Statement

Caplin mentions that, frequently, 'the continuation starts as though it were going to restate the entire basic idea for a third time, but before reaching its conclusion, the idea leads into new material that effects the fragmentation'.[47] After all, according to Schönberg, the continuation of a sentence includes procedures that gradually eliminate some characteristics of the basic idea (liquidation), so that the theme can reach its conclusion, and not an 'unlimited extension'.[48] BaileyShea identifies this type of sentence, in which the continuation begins with the basic idea again, but abandons it before its conclusion, as a special type that he calls 'sentence with a dissolving third statement'.[49] Given that this form is used very often by Williams, it is necessary to refer to it as a particular kind of construction, which could be considered the precursor of the trifold type.

I believe that 'Yoda's Theme' from *The Empire Strikes Back* (Irvin Kershner, 1980) (Fig. 15.5) is an excellent representation of this form. The basic idea (mm. 3–4) (with the tenor voice conveying the melody) is repeated with flourishes in the next two measures (mm. 5–6), supported in both its appearances by an shift between tonic and Lydian supertonic triads moving on a tonic pedal. While m. 7 leads us to anticipate that a second restatement is about to follow, m. 8 interrupts such a course because it sequentially repeats the previous motif (depicting a fragmentation of

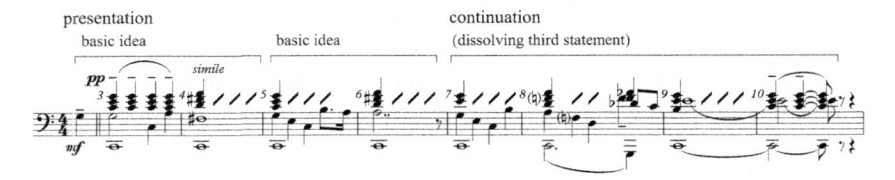

Fig. 15.5 'Yoda's Theme' from *The Empire Strikes Back*. Adapted from '*Star Wars* Suite for Orchestra, IV. Yoda's Theme' (mm. 3–10), © 1980 Warner-Tamerlane Publishing Corp & Bantha Music, Hal Leonard Signature Edition, 04490057

the basic motivic content) and leads to the final cadence. Therefore, what seems to be the third statement of the basic idea (m. 7) is liquidated from the following measure onwards and constitutes the beginning of the continuation of this sentential type, which in this case retains the symmetry of the tightly knit eight-measure sentence: (2 + 2) + (1 + 1 + 2) mm.

Unfolding Sentence

A rare type of sentence encountered in Williams's work, but distinctive enough to be mentioned here, is based on the use of the basic idea as the exclusive building block. In other words, there are successive repetitions of this idea, which is rearranged and altered (mainly regarding its harmonic and intervallic aspects), thus creating the overall impression of a sentence type. For this form, which can be represented as a1-a1-a2-a3 or a1-a2-a3-a4—or using 'a' (representing the basic idea) in any other possible combination[50]—I adopt the term *unfolding sentence*, because the main thematic gesture unfolds and develops as it is stated. After all, this strong structure could be considered the most tightly knit compared to the previous types, since it lacks a new or contrasting content, fragmentation, liquidation or an increase in surface rhythm activity.

This structural model is found in 'Irish Theme' from *Far and Away* (Ron Howard, 1992) (Fig. 15.6): the basic idea[51] is outlined in the first six measures (mm. 5–10) on a tonic pedal, while in mm. 11–6 it is exactly repeated melodically and harmonically, coloured with a Dorian character cadence at the end. The third stated idea (mm. 17–22) is a varied version of the basic idea: the rhythmic patterns remain the same. However, despite the melody following an opposite direction only at the beginning,[52] it rests on A and D notes (mm. 18 and 21) as it did in mm. 6 and 9, but this time transposed an octave up. The special element in this embodiment

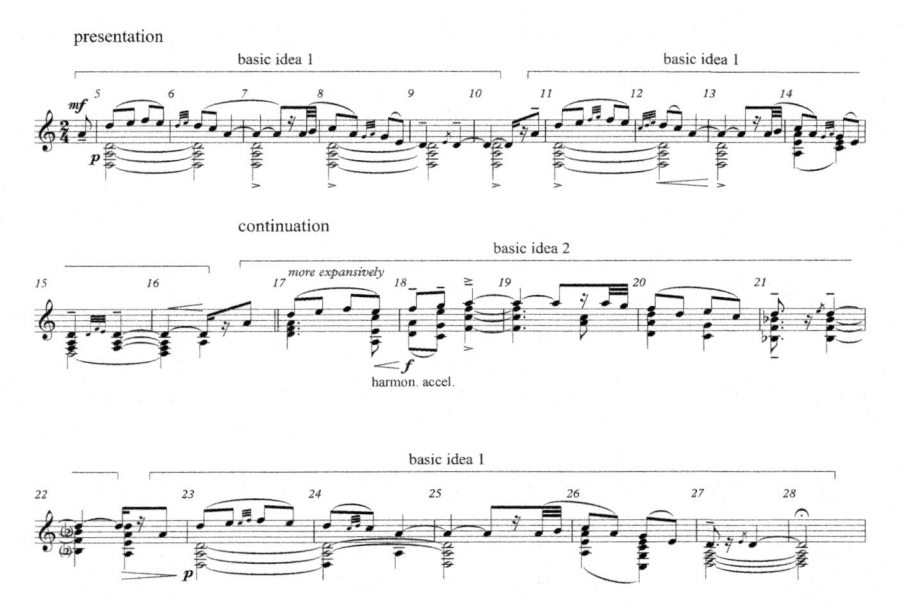

Fig. 15.6 'Irish Theme' from *Far and Away*. Adapted from 'Suite from *Far and Away*' (mm. 5–28), © 1992 Songs of Universal Inc., Hal Leonard Signature Edition, 04490190

of the basic idea is a more energetic harmony supporting it with a quick shift, resulting in an Aeolian submediant chord (m. 21) through stepwise chords, and moving away from the tonic. Eventually, the theme ends with a fourth statement of the basic idea (mm. 23–8), which takes on a function of return and corresponds melodically and harmonically with mm. 11–6. So, the pattern now becomes as follows: a1-a1-a2-a1 (6 + 6 + 6 + 6 measures). How, can the borderline between *presentation* and *continuation* be detected? The harmonic acceleration appearing from measure 17 onwards, as well as the obvious grouping of the first two similar six-measure phrases, is a decisive factor that indicates their point of intersection, as shown in the example.

The study of the syntactic forms found in Williams's themes can be summed up in the following table (Table 15.1). It is a summary of their recurrence in Williams's film scores between 1975 and 2013.[53]

The analysis of the table and the percentage (in brackets) proves beyond doubt that the two main forms of the classical era, namely the sentence (including its different types) and the period, hold a prominent position

Table 15.1 Syntactic forms in John Williams's themes from 66 films (1975–2013)

Sentence	Basic form	44 (12,9%)	107 (31,38%)
	With dissolving third statement	38 (11,15%)	
	Trifold	18 (5,28%)	
	Unfolding	7 (2,05%)	
Period			131 (38,42%)
Other forms (hybrid, small binary, incomplete sentence/ period, etc.)			103 (30,2%)
Total number of themes			**341** (100%)

in the composer's thematic output. This is hardly surprising since these forms contain, and are characterized by, all those elements that, according to Schönberg, contribute to a transparent and intelligible presentation[54] of the musical idea, which leads inevitably to memorability: 'evenness, regularity, symmetry, subdivision, repetition, unity, relationship in rhythm and harmony and even logic'.[55] Williams himself recognizes the importance of memorability in film music and its subsidiary role in the structural unity and functionality of a complete film score.[56]

A second element revealed by the figures in the table is the comparative prevalence of the period over the sentence.[57] There is a practical explanation: the often relentless action and the fast-paced editing in mainstream films typically leave little room for musical themes to be stated completely. A complete statement of a musical theme takes more than a few seconds, so very often only one part of the theme is used, usually the first half.[58] In this particular case, if we compare the first half of a sentence (the *presentation*) with the first half of a period (the *antecedent*), we notice a greater sense of 'completeness' in the *antecedent*, due to the contrasting idea and its final cadence.[59] Consequently, the periods enable the composer to use more complete thematic units as tools for building his music.

A further observation on the different types of the sentence is that the frequency of their occurrence is inversely proportional to the times the basic idea appears in the sentence. In other words, out of 107 sentences, the typical form (which contains two occurrences of the basic idea) can be found in 44 themes, the dissolving third statement type (containing the basic idea a bit more than two or, more rarely, three times) in 38 and so on. When we come to the unfolding sentence with four or more statements of the basic idea, it occurs only in seven themes. Moreover, on the one hand, the repetitions of an idea contribute to the above-mentioned memorability; on the other hand, they risk sounding like a recycling of the motivic content[60] and result in a lack of contrast—contrast is what produces musical variety.[61] In any case, these special sentence forms do not occur in the main themes very often, but mostly in secondary ones or those appearing only once in a film.[62]

Conclusion

I have described and exemplified some of the most important syntactic forms found in John Williams's film music themes. The sentence and the period, at the basis of my approach and derived from classical models, were adopted by Williams as the two main forms of low-level structural organization because they seemed appropriate to capturing the thematic content of his musical language. The 'basic idea', which is the core of these structural models in a dynamic way, through repetition, variation and contrast, is used as the fundamental building block of the theme. I would like to point out that, although the majority of these themes can undoubtedly be classified under these particular types (in the framework of the theoretical system I have adopted), there are still some others that raise interpretive issues. Therefore, the numerical data above are to a small extent subjective, since some themes may also correspond to a different structural model in another researcher's point of view.[63] Despite potential divergent views about this classification, these results have nevertheless spotted and highlighted some considerable syntactic recurrences in Williams's way of constructing his themes. The musicological survey of these lower-level models is only a short introduction to the larger issue of thematic structure in Williams's music and can hopefully trigger a more systematic study of the work of this seminal composer.

Notes

1. Theodor Adorno and Hanns Eisler, *Composing for the Films* (London: The Athlone Press, 1994), 92–3.
2. Nicholas Cook, *A Guide to Musical Analysis* (Oxford: Oxford University Press, 1994), 9.
3. Fred Karlin, *Listening to Movies: The Film Lover's Guide to Film Music* (Belmont, CA: Schirmer, 1994), 26.
4. Claudia Gorbman, *Unheard Melodies* (Bloomington, IN: Indiana University Press, 1987), 27.
5. Moving in this direction, Mark Richards has recently adopted a detailed methodology for the syntactical analysis of a wide range of themes—a wide range both chronologically and stylistically—by

various film composers. See Mark Richards, 'Film Music Themes: Analysis and Corpus Study', *Music Theory Online*, 22: 1 (2016), accessed 2 July 2016, http://www.mtosmt.org/issues/mto.16.22.1/mto.16.22.1.richards.html

6. Adorno and Eisler, *Composing for the Films*, 151.
7. Adorno and Eisler, *Composing for the Films*, 93.
8. A term used by William Earl Caplin in *Classical Form: A Theory of Formal Functions for the Instrumental Music of Haydn, Mozart, and Beethoven* (New York and Oxford: Oxford University Press, 1998), 9. It goes without saying that the themes discussed in this chapter include those that are of a considerable extent (at least four measures) so as to correspond to the types employed here. Therefore, motives and phrase-units of one, two or three measures functioning as themes are not discussed here. Also, the hybrid and small binary form have been omitted. For a detailed study of these forms in Williams see the chapter about 'Form' in Zacharopoulos, 'The Film Music of John Williams', while for their conceptual definition in the classical period see Caplin, *Classical Form*, 59–61 (hybrid 1) and 87–93 (small binary form).
9. See, for example, Per F. Broman, 'In Beethoven's and Wagner's Footsteps: Phrase Structures and Satzketten in the Instrumental Music of Bela Bartók', *Studio Musicologica* 48: 1–2 (2007): 113–31; Debora Rifkin, 'Making it Modern: Chromaticism and Phrase Structure in Twentieth-Century Tonal Music', *Theory and Practice* 31 (2006): 133–58; Avo Somer, 'Musical Syntax in the Sonatas of Debussy: Phrase Structure and Formal Function', *Music Theory Spectrum*, 27: 1 (2005): 67–96. The use of the term 'neoclassical' here should not be confused with Audissino's use referring to the revival of the 'classical' Hollywood style of film scoring in Chapter 14. Here it refers to a 'movement of style in the works of certain 20th-century composers, who […] revived the balanced forms and clearly perceptible thematic processes of earlier styles', that is, the classical style of Haydn, Mozart and Beethoven (Arnold Whittal, 'Neo-classicism', *Grove Music Online*, ed. Deane Root, accessed 17 June 2015, http://www.oxfordmusiconline.com).
10. James Chute, 'John Williams to Premiere Work at SummerFest—"Quartet La Jolla" Takes the Spotlight Friday', 13 August 2011, accessed 20 July 2015, http://www.sandiegouniontribune.com/news/2011/aug/13/La-Jolla-Music-Society-SummerFest-John-Williams

11. Jack Sullivan, 'Conversations with John Williams', *Chronicle of Higher Education*, 53:19, 12 January 2007, 13.
12. Marian Christy, 'Conversations: John Williams' Pursuit of Excellence', *Boston Globe*, 4 July 1989, 21.
13. Arnold Schönberg, *Fundamentals of Musical Composition* (London: Faber and Faber, 1983).
14. Erwin Ratz, *Einführung in die musikalische Formenlehre* (Wien: Universal Edition, 1973).
15. Caplin, *Classical Form*.
16. See mainly Matthew BaileyShea, 'Beyond the Beethoven Model: Sentence Types and Limits', *Current Musicology*, 77 (2004): 5–33; 'The Wagnerian Satz: The Rhetoric of the Sentence in Wagner's Post-Lohengrin Operas' (Ph.D. diss., Yale University, 2003); and 'Wagner's Loosely Knit Sentences and the Drama of Musical Form', *Integral*, 16/17 (2002/2003): 1–34.
17. Mark Richards, 'Viennese Classicism and the Sentential Idea: Broadening the Sentence Paradigm', *Theory and Practice*, 36 (2011): 179–224, and 'Analyzing Tension and Drama in Beethoven's First-Movement Sonata Forms' (Ph.D. diss., University of Toronto, 2011), 25–41 mainly.
18. Schönberg, *Fundamentals of Musical Composition*, 58.
19. See BaileyShea, 'Beyond the Beethoven Model', 5. BaileyShea mentions 11 resources (including two theory textbooks) where Beethoven's prototype example is used (BaileyShea, 'Beyond the Beethoven Model', 29n2), whereas Richards enumerates 18 academic references (outside of textbooks) (Richards, 'Viennese Classicism', 181n7).
20. The term 'basic idea' is drawn on Caplin, who uses it to express the distinctive opening structural part of a classical theme. For more about this term and the different terms used by other theorists such as Schönberg and Ratz, see Caplin, *Classical Form*, 264n11.
21. The term 'sentence' refers here to its simple form, a typical structure of 8 measures (but also of 4 or 16 measures depending on the proportion of real to notated measures. See Caplin, *Classical Form*, 35). This size, of course, can be extended or expanded in various ways, but the typical defining characteristics remain the same.
22. The themes' names appearing in the main text and Appendix come from various sources. In most cases they're coming from reviews, analyses and discussions of film scores on the internet (e.g. www.jwfan.com/forums); in other cases they're coming from more official sources like the liner notes of soundtrack releases (e.g. the

'Shoebridge Theme' mentioned in the Appendix is attributed to Mike Matessino, liner notes for *Family Plot*, CD, Varèse Sarabande, 2010, VCL 1110 1115); on some occasions I have named the themes for easier identification based on the title of the CD track in which they appear or their general character and narrative function in the film (e.g. 'Basket Game Theme', 'Irish Theme'), and on rare occasions they are attributed to Williams himself (e.g. 'Yoda's Theme' appears in the handwritten music sketches of the composer).

23. The musical examples presented here are one-staff personal transcriptions adapted from the corresponding published scores (see 'List of musical examples'), taking certain liberties and making simplifications like changes of register, omitting doublings, simplifying arpeggios to sustained chords (e.g. Fig. 15.2), but always preserving the melody and harmony of the themes. In a couple of cases additional notes (Fig. 15.3) or a bass line (Fig. 15.4) have been transcribed and added because they are important to consider in the analysis. The accuracy of these transcriptions was corroborated with the original handwritten scores, and I'm grateful to the anonymous helpers who made it possible for me to study these.

24. About the concept of prolongation, see Allen Forte and Steven Gilbert, *An Introduction to Schenkerian Analysis* (New York: Norton, 1982), 142–8.

25. The *continuation* does not always elaborate the thematic content of the *presentation* but can resort to new motivic content, which is not at any rate as distinctive as that in the *presentation* (See example 3.15 in Caplin, *Classical Form*, 46–7).

26. While Caplin refers briefly to this, saying that 'a continuation phrase most often begins with a one-measure idea, which is immediately repeated in the following measure' (Caplin, *Classical Form*, 41), BaileyShea dedicates a separate paragraph to this type of sentence, which he calls 'sentences with a sentential continuation'. This construction is noteworthy because it features a potentially 'aggressive [and] accelerated drive to cadence, an option that Beethoven fully exploits' (BaileyShea, 'Beyond the Beethoven Model', 15), while its exceptionally common use in classical music literature is also pointed out by Richards ('Viennese Classicism', 215). In this chapter the distinction between some special types of sentences mentioned below is made by considering the basic idea and the number of its repetitions within a theme; consequently, the adoption of the above-mentioned type as a special type of sentence and its reference in the main text is far from the author's intentions and reasoning.

27. See Appendix for a list of more typical examples of each type in Williams's film music.
28. Schönberg, *Fundamentals of Musical Composition*, 25.
29. Caplin, *Classical Form*, 49.
30. See Table 15.1. We must of course take into consideration that this rate changes if some specific kinds of sentence, and not only the simple ones, are added too. In this case, however, the comparison is made with the typical basic forms.
31. Although the harmonic support of the theme plays a structural and determinative role for the period according to Caplin, such strictness in the rules is not appropriate here and therefore the approach to the harmonic factor in these film-music themes (and likewise in a possible analysis of romantic or post-romantic music themes) is more flexible. For more about cadences in film music see Frank Lehman, 'Hollywood Cadences: Music and the Structure of Cinematic Expectation', *Music Theory Online*, 19:4 (2013), accessed 20 July 2015, http://www.mtosmt.org/issues/mto.13.19.4/mto.13.19.4.lehman.php
32. Supposing that in such a theme there are four consecutive ideas, then the third resembles the first more than the second compared to the first: in this case the theme is identified as a period. A form that may correspond to this structure would be: a1-a2-a1-a3/b (letter 'a' corresponds to two-measure units in a typical eight-measure period). Thus, although a2 resembles a1, the return to a1 in the third idea divides the theme into two phrases, the *antecedent* (although weak) and the *consequent*, as already seen. The concluding idea can be another modification of a1 (a3) or even new motivic content (b). Mark Richards adopts the terms *sentential* and *developing period* for themes with similar forms (See Richards, 'Film Music Themes', Example 1), indicating the flexibility of the contrasting idea that can resemble the basic idea. Nevertheless, in my framework, and according to the needs of this chapter, I do not think a further subdivision of the period form is necessary.
33. Such a case is also mentioned by Caplin (see example 4.4 in *Classical Form*, 49–51).
34. The not so essential differentiation is more evident in the second and third beat of m. 6 (cf. m. 4) where the melody changes direction.
35. An additional detail that differentiates the 'contrasting idea' is the offbeat accents of tonic and subdominant degree on the bass in mm. 5 and 9.
36. BaileyShea, 'Beyond the Beethoven Model', 7.

37. Caplin states this view as one of the initial principles of his book in the introductory chapter. See Caplin, *Classical Form*, 4.
38. BaileyShea, 'The Wagnerian Satz'.
39. BaileyShea, 'Beyond the Beethoven Model', 8.
40. Richards, 'Viennese Classicism', 182.
41. Richards, 'Viennese Classicism', 192–6.
42. Caplin, *Classical Form*, 99. The precursor of this structure is also found in the form (3xa) + b, noticed by Dahlhaus (Carl Dahlhaus, 'Satz und Periode: Zur Theorie der musikalischen Syntax', *Zeitschrift für Musiktheorie*, 9:2 (1978), 25 [unofficial English translation by Mark Richards]) in classical repertory (as in the subordinate theme of the finale in Beethoven's sonata op. 2/1). Although it differs from a dualistic typology, it is recognized as an independent and closed syntactic structure related to the concepts of the sentence and the period.
43. Richards, 'Viennese Classicism', 190.
44. At this point I would like to diverge from Richards, since, as shown in the examples of trifold sentences in the classical repertory he lists (Richards, 'Viennese Classicism and the Sentential Idea', 224), and as I gathered from our email conversation, he adopts a rigid concept regarding the 'repetition' of an idea, where the idea must be intact or slightly varied. Therefore, a greater deviation from the basic idea leads him to the invention of new types (developing sentence, developing period, developing clause and clause; see Richards, 'Film Music Themes', Example 1). The reason for my different view, as well as the reason why I have not created subdivisions of the basic forms based on variation, is that it is often difficult to clearly draw the line that distinguishes the more (varied) from the less varied ideas.
45. Except for the fragmentation of the basic idea, the last two-measure phrase is also motivically linked with it through the augmentation of the secondary motif formed by the triplets in m. 9:

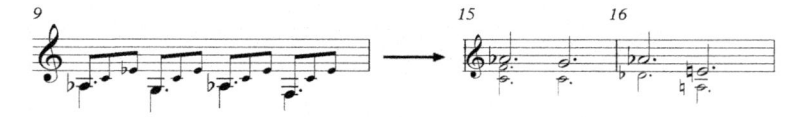

46. According to Caplin, the third statement of the initial idea creates a 'functional redundancy', which, in combination with the asymmetry of the sentence, contributes to a loose organization (Caplin, *Classical Form*, 99).

47. Caplin, *Classical Form*, 41.
48. Schönberg, *Fundamentals of Musical Composition*, 58.
49. BaileyShea, 'Beyond the Beethoven Model', 11–2. In fact, one of the examples that he uses to illustrate this form is a theme from *Ligeti's String Quartet no.1* ('Beyond the Beethoven Model', 13), which features the release of the sentence and its particular types from the typical harmonic procedures of tonal music.
50. These types are reminiscent of the *clause* and the *developing clause* suggested by Richards ('Film Music Themes'). There they take the form of a1-a1-a2-x and a1-a2-a3-x, with x consisting of new thematic material or another variation of a. The author, however, distinguishes this type from the sentence, terming its second half 'divergence' and not 'continuation'. This is the reason why I have chosen not to adopt this term.
51. In fact, it is a *compound basic idea* because it can be divided into the ideas of measures 5–7 and 8–10 (see Caplin, *Classical Form*, 61. In this case I don't consider the absence of cadence that Caplin mentions as a necessary element of a compound basic idea but I use the term in relation to the motivic division of this large idea into two parts).
52. Cf. mm. 6 and 18.
53. Here follows a complete list of the 66 theatrical films for which Williams composed original music between 1975 and 2013: *Jaws* (1975), *Family Plot* (1976), *The Missouri Breaks* (1976), *Midway* (1976), *Black Sunday* (1977), *Star Wars* (1977), *Close Encounters of the Third Kind* (1977), *The Fury* (1978), *Jaws 2* (1978), *Superman—The Movie* (1978), *Dracula* (1978), *1941* (1979), *The Empire Strikes Back* (1980), *Raiders of the Lost Ark* (1981), *Heartbeeps* (1981), *E.T. The Extra Terrestrial* (1982), *Monsignor* (1982), *Return of the Jedi* (1983), *Indiana Jones and the Temple of Doom* (1984), *The River* (1984), *SpaceCamp* (1986), *The Witches of Eastwick* (1987), *Empire of the Sun* (1987), *Superman IV—The Quest for Peace* (1987) (three themes), *The Accidental Tourist* (1988), *Indiana Jones and the Last Crusade* (1989), *Born on the Fourth of July* (1989), *Always* (1989), *Stanley and Iris* (1990), *Presumed Innocent* (1990), *Home Alone* (1990), *Hook* (1991), *JFK* (1991), *Far and Away* (1992), *Home Alone 2: Lost in New York* (1992), *Jurassic Park* (1993), *Schindler's List* (1993), *Sabrina* (1995), *Nixon* (1995), *Sleepers* (1996), *Rosewood* (1997), *The Lost World: Jurassic Park* (1997), *Seven Years in Tibet* (1997), *Amistad* (1997), *Saving Private Ryan* (1998), *Stepmom* (1998), *Star*

Wars—Episode I: The Phantom Menace (1999), *Angela's Ashes* (1999), *The Patriot* (2000), *A.I.: Artificial Intelligence* (2001), *Harry Potter and the Sorcerer's Stone* (2001), *Star Wars—Episode II: Attack of the Clones* (2002), *Minority Report* (2002), *Harry Potter and the Chamber of Secrets* (2002), *Catch Me if You Can* (2002), *Harry Potter and the Prisoner of Azkaban* (2004), *The Terminal* (2004), *Star Wars—Episode III: Revenge of the Sith* (2005), *War of the Worlds* (2005), *Memoirs of a Geisha* (2005), *Munich* (2005), *Indiana Jones and the Kingdom of the Crystal Skull* (2008), *The Adventures of Tintin: The Secret of the Unicorn* (2011), *War Horse* (2011), *Lincoln* (2012), *The Book Thief* (2013).

There are two reasons for the exclusion of his film music before 1975. The first is practical. I did not have access to scores composed before 1975. Because of the complexity of Williams's music, the access to scores is an important prerequisite for a serious musicological analysis, and I have had access to most themes composed after 1975 in written form (although the analysis of a very few themes have been based on my own transcriptions). The second reason is that 1975 was a crucial point in Williams's career. The composer himself referring to his wife's death in 1974 says: "Before that point in my life, I didn't know what I was doing. But after that point, in my writing, in my approach to music, and everything I was doing, I felt clear about what it is I was trying to do and how I could do with whatever small gift I may have been given. It was a huge emotional turning point in my life […] but one that resonates with me still and taught me about who I was, what I was doing and what it meant" ("John Williams: A Pivotal Moment in his life and work," Youtube video, 2:21, posted by "Oscars", July 22, 2014, https://www.youtube.com/watch?v=bE9IWvLz6Dk). Certainly this "pivotal moment" (as he calls it) in his life had a great impact on his music by rounding-off and establishing his distinctive style, resulting the next year (1975), in his first Academy Award win for the original score of *Jaws*. I've also omitted the film *Yes, Giorgio* (1982) for which Williams composed only the title song while the rest of the score was composed by Michael J. Lewis and *The Eiger Sanction* (1975) released before *Jaws*, since I chose the latter as a starting point.

54. Confusion with the term 'presentation' of the sentence should be avoided here.
55. Schönberg, 'Brahms the Progressive', in *Style and Idea: Selected Writings* (Berkeley, CA: University of California Press, 2010), 399.

56. David Thomas, 'Point Black—The Total Film interview: John Williams', *Total Film Magazine*, September 1997, 76.
57. This ratio increases in favour of the period, taking also into account the A section of small binary forms, which is usually formed as a period, as I have discovered analysing Williams's small binary themes (e.g. the 'Midway March Theme', in John Williams, *Midway*, Compact Disc, Varèse Sarabande Cd Club, 2011, VCL 1011 1124, track 20: 0.07″–0.39″). Besides, as mentioned above, if we just compare the number of typical sentences (44) to the periods (131), the vast majority of the latter is evident.
58. An example of this can be found in the film *Indiana Jones and the Last Crusade* (Steven Spielberg, 1989). The 'Grail Theme' (see Appendix), in its first appearance (at 10.34″ in *Indiana Jones and the Last Crusade*, Paramount Home Entertainment, Blu-ray, 2012), is stated only in its first half, since the way the scene has been edited does not allow its completion. (See Peter Moormann, *Spielberg-Variationen: Die Filmmusik von John William* [Baden-Baden: Nomos Verlag, 2010], 507 for a scene description and melodic transcription of the complete theme). At this point of the plot we are not aware we are about to see a quest for the Grail; however, the close-up of Indy's father's Grail-diary, which lasts a few seconds and is accompanied by the phrase 'May he who illuminated this illuminate me', gives the narrative opportunity for the appearance of this particular theme, but it does not last long enough for it to have time to complete syntactically.
59. Cf. for example, the first four measures of the 'Superman Theme' with the corresponding ones of the 'Remembrances Theme' discussed in this chapter.
60. This is especially evident in the 'Book Thief Theme' (see Appendix) in my opinion, despite the harmonic divergences. See also Mark Richards, 'Oscar Nominees 2014, Best Original Score (Part 1 of 6): John Williams' The Book Thief', accessed 20 July 2015, http://www.filmmusicnotes.com/oscar-nominees-2014-best-original-score-part-1-of-6-john-williams-the-book-thief, for an analysis of this theme ('Liesel's Theme').
61. See Schönberg, 'Criteria for the Evaluation of Music', *Style and Idea*, 129, in which he criticizes the technique of intact sequential repetitions as a tool of construction in music composition. Although in the basic form of the sentence, in Williams the repetition

of the basic idea is usually exact or slightly varied; in the three other sentence forms, as seen above, there is room for variation of the basic motivic content, particularly from the third statement of an idea onwards.

62. This has also been noticed by Caplin (*Classical Form*, 99), who identifies the 'trifold sentence' mainly in subordinate themes of the classical repertoire.
63. A sentence would be difficult to misinterpret as a period and vice versa, so any contrasting opinions are likely to focus on the related types, such as a sentence with dissolving third statement and a trifold sentence. Besides, the former could also contain a motivically complete third statement of the basic idea, as Richards points out too ('Viennese Classicism', 195).

Appendix

As the analysis in this article is limited to one or two themes of each type, the appendix lists a more extensive selection of themes. It is a guide both for the general reader, who can listen to the themes and get a richer understanding of the issues discussed in the essay, and the scholar who can check my claims through a study of other representative themes.

Sentence

Darth Vader's Theme (Imperial March), in John Williams, *John Williams Conducts John Williams: The Star Wars Trilogy*, Sony Classical, 1990, SK 46947, track 4: 0.09–0.36

Medallion Theme, in John Williams, *Raiders of the Lost Ark*, CD, DCC Compact Classics, 1995, DZS-090, track 6: 0.00–0.31

Phil's Theme, in John Williams, *Heartbeeps*, CD, Varèse Sarabande, 2001, VCL 1101 1001, track 9: 0.30–0.45

Stanley and Iris Theme, in John Williams, *Stanley and Iris*, CD, Varèse Sarabande, 1990, VSD-5255, track 1: 0.35–1.05

JFK Theme, in John Williams, *JFK*, CD, Elektra, 1992, 7559-61293-2, track 1: 0.19–1.23

Piano Theme, in John Williams, *Angela's Ashes*, CD, Sony Classical, 1999, SK 89009, track 1: 2.09–2.28

'Lost' Theme, in John Williams, *A.I.: Artificial Intelligence*, CD, La-La Land Records, 2015, LLLCD 1353, disc 3, track 13: 0.06–0.33

Sean's Theme, in John Williams, *Minority Report*, CD, Dreamworks Records, 2002, 450 385-2, track 9: 0.23–0.53

Dobby Theme, in John Williams, *Harry Potter and the Chamber of Secrets*, CD, Warner Sunset/Nonesuch/Atlantic, 2002, 83574-2, track 9: 0.10–0.27

The Past Theme, in John Williams, *Harry Potter and the Prisoner of Azkaban*, CD, Atlantic Records, 2004, 7567837115, track 7: 1.09–1.34

Sentence with Dissolving Third Statement

Leia's Theme, in John Williams, *John Williams Conducts John Williams: The Star Wars Trilogy*, Sony Classical, 1990, SK 46947, track 2: 0.15–1.12

Superman Theme B, in John Williams, *Superman*, CD, Warner Archives/Rhino, 2000, R2 75874, disc 1, track 1: 2.15–2.31

Dracula Theme, in John Williams, *Dracula*, CD, Varèse Sarabande, 1990, VSD-5250, track 11: 0.41–1.21

Cherry Theme, in John Williams, *The Witches of Eastwick*, CD, Collector's Choice Music, 2006, CCM-685-2, track 9: 0.00–0.17

Main Title/House Theme B, in John Williams, *Home Alone*, CD, La-La Land, 2010, LLLCD 1158, track 3: 0.29–0.47

Prologue Theme, in John Williams, *Hook*, CD, Epic Records, 1991, 469349-2, track 1: 0.06–0.21

Sabrina Theme, in John Williams, *Sabrina*, CD, A&M Records, 1995, 540456-2, track 1: 0.12–0.34

Angela's Ashes Theme, in John Williams, *Angela's Ashes*, CD, Sony Classical, 1999, SK 89009, track 1: 0.10–0.40

Duelling Theme, in John Williams, *The Adventures of Tintin: The Secret of the Unicorn*, CD, Sony Classical, 2011, 88697975882, track 18: 0.06–0.20

Death Theme, in John Williams, *The Book Thief*, CD, Sony Masterworks, 2013, 379707, track 1: 0.06–0.36

Trifold Sentence

Military Theme, in John Williams, *Close Encounters of the Third Kind*, CD, Arista Records, 1998, 07822-19004-2 3, track 15: 0.00–0.15

The Fury Theme, in John Williams, *The Fury*, CD, La-la Land Records, 2013, LLLCD 1238, disc 1, track 1: 0.09–0.54

Friendship Theme, in John Williams, *E.T. The Extra Terrestrial*, CD, MCA Records, 2002, 088 112 819-2, track 7: 0.00–0.44

Main Title/House Theme A, in John Williams, *Home Alone*, CD, La-La Land, 2010, LLLCD 1158, track 3: 0.10–0.28

Charleston Theme, in John Williams, *The Patriot*, CD, Hollywood Records/Edel, 2000, 0112442HWR, track 3: 0.54–1.12

Love Theme, in John Williams, *Far and Away*, CD, MCA Records, 1992, MCAD-10628, track 19: 1.50–2.20

American Cause Theme, in John Williams, *The Patriot*, CD, Hollywood Records/Edel, 2000, 0112442HWR, track 1: 5.25–6.05

Flying Car Theme, in John Williams, *Harry Potter and the Chamber of Secrets*, CD, Warner Sunset/Nonesuch/Atlantic, 2002, 83574-2, track 5: 0.09–0.19

Dartmoor Theme, in John Williams, *War Horse*, CD, Sony Classical, 2011, 88697975282, track 1: 2.09–2.28

Unfolding Sentence

Schindler's List Theme, in John Williams, *Schindler's List*, CD, MCA Records, 1993, MCAD 10969, track 1: 0.17–1.05

Sayuri's Theme, in John Williams, *Memoirs of a Geisha*, CD, Sony Classical, 2005, SK 74708, track 1: 0.09–0.46

Chiyo's Theme, in John Williams, *Memoirs of a Geisha*, CD, Sony Classical, 2005, SK 74708, track 2: 2.41–3.13

Book Thief Theme, in John Williams, *The Book Thief*, CD, Sony Masterworks, 2013, 379707, track 1: 0.40–1.11

Period

Schoebridge Theme, in John Williams, *Family Plot*, CD, Varèse Sarabande, 2010, VCL 1110 1115, track 3: 0.17–0.34

Ark Theme, in John Williams, *Raiders of the Lost Ark*, CD, DCC Compact Classics, 1995, DZS-090, track 9: 0.00–0.37

Monsignor Theme, in John Williams, *Monsignor*, CD, Intrada, 2007, Special Collection Volume 51, track 1: 0.18–1.22

Anakin's Theme, in John Williams, *Star Wars—Episode I: The Phantom Menace*, CD, Sony Classical/Sony Music Soundtrax, 1999, SK 61816, track 3: 0.23–0.49

Rosewood Theme, in John Williams, *Rosewood*, CD, La-La Land, 2013, LLLCD 1244, disc 1, track 24: 0.00–0.32
Grail Theme, in John Williams, *Indiana Jones and the Last Crusade*, CD, Warner Bros, 1989, 925 883-2, track 13: 0.41–1.06
Kovic's Theme B, in John Williams, *Born on the Fourth of July*, CD, MCA Records, 1989, MCAD 6340, track 10: 0.56–1.35
Holiday Flight Theme, in John Williams, *Home Alone*, CD, La-La Land, 2010, LLLCD 1158, track 7: 0.06–0.18
Island Theme, in John Williams, *Jurassic Park*, CD, MCA Records, 1993, MCAD-10859, track 4: 1.23–1.46
Nordic Theme, in John Williams, *Seven Years in Tibet*, CD, Mandalay Records, 1997, SK 60271, track 3: 0.00–0.38

Bibliography

Adorno, Theodor, and Eisler Hanns 1947. *Composing for the Films*. London: The Athlone Press. Reprint 1994.

BaileyShea, Matthew. 2002–2003. Wagner's Loosely Knit Sentences and the Drama of Musical Form. *Integral* 16(17): 1–34.

———. 2003. *The Wagnerian Satz: The Rhetoric of the Sentence in Wagner's Post-Lohengrin Operas*. PhD diss., Yale University.

———. 2004. Beyond the Beethoven Model: Sentence Types and Limits. *Current Musicology* 77: 5–33.

Broman, Per F. 2007. In Beethoven's and Wagner's Footsteps: Phrase Structures and Satzketten in the Instrumental Music of Bela Bartók. *Studio Musicologica* 48(1-2): 113–131.

Caplin, William Earl. 1998. *Classical Form: A Theory of Formal Functions for the Instrumental Music of Haydn, Mozart, and Beethoven*. New York and Oxford: Oxford University Press.

Christy, Marian. 1989. Conversations: John Williams' Pursuit of Excellence. *Boston Globe*, 4 July.

Chute, James. 2011. John Williams to Premiere Work at SummerFest—'Quartet La Jolla' Takes the Spotlight Friday, 13 August. http://www.sandiegouniontribune.com/news/2011/aug/13/La-Jolla-Music-Society-SummerFest-John-Williams. Accessed 20 July 2015.

Cook, Nicholas. 1994. *A Guide to Musical Analysis*. Oxford: Oxford University Press.

Dalhaus, Carl. 1978. Satz und Periode: Zur Theorie der musikalischen Syntax. *Zeitschrift für Musiktheorie* 9(2): 16–26.

Forte, Allen, and Gilbert Steven. 1982. *An Introduction to Schenkerian Analysis*. New York: Norton.

Gorbman, Claudia. 1987. *Unheard Melodies*. Bloomington, IN: Indiana University Press.
Karlin, Fred. 1994. *Listening to Movies. The Film Lover's Guide to Film Music*. Belmont, CA: Schirmer.
Lehman, Frank. 2013. Hollywood Cadences: Music and the Structure of Cinematic Expectation. *Music Theory Online* 19: 4. http://www.mtosmt.org/issues/mto.13.19.4/mto.13.19.4.lehman.php. Accessed 20 July 2015.
Matessino, Mike. 2010. Family Plot, CD (Liner Notes). Varèse Sarabande, VCL 1110 1115.
Moormann, Peter. 2010. *Spielberg-Variationen: Die Filmmusik von John William*. Baden-Baden: Nomos Verlag.
Ratz, Erwin. 1973. *Einführung in die musikalische Formenlehre*. Wien: Universal Edition.
Richards, Mark. 2011a. *Analyzing Tension and Drama in Beethoven's First-Movement Sonata Forms*. PhD. diss., University of Toronto.
———. 2011b. Viennese Classicism and the Sentential Idea: Broadening the Sentence paradigm. *Theory and Practice* 36: 179–224.
———. 2014. Oscar Nominees 2014, Best Original Score (Part 1 of 6): John Williams' The Book Thief. http://www.filmmusicnotes.com/oscar-nominees-2014-best-original-score-part-1-of-6-john-williams-the-book-thief. Accessed 20 July 2015.
———. 2016. Film Music Themes: Analysis and Corpus Study. *Music Theory Online* 22: 1. http://www.mtosmt.org/issues/mto.16.22.1/mto.16.22.1.richards.html. Accessed 2 July 2016.
Rifkin, Debora. 2006. Making it Modern: Chromaticism and Phrase Structure in Twentieth-Century Tonal Music. *Theory and Practice* 31: 133–158.
Schönberg, Arnold. 1967. *Fundamentals of Musical Composition*. London: Faber and Faber. Reprint 1983.
———. 1975a. Brahms the Progressive. *Style and Idea: Selected Writings*. Berkeley, CA: University of California Press. Reprint 2010, 398–441.
———. 1975b. Criteria for the Evaluation of Music. *Style and Idea: Selected Writings*. Berkeley, CA: University of California Press. Reprint 2010, 124–136.
Somer, Avo. 2005. Musical Syntax in the Sonatas of Debussy: Phrase Structure and Formal Function. *Music Theory Spectrum* 27(1): 67–96.
Sullivan, Jack. 2007. Conversations with John Williams. *Chronicle of Higher Education* 53:19, 12 January, B12–B13.
Thomas, David. 1997. Point Black—The Total Film Interview: John Williams. *Total Film Magazine*, September.
Whittall, Arnold. 1980. Neo-classicism. *Grove Music Online*, ed. Deane Root. http://www.oxfordmusiconline.com. Accessed 17 June 2015.
Zacharopoulos, Konstantinos. Forthcoming. *The Film Music of John Williams (1975–2015)*. PhD diss., University of Athens.

INDEX[1]

A
Aadahl, Erik, 116
Abbate, Carolyn, 131, 132, 134
Abrams, J. J., 229
Accidental Tourist (1988), 227, 255n53
Addinsell, Richard, 65, 84n47
Adorno, Theodor, 237, 238
Adventures of Robin Hood, The (1938), 6
Adventures of Tintin, The (2011), 228, 256n53, 259
Aerosmith, 222
A.I.: Artificial Intelligence (2001), 256n53, 258
Ailsa (1994), 142
Alger, Horatio, 2
Altered States (1980), 87, 116
Altman, Rick, 30, 108
Altman, Robert, 226
Always (1989), 255n53
Amadeus (1984), 66–7, 82n10

Amazing Spider-Man 2, The (2014), 5
American Beauty (1999), 222
Amistad (1997), 227, 255n53
Angela's Ashes (1999), 256n53, 258, 259
Anna Karenina (2012), 139
Armageddon (1998), 222
Arnold, David, 222
Arun, Ila, 49
Atonement (2007), 11, 139, 141, 155, 157, 167–81
At Play in the Fields of the Lord (1991), 57
Austen, Jane, 120, 127–9, 134, 135, 158
Avengers, The (2012), 152

B
Babenco, Hector, 57
Bach, Johann Sebastian, 122, 140, 189

---

[1] Note: Names of actors/actresses and directors are not indexed if they only appear in brackets after the names and titles of their characters and films.

© The Author(s) 2017
L. Coleman, J. Tillman (eds.), *Contemporary Film Music*,
DOI 10.1057/978-1-137-57375-9

Bach, P. D. Q., 66
Bacon, Francis (artist), 142–3
Badelt, Klaus, 223
Badlands (1973), 94
BaileyShea, Matthew, 239, 240, 243, 245, 251n19, 252n26, 255n49
Balasubrahmaniyan, B., 29, 37
Balasubrahmanyam, S. P., 38
Baragwanath, Nicholas, 102
Barbieri, Gato, 116
Bardem, Javier, 91
Bartók, Béla, 238
Batman (1989), 3
Batman v Superman: Dawn of Justice (2016), 5
Bazin, André, 198
Beatles, the, 72
Beethoven, Ludwig van, 12, 23, 88–9, 122, 130–3, 135, 143, 145, 149, 158, 159, 166, 218n24, 238, 239, 243, 252n26, 254n42
Beloved (1998), 119
Berg, Alban, 102
Berkey, Craig, 116
Berlioz, Hector, 155, 172, 216
Bernstein, Elmer, 12
Bertolucci, Bernardo, 116
Best Years of Our Lives, The (1946), 101, 102
Blacking, John, 34
Black Sunday (1977), 255n53
Blood Simple (1984), 115
Blur, 44
Bombay (1995), 9, 17, 20, 28, 30, 32, 33, 36–41, 43, 44, 48, 52n25, 54n56
Bon Jovi, Jon, 222
Book Thief, The (2013), 225, 234n22, 256n53, 257n60, 259, 260
Booth, Greg, 30
Born on the Fourth of July (1989), 255n53, 261

Bouyamourn, Adam, 8
Boyle, Danny, 9, 17, 22, 27, 28, 31, 44–6, 48, 49
Branigan, Edward, 156, 173
Breaking Bad (2008–13), 116
Bride of Frankenstein (1935), 100, 111
Bridges, Jeff, 108
Brown, Blair, 87
Brown, Royal S., 34, 196, 198, 199
Broxton, Jonathan, 64
Buecker, Brad, 144
Burgess, Anthony, 65, 82n9
Burwell, Carter, 9, 10, 87–118, 119
Buscemi, Steve, 94, 104
Byrne, Gabriel, 87, 99, 105, 117n5

C
Cain, James M., 92
Cameo, 40
Campbell, Joseph, 95
Caplin, William, 239, 241, 243–5, 251n20, 252n26, 253n31, 254n37, 254n46, 255n51, 258n62
Captain America: Civil War (2016), 5
Carlos, Wendy, 2
Carol (2015), 87
Carter, Elliot, 238
Cartmell, Deborah, 158, 162
Casablanca (1942), 104
Catch Me if You Can (2002), 227, 256n53
Chemical Brothers, The, 4, 147
Chion, Michel, 223
Chithra, K. S., 38
Chopin, Fryderyk, 83n28, 161–2, 182n23
Cider House Rules, The (1999), 10, 119, 121, 123
Citizen Kane (1941), 2
Clarida, Bob, 34

Clemmensen, Christian, 133
Close Encounters of the Third Kind (1977), 255n53, 259
Clueless (1995), 129
Coen, Ethan, 95, 102, 108, 114
Coen, Joel, 95, 102, 108, 109
Coen brothers, 87–9, 91, 94–6, 99, 100, 102, 111, 112, 113, 115, 116, 117–8n16
Condon, Bill, 87, 100
Constellation, La, 79
Cook, Nicholas, 238
Copland, Aaron, 103
Coppola, Francis Ford, 58, 147
Corigliano, John, 87, 116
Covach, John, 72, 82n7
Cowboys, The (1972), 226
Cronenberg, David, 89
Cutthroat Island (1995), 222

D
Dadié, Bernard, 227
Dahlhaus, Carl, 131, 132, 254n42
Damage (1992), 57, 59
Dangerous Liaisons (1988), 2
Dangerous Moonlight (1941), 65
Danna, Jeff, 187
Danna, Mychael, 9, 11, 22, 103, 123, 187–219
Danny the Dog (2005), 4
Dante, 62, 174
Dark Knight, The (2008), 3–5
Dark Victory (1939), 198–9
Davis, Bette, 198–9
Days of Heaven (1978), 94
Debney, John, 222
Debussy, Claude, 190, 238
Decalogue I (1989), 77
Decalogue II (1990), 65
Decalogue IX (1990), 61, 65, 69, 73, 74, 77

De Laurentiis, Dino, 58
Delerue, Georges, 116, 146
Desplat, Alexandre, 8, 116
Despotopolou, Anna, 129
Devil's Knot (2013), 187
Dido, 19–20, 45
Dil Se (1998), 17
Divecha, Sanjay, 46
D'Mello, Suzanne, 47
Doctor Zhivago (1965), 2, 3
Double Life of Véronique, The (1991), 60, 61–2, 64–71, 73–4, 77, 79, 81
Dovzhenko, Alexander, 148
Downey Jr, Robert, 122
Doyle, Patrick, 8
Dracula (1978), 255n53, 259
Duchess, The (2008), 119, 121
Dun, Tan, 20
Du Pré, Jacqueline, 125, 126

E
Earth (1930), 148
Earth (1998), 17
Earthquake (1974), 226
Eat Pray Love (2010), 144
Eeden, Frederik van, 61
Egoyan, Atom, 187, 196, 197
Eiger Sanction, The (1975), 256n53
Eisenstein, Sergei, 115, 198
Eisler, Hanns, 237, 238
Elfman, Danny, 3
Elgar, Edward, 125, 126
Eliot, T. S., 234n34
Emma (1996), 10–11, 119, 120, 125–38
Emma (novel), 120, 127–9, 132, 135
Empire of the Sun (1987), 255n53
English Patient, The (1996), 173
Eno, Brian, 44

E.T. the Extra-Terrestrial (1982), 5, 221, 255n53, 260
Europa Europa (1990), 57
Event Horizon (1997), 4
Exotica (1994), 187, 197

F

Family Plot (1976), 252n22, 255n53, 260
Family Viewing (1987), 197
Far and Away (1992), 246–7, 255n53, 260
Fargo (1996), 10, 90, 91, 93–5, 98, 99, 104, 106, 108, 112–14
Farrow, John, 104
Farrow, Mia, 104
Fellini, Federico, 147
Fenton, George, 2
Fielding, Jerry, 226
Files, Will, 116
Fincher, David, 3, 4
Finding Nemo (2003), 146
Fire (1996), 9, 17, 18, 28, 42–4, 48, 54n56
First Impressions (original title of Jane Austen's *Pride and Prejudice*), 159
Firth, Colin, 157
Frankenstein (1931), 100
Frazier, Jane, 169
Free Blood, 46
Friedhofer, Hugo, 101
Fury, The (1978), 255n53, 259

G

Genette, Gérard, 11, 156
Gerrard, Lisa, 222
Getter, Joseph, 29, 37
Gilmour, David, 59
Girl With the Dragon Tattoo, The (2011), 4

Gladiator (2000), 222, 223
Godard, Jean-Luc, 108, 116
Gods and Monsters (1998), 10, 87, 98, 100, 109–11
Goldenthal, Elliot, 23, 189
Goldsmith, Jerry, 89
Gone Girl (2014), 4
Good, the Bad and the Ugly, The (1966), 52n23
Goodbye Bafana (2007), 145
Gorbman, Claudia, 156, 207, 212, 238
Goulding, Edmund, 198
Great Beauty, The (2013), 62
Gregson-Williams, Harry, 5
Guru (2007), 18

H

Hallström, Lasse, 22
Hamilton, Kenneth, 161
Hanna (2011), 4, 147
Hannibal (2013–15), 116
Harry Potter (film series), 7, 8, 9, 226
Harry Potter and the Chamber of Secrets (2002), 227, 256n53, 259, 260
Harry Potter and the Prisoner of Azkaban (2004), 256n53, 259
Harry Potter and the Sorcerer's Stone (2001), 256n53
Haydn, Joseph, 12, 238, 250n9
Haynes, Todd, 87, 93
Heartbeeps (1981), 226, 255n53, 258, 260, 261
Heldt, Guido, 29, 30, 67, 156–7
Herrmann, Bernard, 3, 32, 226
Hi-Lo Country, The (1998), 93
Hobbit, The: An Unexpected Journey (2012), 7
Hobbit, The: The Desolation of Smaug (2013), 7–8
Hoffman, Elisha, 100

Holland, Agnieszka, 57, 58
Home Alone (1990), 255n53, 259
Home Alone 2: Lost in New York (1992), 255n53
Hook (1991), 228, 255n53, 259
Hooper, Nicholas, 8
Horner, James, 2
Hotel Rwanda (2004), 143
Human Stain, The (2003), 119

I
Ice Storm, The (1997), 11, 103, 196, 199–205, 209, 214
Iglesias, Alberto, 146, 153
Ilayaraja, 27, 33
Images (1972), 226
Inception (2010), 5–6, 8
Independence Day (1996), 222
Indiana Jones (film series), 6, 7, 226
Indiana Jones and the Kingdom of the Crystal Skull (2008), 255n53
Indiana Jones and the Last Crusade (1989), 255n53, 257n58, 261
Indiana Jones and the Temple of Doom (1984), 255n53
Invisible Man, The (1933), 100
Ives, Charles, 66
I Went Down (1997), 141–2
Iyer, Mahalaxmi, 50

J
Jackman, Henry, 5
Jackson, Michael, 40
Jackson, Peter, 8
Jagger, Mick, 28
Jane Eyre (1970), 226
Jane Eyre (2011), 139, 151, 155, 156
Jarre, Maurice, 2
Jaws (1975), 105, 226, 255n53, 256n53

Jaws 2 (1978), 255n53
Jayashri, Bombay, 210
JFK (1991), 255n53, 258
Jim Thorpe, All-American (1951), 205
John Paul Jones (1959), 104
Jullier, Laurent, 223
Junkie XL (Tom Holkenborg), 5
Jurassic Park (1993), 255n53, 261

K
Kaczmarski, Jacek, 69
Kalinak, Kathryn, 31, 180
Kamen, Michael, 4, 155
Karlin, Fred, 155
Karmitz, Marin, 58
Kassabian, Anahid, 30
Kayirebwa, Cecile, 144
Khan, Nusrat Fateh Ali, 23
Kickasola, Joseph, 69
Kieślowski, Krzysztof, 10, 57, 58, 60, 61, 63–85
Knightley, Keira, 157
Koirala, Manisha, 21
Korngold, Erich Wolfgang, 6, 33, 216, 224, 228, 231n4
Kramer, Lawrence, 134
Kurosawa, Akira, 116

L
Last Tango in Paris (1972), 116
Lawrence of Arabia (1962), 2
Lee, Ang, 103, 187, 196, 199–203, 209, 213–15
Leone, Sergio, 52n23
Lethal Weapon (1987), 155
Levinson, Jerrold, 133
Lewis, Michael, J., 256n53
Life of Pi (2012), 11, 22, 187–93, 196, 197, 209–16
Lincoln (2012), 225, 234n22, 256n53

Liszt, Franz, 126
Little Miss Sunshine (2006), 187, 188
Livingston, Paisley, 64–6
Llach, Lluis, 69
Long Goodbye, The (1973), 226
Lord of the Rings (film trilogy), 89–90
Lord of War (2005), 18, 52n25
Lost World: Jurassic Park, The (1997), 255n53
Lucas, George, 229

M
Machado, Antonio, 152
Macy, William H., 105
Madosini, 145
Mahler, Gustav, 122, 132
Malick, Terrence, 62, 94, 116
Malkovich, John, 2
Malle, Louis, 57, 58
Manchurian Candidate, The (2004), 119
Mancini, Henry, 230
Mandela, Nelson, 145
Mann, Thomas, 65
Man of Steel (2013), 5
Mansell, Clint, 153
Man Who Loved Cat Dancing, The (1973), 226
Man Who Wasn't There, The (2001), 87, 88, 93
Marianelli, Dario, 4, 9, 11, 88, 139–86
Massive Attack, 4
McCreary, Bear, 116
McDormand, Frances, 94, 105
McEwan, Ian, 167, 180
McGarvey, Seamus, 140
McGrath, Douglas, 129
McKellen, Ian, 100
Media Ventures, 6, 223
Mehta, Deepa, 9, 17, 28, 42, 43

Memoirs of a Geisha (2005), 227, 256n53, 260
Men in Black (1997), 152
Mépris, Le (1963), 116
M.I.A., 45
Miceli, Sergio, 227
Midway (1976), 255n53, 257n57
Mildred Pierce (2011), 87, 92–3
Miller, Bennett, 196, 206, 208, 209
Miller's Crossing (1990), 10, 87–8, 98, 99–100, 102, 105–8, 113, 117n5
Minghella, Anthony, 173
Minority Report (2002), 256n53, 259
Mission, The (1986), 139
Missouri Breaks, The (1976), 226, 255n53
Moggach, Deborah, 157
Moneyball (2011), 11, 195, 196, 205–9
Monsignor (1982), 255n53, 260
Monsoon Wedding (2001), 197
Moody, Rick, 199
Morricone, Ennio, 52n23, 139, 146
Morross, Jerome, 226
Mozart, Wolfgang Amadeus, 12, 23, 66, 67, 82n10, 122, 189–90, 238, 250n9
Munich (2005), 227, 256n53
Murch, Walter, 200, 202, 208, 209, 217

N
Nair, Mira, 196, 197
Nashville (2012–), 65
Nattiez, Jean-Jacques, 125, 131–2, 132, 135
Never Let Me Go (2010), 119, 121
Newcomb, Anthony, 132
Newman, Alfred, 216, 226
Newman, Thomas, 9, 90, 146, 222

Newton Howard, James, 4–5, 217
Nightcrawler (2014), 217
1941 (1979), 255n53
Nixon (1995), 255n53
Nixon, Richard, 199
No Country for Old Men (2007), 90, 91
No End (1985), 63, 69, 70, 72, 79, 80
Nolan, Christopher, 4, 7
Nyman, Michael, 2

O
Olivier, Laurence, 157
One Day (2011), 123–4
127 Hours (2010), 9, 17, 18, 19, 28, 32, 35, 37, 44–50
Only You (1994), 122
Oranges Are Not the Only Fruit (1990), 120
Orbital, 4
Ostaszewski, Jacek, 77
OuterSpace, 79

P
Patel, Dev, 21, 22
Patriot, The (2000), 256n53, 260
Patterson, Frank, 107
Peabody, Paul, 90–1
Penderecki, Krzysztof, 73, 75, 76
Pi (1998), 153
Piano, The (1993), 2–3
Picasso, Pablo, 234n34
Pink Floyd, 59
Pirates of the Caribbean: The Curse of the Black Pearl (2003), 222, 223, 228
Planet of the Apes (1968), 89
Ponti, Carlo, 58
Ponti, Edoardo, 59
Pop, Iggy, 44

Pope, Conrad, 234n22
Porter, Dave, 116
Portman, Rachel, 9, 10–11, 119–38
Poseidon Adventure, The (1972), 226
Preisner, Zbigniew, 9, 10, 57–85
  Requiem for My Friend, 59, 62, 63, 76–9
  Silence, Night & Dreams, 63, 77
  Ten Easy Pieces for Piano, 77
  Ten Pieces for Orchestra, 63, 81n2
Presumed Innocent (1990), 227, 244–5, 255n53
Pride & Prejudice (2005), 11, 139, 140, 150–1, 155–68, 171, 173, 180–1, 182n23
Primal Scream, 44
Prince, 40
Prokofiev, Sergei, 238
Psycho (1960), 3, 226
Puccini, Giacomo, 167, 176, 177, 179
Purcell, Henry, 189

Q
Quai des Brumes, Le (1938), 172

R
Rabin, Trevor, 222
Rabinowitz, Peter J, 66, 80–1, 82n9, 82n10
Rachmaninov, Sergei, 121, 122
Rahman, A.R., 9–10, 17–55, 123
Raiders of the Lost Ark (1981), 5, 221, 228, 242–3, 255n53, 258, 260
Raksin, David, 12
Ran (1985), 116
Ratnam, Mani, 9, 17, 18, 20, 21, 24, 27, 28, 33, 36, 37, 40, 43
Ratz, Erwin, 239
Rea, Stephen, 149
Reed, Lou, 44

Reivers, The (1969), 226
Reyland, Nicholas, 67–70, 72, 73, 75, 79, 80, 82n13, 83n31, 84n34, 84n35
Reznor, Trent, 3, 4, 6, 153
Richards, Mark, 239, 243, 244, 249–50n5, 251n19, 252n26, 253n32, 254n44, 255n50, 258n63
River, The (1984), 227, 255n53
Roberts, Julia, 144
Rob Roy (1995), 87
Rodman, Ronald, 33
Roja (1992), 9, 17, 20, 24, 27, 28, 30, 37–41
Rolland, Romain, 130–3, 136
Rollo, 20
Ronan, Saoirse, 147
Rosewood (1997), 227, 255n53, 261
Ross, Atticus, 3
Rostropovich, Mstislav, 140
Rota, Nino, 146, 147
Rózsa, Miklós, 222
Rudy (1993), 205
Russ, Patrick, 233n16
Russell, Ken, 116
Rutles, The, 72

S
Sabrina (1995), 227, 255n53, 259
Same, The, 97
Saving Private Ryan (1998), 255n53
Schickele, Peter, 66
Schindler's List (1993), 241–2, 255n53, 260
Schönberg, Arnold, 239, 240, 241, 245, 248, 257n61
Schowalter, Anthony, 100
Schubert, Franz, 110
Serious Man, A (2009), 89

Seven Years in Tibet (1997), 227, 255n53, 261
Shah, Tanvi, 50
Shawshank Redemption, The (1994), 146
Shearer, Joel, 19, 46
Shekhar, R. K., 27
Shooting Dogs (2005), 143
Shore, Howard, 7, 89–90
Sigur Ros, 18–19, 49
Singh, Sukhvinder, 50
Skyfall (2012), 9
Sleepers (1996), 255n53
Slumdog Millionaire (2008), 9, 17, 21, 27, 28, 30, 32, 37, 44–50
Smith, Jeff, 30
Smith, Patty, 222
Social Network, The (2010), 2–4, 8
Soloist, The (2009), 88, 143, 145, 149
Sorrentino, Paolo, 62
Southall, James, 6, 64
South Park, 5
SpaceCamp (1986), 226, 255n53
Spax, 79
Spectre (2015), 9
Spielberg, Steven, 95
Stack, Robert, 104
Stanley and Iris (1990), 227, 255n53, 258
Star Wars (film series), 5, 7, 101, 226, 258, 259
Star Wars: Episode I—The Phantom Menace (1999), 8, 228–9, 234n27, 256n53, 260
Star Wars: Episode II—Attack of the Clones (2002), 227, 234n27, 256n53
Star Wars: Episode III—Revenge of the Sith (2005), 227, 228, 232n14, 234n27, 256n53
Star Wars: Episode IV—A New Hope (1977), 5, 52n23, 221, 222, 226, 228

INDEX 271

Star Wars: Episode V—The Empire Strikes Back (1980), 228, 245–6, 255n53
Star Wars: Episode VI—Return of the Jedi (1983), 255n53
Star Wars: Episode VII—The Force Awakens (2015), 8, 225, 229, 233n19, 234n22
Steiner, Max, 33, 104, 198–9, 216
Steinfeld, Hailee, 108
Stepmom (1998), 255n53
Stewart, Dave, 28
Strauss, Richard, 155, 172, 216
Stravinsky, Igor, 230, 234n34
Superman (1978), 6, 221, 226, 239–40, 255n53, 257n59, 259
Superman IV–The Quest for Peace (1987), 255n53
Swami, Arvind, 21
Sweet Hereafter, The (1997), 187

T
Tagg, Phillip, 34
Takemitsu, Toru, 116
Tarasti, Eero, 10–11, 125–7, 136
Tchaikovsky, Pyotr, 149
Terminal, The (2004), 227, 256n53
Thibaudet, Jean-Yves, 168
Thick Pigeon, 97
Thin Red Line, The (1998), 94
This Is Spinal Tap (1984), 65, 82n7
Thornton, Billy Bob, 88
Three Colours: Blue (1993), 10, 57, 59–61, 65–81
Three Colours: Red (1994), 57, 63, 65, 73, 77
Three Colours: White (1994), 57, 69, 83n27
Tiomkin, Dimitri, 226
Titanic (1997), 2
Tolkien, J. R. R., 7
Torn, David, 90

Towarnicka, Elżbieta, 59, 77
Towering Inferno, The (1974), 226
Trainspotting (1996), 44, 46
Tree of Life, The (2011), 62, 116
True Grit (2010), 10, 87, 95, 98, 100, 108–9, 113–15
Twilight (film series), 87

U
Underworld, 44

V
Vairamuthu, 30
Van den Budenmayer, 10, 61, 64–70, 72–4, 76, 77, 79, 80, 83n31, 85n53
Vaughan Williams, Ralph, 226
Vertigo (1958), 32
V for Vendetta (2005), 139, 148–9

W
Wagner, Richard, 31–2, 102, 106, 216, 243
    Meistersinger von Nürnberg, Die, 65
    Ring, The, 102
    Tristan und Isolde, 159
Walking Dead, The (2010), 116
Wall-E (2008), 146
Walton, Kendall, 80, 85n50
War Horse (2011), 256n53, 260
War of the Worlds (2005), 227, 256n53
Water (2005), 17
Waxman, Franz, 226
Webber, Andrew Lloyd, 28
Wesson, Mel, 223
Whale, James, 100, 109–11, 116
Wierzbicki, James, 14n11, 31, 222
Wilcox, Larry, 107
Wild Bunch, The (1969), 226

Williams, John, 5, 6, 7, 8, 11, 12–13, 14n9, 18, 52n23, 221–62
Wilson, Alexandra, 167, 176, 177, 179, 180
Winfrey, Oprah, 22
Winters, Ben, 85n50
Witches of Eastwick, The (1987), 255n53, 259
Wright, Joe, 4, 139, 147, 150, 157–9, 164–70, 172, 175–81, 182n25

Y
Yagnik, Alka, 49
Yared, Gabriel, 153
Yes, Giorgio (1982), 256n53

Z
Zaentz, Saul, 58
Zimmer, Hans, 3–7, 94, 153, 222–3, 233n19